CLASSICS
OF
ANCIENT
CHINA

I CHING

THE CLASSIC OF CHANGES

TRANSLATED
WITH AN INTRODUCTION AND
COMMENTARY BY

EDWARD L. SHAUGHNESSY

BALLANTINE BOOKS · NEW YORK

http://www.randomhouse.com

Library of Congress Cataloging-in-Publication Data
I ching.   English
I Ching : The classic of changes / translated with an introduction
and commentary by Edward L. Shaughnessy.
p.   cm.—(Classics of ancient China)
Includes bibliographical references and index.
ISBN 0–345–36243–8
I. Shaughnessy, Edward L., 1952–   . II. Series
PL2478.I1613   1996
299'.51282—dc20   96–30598

Text design by Holly Johnson

Manufactured in the United States of America

First Edition: January 1997

10   9   8   7   6   5   4   3   2   1

CONTENTS

ACKNOWLEDGMENTS

When as a graduate student in the early 1980s I decided to write my doctoral dissertation on the early history of the *I Ching* (hereafter *Yijing*) or *Classic of Changes*, I was of course aware that a manuscript of the text had been discovered some years earlier at Mawangdui, Changsha, Hunan. It was frustrating that the text was not published before I finished the dissertation ("The Composition of the *Zhouyi*," Stanford University, 1983), but I consoled myself that my own study concerned an earlier period of the *Yijing*'s history than that for which the Mawangdui manuscript would be directly pertinent. Thereafter I continued to watch the scholarly press for publication of the manuscript and, on each visit to China, to ask colleagues there about any progress toward that end, but (with the exception of a simplified character transcription of the text of the hexagram and line statements of the sixty-four hexagrams that was published in 1984 in the journal *Wenwu*) I continued to be frustrated.

It was not until the early autumn of 1992 when friends returning from a conference in Changsha marking the twentieth anniversary of the first excavations at Mawangdui provided me with a copy of *Mawangdui Han mu wenwu* (*Cultural Relics from the Mawangdui Han Tomb*), which included complete photographs of the text of the sixty-four hexagrams and also that of the *Xici* or *Appended Statements*, that it seemed possible to begin working with the manuscript. Other scholars were equally excited by the possibilities. When, in 1994, volume 3 of *Daojia wenhua yanjiu* (Research on Daoist Culture) appeared with complete transcriptions of all but one of the commentarial texts included in the manuscript,

ix

I scheduled a seminar at the University of Chicago to read the texts with my students.

While teaching that seminar, for which I began preparing my own draft translations, I received a telephone call from Owen Lock of Ballantine Books asking if I would be interested in publishing a complete translation. My first thought was that this was a really happy coincidence; I would just need to polish my draft translations. Surprise of surprises, I still think that it was a happy coincidence; though the translations that I had done at that point needed more than just a little polishing, I have enjoyed doing it and through it have come to a deeper appreciation of the content of the various texts. What is more, Owen has been a delightful editor, and it is a pleasure here to express my appreciation to him.

Others I would like to thank include my students in the seminar at the University of Chicago, Li Feng, Peng Ke, and Tseng Lan-ying, as well as my friends and colleagues Bill Boltz, Fangpei Cai, Don Harper, Michael Puett, and Qiu Xigui, all of whom have improved in one way or another the present translation. Fangpei Cai has also typed the Chinese text, for which he had to create almost two hundred characters; as always, I am extraordinarily grateful to him for the care and expertise that he brought to this task. Finally, I should also like to thank Chen Guying, editor of *Daojia wenhua yanjiu*, for presenting me with an advance copy of volume 6 of that serial, the volume containing the transcription of the commentary *Mu He/ Zhao Li*; without his thoughtfulness the production of this book would not have been so smooth.

for elena

THE ORIGINS
AND EARLY DEVELOPMENT
OF THE *YIJING*

For the last two thousand and more years, the *Yijing* (*I Ching*) or *Classic of Changes* has been, with the Bible, the most read and commented upon work in all of world literature. Since the Han dynasty (206 B.C.–A.D. 220), virtually every major figure in China's intellectual tradition has had something, and often quite a lot, to say about the text. The enigmatic images of its hexagram and line statements have been adapted to every imaginable life situation, while the worldview of its *Xici* or *Appended Statements* commentary—integrating man and nature through the medium of the *Yijing*—is arguably the most sophisticated (it is certainly the most subtle) statement of the correlative thought that has been so fundamental to all of China's philosophical systems. Indeed, so central has the *Yijing* been to Chinese thought over these two millennia that a history of its exegetical traditions would require almost a history of Chinese thought. That is not a topic for this brief introduction.

Despite the volume of writing the *Yijing* has inspired, until very recently it had seemed that the text itself emerged—over the course of the preceding millennium—as if by revelation; that is to say, it seemed to be unique within the intellectual context of Zhou China (1045–256 B.C.). Supposed to have been created by the three greatest of China's historical figures—King Wen (r. 1099–1050 B.C.), the Duke of Zhou (d. 1032 B.C.), and Confucius (551–479 B.C.)—the text, itself very brief, is little noted in the received literary record of the period. A few references in the *Zuo zhuan* or *Mr. Zuo's Tradition* of the *Spring and Autumn Annals* indicate that, as later tradition would hold, the *Yijing* was first used as a diviner's prompt book. On the other hand, one or two passages

1

in the *Analects* of Confucius suggest, as later tradition would also hold, that Confucius was not content to use the book just for divination, but rather saw in it—and perhaps imbued it with—a more general philosophical significance. These are both important aspects of the *Yijing* tradition, but they only hint at the origins of the tradition.

Fortunately, the present century has been—in the development of the *Yijing* tradition as also in Chinese literary and intellectual history in general—dominated by archaeological discoveries. For the *Yijing* specifically, the most momentous discovery has probably been the second-century B.C. manuscript of the text unearthed in 1973 at Mawangdui in Changsha, Hunan, that will be the focus of this book. But other discoveries have also been important for illustrating the intellectual and social context in which the *Yijing* originally developed. It is owing to these other discoveries that we are now in a position to begin to describe the origins and early development of the *Yijing*.

TURTLE-SHELL DIVINATION

The nineteenth century ended in China with a discovery that would prove to have very great significance for all aspects of our developing understanding of ancient China. Whether by happenstance or not, in 1899 the noted antiquarian and paleographer Wang Yirong (1845–1900) bought several specimens of "dragon bones"—ancient bones used by apothecaries in the preparation of traditional Chinese medicines. Wang noticed that on the bones he bought was a type of writing similar to, but even older than, the inscriptions on ancient bronze vessels with which he was already familiar. Over the next year, he managed to buy a sizable collection of these inscribed bones, a collection that after his death in 1900 passed into the hands of his friend, the famous author Liu E (1857–1909). Liu's publication in 1903 of more than one thousand of these pieces, *Tieyun's Collected Turtles*, established a new field of learning in China: the study of bones and shells or, as they are better known in the West, oracle bones.

Now, almost a century after this first discovery, well over one hundred thousand pieces of inscribed oracle bones have been discovered in the vicinity of Anyang, Henan, the last capital of the Shang dynasty (c. 1600–1045 B.C.). From the inscriptions on these bones, which are the earliest form of writing in China and which we now know to have been produced in the course of divinations (attempts to determine the future), the history of this dynasty has emerged from the mists of legend. The range of topics about which divinations were performed, particularly during the rule of King Wu Ding (r. c. 1200 B.C.), the earliest reign from which oracle bones are known, is amazingly varied. The weather and the harvest are of course common topics, as are sacrifices to the ancestors and attacks against or by enemy states; but also divined were the king's health, and that of his consorts and relatives, his hunts, his dreams, the building of cities, the giving of orders, and the receipt of tribute.[1] The fullest of these inscriptions indicates the date and name of the divination official presiding, the "charge" to the turtle (i.e., the topic of the divination), the king's prognostication, and—showing that the inscriptions were engraved after the fact—a verification, almost invariably corroborating the king's prognostication. Two sets of inscriptions from this period (which at this time were usually divined in positive and negative pairs) will give some flavor of these divinations, and perhaps also a little sense of their role in the intellectual context of the day.

> Crack-making on *guichou* (day 50), (diviner) Zheng determined: "From today until *dingsi* (day 54), we will harm Xi." The king prognosticated and said: "On *dingsi* we ought not to harm them; on the coming *jiazi* (day 1), we will harm them." On the eleventh day *guihai* (day 60), Zhu did not harm them; that evening cleaving into *jiazi*, he really did harm them.
> Crack-making on *guichou* (day 50), (diviner) Zheng determined: "From today until *dingsi* (day 54), we will not perhaps harm Xi."[2]

> Crack-making on *renyin* (day 39), (diviner) Que determined: "Consort Hao will give birth and it will be advantageous." On *renchen* (day 29) cleaving into *guisi* (day 30), she gave birth; it was a girl.[3]
> Crack-making on *renyin* (day 39), (diviner) Que determined: "Consort Hao will give birth but it will not perhaps be advantageous." The king prognosticated and said: "Pray that it not be advantageous. If it is advantageous, it will not be auspicious; it is in breech. Like this, then she will die."[4]

Toward the end of the Shang dynasty, something of a theological constriction took place in the Shang kings' performance of divination. No longer was the broad range of royal life open to determination, nor

3

were negative consequences entertained. Instead, divinations were routinely performed on *gui* days, the tenth and final day of the Shang ten-day week, announcing the desire that there be no misfortune in the coming week. Also unlike the earlier divinations of King Wu Ding in which the king often anticipated baleful results, now the king's prognostications were uniformly auspicious. The following inscription is just one of literally thousands of virtually identical examples:

> On *guiwei* (day 20), the king made a crack and determined: "In the coming ten-day week there will be no misfortune." The king prognosticated and said: "Auspicious." In the fourth month.[5]

The optimism of the last Shang kings, at least insofar as their divinations were concerned, did not prevent the rise of a new power—the Zhou—that was destined soon to replace them as the dominant power in the north China plain, and thus to become in the eyes of later Chinese the next legitimate dynasty in Chinese history. The Zhou were led at this time by several remarkable figures: King Wen, who died just before the Shang were finally overthrown; his son King Wu, who defeated the Shang at the battle of Muye in 1045 B.C. and thus formally established the new dynasty; and King Wu's younger brother, Dan, better known as the Duke of Zhou, who also ruled briefly after King Wu's untimely death two years after the conquest. It is particularly King Wen and the Duke of Zhou who are revered in the Chinese tradition (King Wu, after all, by virtue of being a conqueror, had the blood of the last Shang king on his hands), and it is they to whom the writing of the basic statements of the *Yijing* is attributed. With the discovery of the Shang oracle bones, some historians in the earlier part of this century had surmised that this attribution had at least some basis in fact; they contended that whereas the Shang divined by causing cracks to appear in bones and shells, since no such artifacts had been found in Zhou contexts this showed that the Zhou used a different medium in their divinations: yarrow or milfoil stalks, which were manipulated in such a way as to produce a numerical result that was then expressed as one of the sixty-four possible configurations of six solid or broken lines, the so-called hexagrams (e.g., ☰, ☱, etc.). Although it is likely that the Zhou were indeed performing milfoil divinations at that time, they also continued to perform turtle-shell divination, as was proven in 1976 by the discovery of a cache of inscribed oracle bones in the remains of a temple or palace located in the Zhou homeland at the foot of Mount Qi in Shaanxi province. The inscriptions on these shells (unlike the Shang, who used both turtle shells and ox bones, the Zhou seem to have used only turtle shells in this form of divination) are generally similar to those of Shang oracle-bone divination, yet they also display certain important Zhou innovations. Among these, perhaps the most important is the routine phrasing of the divination in the form of a prayer, as seen in the following example:

> On *guisi* (day 30), determining at the temple of the cultured and martial Di Yi: "The king will summon and sacrifice to Cheng Tang, performing a cauldron exorcism of the two surrendered women; he will offer the blood of three rams and three sows. May it be correct."[6]

The Zhou oracle bones are generally too fragmentary to shed much light on their divinational context, but one complete turtle shell discovered three years later (1979), again in the Zhou ancestral homeland, seems to suggest that Zhou divination, somewhat like that of the early Shang, entailed a two-step procedure. However, unlike the Shang, in which the two steps were related as positive and negative, the second Zhou divination seems perhaps to be an elaboration of the first. This shell includes five discrete inscriptions, two pairs of which are related in this way:

1a. May it lead to an eternal end.
1b. May it lead to a beneficent mandate.
 2. The Protector determines about the palace; auspicious.
3a. Use this omen to catch the wife.
3b. This omen is also that this one is missing.[7]

As we will see in divinations from later contexts, this two-stage divination process seems to have become a standard feature. It may also have important implications for the early development, and use, of the *Yijing*.[8]

Finally, these Zhou oracle-bone inscriptions perhaps also reflect, even if only indirectly, the Zhou use of milfoil divination, the form of divination associated with the *Yijing*. Several of these shell fragments, as also a number of Zhou bronze vessels, contain groupings of numerals, almost always in sets of six. Although it is unclear just how these numerals should be interpreted, it does seem likely, as proposed in a celebrated article by Zhang Zhenglang, the leader of the official Mawangdui *Yijing* team, that they were produced in the course of milfoil divination akin to that with which the *Yijing* was used.[9]

Unfortunately, milfoil does not survive long burial the way that shells and bones do, and thus the milfoil divination of the early Zhou period has not left any other trace besides the *Yijing* itself. However, an important discovery in 1987 of divination records from near the end of the Zhou dynasty shows that both turtle-shell divination and milfoil divination using the *Yijing* were used in similar contexts and interpreted in similar ways. These records were written on bamboo strips found in the tomb of one Zuoyin Tuo, apparently an administrator of the southern state of Chu who died in 316 B.C. The divinations were performed during the last year of his life in an attempt to determine how to alleviate the life-threatening illness from which he was suffering. The first of the divinations quoted below, using turtle-shell divination, was performed in the fifth month of 317 B.C., while the second, using milfoil divination resulting in a pair of hexagrams, was performed in the fourth month of 316 B.C. In both cases, the divinations involved two stages, the first producing an initial prognostication—a "long-term determination" that seems invariably to have diagnosed certain problems—and then a second, exorcistic rite intended to resolve those problems.

It was the year that the emissary Wu Cheng from East Zhou returned to serve in the capital Ying (317 B.C.); in the Summer Presentation month (i.e., the fifth month of the Chu calendar), on the day *yichou* (day 2), Ke Jia used the Long Model (turtle shell) to determine on behalf of Zuoyin Tuo: "In exiting and entering to wait upon the king, from this Summer Presentation month until the next full year's Summer Presentation month, throughout the year would that his body have no trouble." Prognosticating it, the long-term determination is auspicious, but there is a little anxiety in his body, and there are some incongruities without. For these reasons, they exorcised it, offering prayer to the Chu ancestors Lao Tong, Zhu Rong, and Yu Yin, each one sheep; "May it attack and resolve his guiltlessness." Ke Jia prognosticated it, saying: "Auspicious."[10]

It was the year that the Great Supervisor of the Horse Shao Zhi dispatched the Chu state's troops and infantry to rescue Fu (316 B.C.); in the Formal Presentation month (i.e., the fourth month of the Chu calendar), on the day *jimao* (day 16), Wu

Sheng used the Assisting Virtue (stalks) to determine on behalf of Zuoyin Tuo: "In exiting and entering to attend the king, from this Formal Presentation month until the next full year's Formal Presentation month, throughout the year would that his body have no trouble": ䷀ ䷀. Prognosticating it, the long-term determination is auspicious, but there is a little anxiety in the palace chambers' infirmary. For this reason, they exorcised it, offering prayers to the Palace Lord's Earth Altar, one ram; offering prayers to the road, one white dog, and wine to drink; and killing at the main gate one white dog. Wu Sheng prognosticated it, saying: "Auspicious."[11]

While this second pair of divinations performed on behalf of Zuoyin Tuo appears to have involved the *Yijing* (or at least to have resulted in *Yijing*-like hexagrams), it does not tell us how the *Yijing* was used in divination. Indeed, no archaeological evidence yet discovered seems to provide this information. However, there are accounts of divination in the traditional literary record that, when reconsidered in the light of the sorts of archaeological discoveries discussed above, may tell us both how such divinations were performed and even how they influenced the form of the *Yijing* itself.

DIVINATION WITH THE *YIJING*

Probably the most complete description of divination using the *Yijing* that we have from the Zhou dynasty is found in the *Zuo zhuan*. It purports to recount a divination performed in the year 535 B.C. on behalf of Duke Xiang of Wei to determine which of his two sons should succeed him as duke of Wei.

> The wife of Duke Xiang of Wei had no son, but his concubine Zhou Ge bore to him Meng Zhi. Kong Chengzi (the grand minister of Wei) dreamt that Kangshu (i.e., the first lord of Wei) told him to establish Yuan (the primary one). . . . Zhou Ge bore him a second son and named him Yuan. The feet of Meng Zhi were disabled so that he was feeble in walking. Kong Chengzi used the *Zhouyi* to determine it by milfoil, saying: "Would that Yuan enjoy the state of Wei and preside over its altars." He met the hexagram *Zhun* ䷂. He next said: "I want to

7

establish Zhi; would that he be capable of enjoying it." He met the *Bi* ䷇ (line) of *Zhun* ䷂ (i.e., its Initial Nine line). He showed these to Scribe Chao. Scribe Chao said: " 'Primary receipt' (*yuan heng*); what further doubt can there be?" Chengzi said: "Is it not said of the elder?" (Scribe Chao) replied: "Kangshu named him (i.e., Yuan), so that he can be said to be the elder. And Meng is not a complete man (because of his disability); he will not be placed in the ancestral temple and cannot be said to be the elder. Moreover, its omen-statement says: 'beneficial to establish a lord.' If the heir were auspicious, what need would there be to 'establish' one? To 'establish' is not to inherit. The two hexagrams both say it. The younger one should be established."[12]

This interesting passage suggests three distinct features about divination using the *Yijing*. First, just as with turtle-shell divination, the topic of the divination was expressed in the form of a "charge," a statement indicating a desire on behalf of the person for whom the divination was being performed. Second, the divination involved two stages, in this case the first resulting in a single hexagram (the hexagram statement of which is quoted) and the second resulting in one of the lines of that same hexagram (the line statement of which is quoted). Third, as we might expect, the hexagram and line statements of the *Yijing* that are quoted provide the basis for the prognostication.[13] With this, we have probably come as close to the original use of the text as is possible, at least until new evidence is unearthed. Nevertheless, by examining yet another divination account in the *Zuo zhuan*, this time involving turtle-shell divination, it may be possible to delve even further back into the process by which the *Yijing* developed, to see how divination may have shaped the creation of an *Yijing* line statement.

This divination was performed in 563 B.C. for Sun Wenzi, another lord of the state of Wei, as he contemplated countering an attack on his state made by Huang'er of Zheng. Once again let us begin by quoting the *Zuo zhuan* account of the divination.[14]

Sun Wenzi divined by turtle-shell about pursuing them. He presented the crack to Ding Jiang. Madame Jiang asked the omen-verse. He said:
The crack is like a mountain peak (*ling*/*ljəŋ):
There is a fellow who goes out to campaign (*zheng*/*tsjəŋ),

But loses his leader (*xiong*/*gwjəŋ).

Madame Jiang said: "That the campaigner loses his leader is the benefit of resisting robbers." The great ministers planned it, and the men of Wei pursued (Zheng). Sun Peng captured Huang'er of Zheng at Quanqiu.[15]

This account includes two different types of divination results. The first, about which Ding Jiang inquired, suggesting that it was produced before her services were enlisted, is in the form of three rhyming lines of four characters each; it begins with a description of the crack in the turtle shell, and then follows that with a couplet that apparently relates the meaning of the crack to the topic of the divination. This result is here explicitly referred to as an "omen-verse" (*yao*), the same word used to refer to *Yijing* hexagram and line statements.

This initial divination result, doubtless extemporized by the official who performed the divination based on the topic chosen and the shape of the crack produced in the turtle shell, was apparently subject to different interpretations; otherwise there would have been no need to ask Ding Jiang for her prognostication. It might not be too impressionistic to suppose that the diviner would have perceived a crack in the shape of a "mountain peak" to be an omen of danger. Nevertheless, it may not have been clear to him for whom it would be dangerous, so that the couplet he extemporized, "There is a fellow who goes out on campaign, But loses his leader," must certainly have been as ambiguous to Sun Wenzi as it seems to us today: would it be dangerous for the attackers from Zheng or for the counterattackers from Wei? This must have been the primary reason why Ding Jiang was enlisted to provide a more definitive interpretation.

Her prognostication, "That the campaigner loses his leader is the benefit of resisting robbers," shows that the omen-verse itself could then stand as an image or omen to be interpreted. She obviously interpreted its reference to a "campaigner" to refer to the troops of Zheng rather than to the counterattackers of Wei, and so advised Sun Wenzi that this referred to "the benefit of resisting robbers." It is interesting that this is a clear transformation of an injunction, "beneficial to resist robbers," that occurs twice in the line statements of the *Yijing*.

One of the *Yijing*'s occurrences of this injunction is found in a line statement that begins with a poetic triplet very similar to these omen-verses of turtle-shell divination. The third line of *Jian*, "Advancing," hexagram reads as follows:

9

The wild goose advances to the land (*lu*/*ljəkw):
The husband campaigns but does not return (*fu*/*bjəkw);
The wife is pregnant but does not give birth (*yu*/*rəkw).
    Inauspicious. Beneficial to resist robbers.[16]

This seems to combine two of the types of divination results seen in the turtle-shell divination performed for Sun Wenzi: an omen-verse and an advisory interpretation that I refer to as an "Injunction." (There is also an added technical divination prognostication, "inauspicious," of the sort seen in the excavated records of turtle-shell divination.) Like that of the turtle-shell divination performed for Sun Wenzi, the omen-verse here, "The wild goose advances to the land: The husband campaigns but does not return; The wife is pregnant but does not give birth," begins with a four-character phrase describing the omen, in this case one in the natural world; this omen apparently evoked the following couplet of rhyming four-character phrases that relate it to the human realm (presumably to the topic of an original divination).

Given the long tradition that the *Yijing* originated as a manual of divination, there would seem to be no doubt that the creation of this sort of line statement derives from the same intellectual context as turtle-shell divination. However, whereas it is perhaps easy enough to imagine how a crack in a turtle shell could resemble a "mountain peak," and moreover how this might evoke notions of danger, it is not immediately clear how the omen "The wild goose advances to the land" of the line statement's omen-verse could have been derived from the third line of *Jian* ䷴ hexagram. Below I will offer some speculations first on what this omen must have evoked to the diviner and then, more tentatively, on how it may have come to be associated with *Jian* hexagram.

In the worldview of Zhou China the wild goose seems to have been a natural omen evoking marital separation.[17] This was perhaps because military campaigns in ancient China were typically launched at the onset of winter, thus avoiding the summer monsoon rains and coming after the autumn harvests had been collected. The seasonal coincidence of soldiers marching off in formation with wild geese flying off—also in formation—must have suggested to observers convinced that the natural world and the human world were but two aspects of the same system of changes that the flight of geese was invariably associated with the march of soldiers (but not in any cause-effect relationship; rather, the two phenomena were viewed as necessarily coincidental). And, by yet one further association, since all too many of the soldiers did not return from their campaigns, the appearance of the geese predicted the disappearance of the men. For wives, in particular, this could not have been an auspicious omen.

Given this understanding of the meaning wild geese had for the people of Zhou China, I think we can imagine a scenario wherein a husband proposing to leave his wife to go off on campaign had a milfoil divination performed to determine whether this action would be auspicious. The diviner met with the hexagram ䷴ that would come to be called Jian, "Advancing." In the text of the Yijing, the principal omen of Jian hexagram is a wild goose; each of the six line statements describes its "advance" from one natural place to another, each of the places referred to being slightly higher as one rises through the positions of the hexagram.

> The wild goose advances to the depths.
> The wild goose advances to the slope.
> The wild goose advances to the land.
> The wild goose advances to the tree.
> The wild goose advances to the mound.
> The wild goose advances to the hill.[18]

There seems to be nothing in the hexagram picture of Jian to evoke the image of a wild goose. Could it be that as the divination was in progress a flock of geese flew overhead? (As noted above, it is likely that a divination about beginning a military campaign would have taken place at the onset of the winter campaign season, so that the possibility of geese flying overhead at just that time cannot be discounted.) Since wild geese were recognized as an omen particularly relevant to the topic of the divination, the diviner would have associated it with the result of the divination: the hexagram ䷴. When that result was further specified as the third line of the hexagram, given the bottom-to-top low-to-high organization of the hexagram's images (an organization seen in several other hexagrams as well[19]), the position must have required in some sense the goose's advance to the "land" (lu/*ljəkw). With the omen thereby described, the diviner then would have gone on to extemporize the rhyming rejoinder couplet relating this omen to the topic of the divination:"The husband campaigns but does not return (fu/*bjəkw); The wife is pregnant but does not give birth (yu/*rəkw)."

The person for whom the divination was performed may have questioned this result and, as in the case of Sun Wenzi, sought a second opinion, which would have led to the injunction "beneficial to resist robbers" and perhaps also to the technical prognostication "inauspicious" being added to the line statement. (It is of course also possible that the composition process entailed more than a single divination. The omen-verse must surely have been created at one time, and would subsequently have come to be associated with that line of *Jian* hexagram. Perhaps at some later date, another divination resulted in the same line, and the then existent omen-verse required further explication, at which time the prognostication "inauspicious" and/or the injunction "beneficial to resist robbers" might have been added.) It could be that the divination result proved to be so apt in this particular case that the image of wild geese and the hexagram ䷴ came to be permanently associated; thereafter, just as the appearance of geese evoked the marching of troops, so too must the appearance of this hexagram have evoked the appearance of the geese.

I readily admit the speculative nature of the above discussion about how ䷴ hexagram came to be associated with the image of wild geese and thus to be called *Jian,* "Advancing." However, other *Yijing* hexagrams suggest associations that are more readily apparent. Perhaps the most manifest association is that between the hexagram *Ding* ䷱, "Cauldron," and the image of a cauldron, the pictograph of which in oracle-bone script is 鼎. Chinese commentators of all periods have seen in the broken bottom line of the hexagram picture a representation of the legs of the cauldron; in the three solid lines in the second, third, and fourth positions (counting from the bottom) its solid belly section; in the broken line in the fifth position the cauldron's two handles or "ears"; and in the solid top line a representation of the pole by which a cauldron was carried. The images or omens of the line statements of *Ding* hexagram in the text of the *Yijing* suggest that whoever composed the line statements must have also had these associations in mind. Thus, the first line statement, corresponding to the broken bottom line of the hexagram picture, refers to the cauldron's legs ("the cauldron's upturned legs"); the second line statement, corresponding to the first of the three solid lines perceived to figure the belly of the cauldron, refers to the contents of the cauldron ("the cauldron has substance"); the fifth line statement, corresponding to the broken line figuring the handles of the cauldron, refers to those handles or "ears" ("the cauldron's yellow ears"); and the solid top line refers to the solid bar used to carry it ("the cauldron's jade bar").

These images *qua* omens may have derived naturally from the shape of the hexagram picture. In turn, they evoked omen-verses similar to those examined above that must have derived from the contexts of specific divinations. For instance, the second line statement reads in its entirety:

> The cauldron has substance (*shi*/*djit):
> My enemy has an illness (*ji*/*dzjət),
> It is not able to approach me (*jie*/*tsiet);
>   auspicious.[20]

I think we can easily imagine here a scenario in which someone concerned about his health (perhaps at the time of an epidemic) performed a milfoil divination that concluded by expressing the desire "Would that I not be infected." The divination may then have resulted in the hexagram ䷱, evoking the image of a cauldron to the diviner. If diviners could see in the crack in a turtle shell the image of a mountain peak, then I think it is not hard to imagine that they could see the image of a cauldron in the picture ䷱. When the next stage of the divination specified the second line of the hexagram as that on which the result of the divination was to be based, the diviner would also have wanted to introduce that aspect of the cauldron, its full belly section, into his description of the image or omen: "the cauldron has substance." Needing next to relate this image to the topic of the divination, the lord's desire that he not be infected by the epidemic, the diviner must then have composed the rhyming couplet "My enemy has an illness, it is not able to approach me." If this result were not clear enough, it may have been shown to yet another prognosticator, who would then have pronounced the obvious prognostication: "Auspicious."

This, I think, is the process by which individual line statements of the *Yijing* were produced, and how they must have originally been understood. Of course, this still leaves us far short of understanding either how the 386 line statements (not to mention the 64 hexagram statements) were organized into the text that we have today, or how they came to be understood in later times. The first of these two questions is a topic that will have to be left for a future book. As for the second question, however, we are fortunate today to have important new evidence with which to reconsider the development of the *Yijing*'s exegetical tradition: the Mawangdui manuscript from about 190 B.C., which will be the focus of the remainder of this book.

THE MAWANGDUI *YIJING* MANUSCRIPT

In December 1973, archaeologists excavating Han tomb #3 at Mawang-dui, in Changsha, Hunan, made probably the greatest discovery of early Chinese manuscripts since the opening of cave #17 at Dunhuang in 1900. They discovered, neatly folded in a lacquer hamper placed in the tomb of Li Cang, Lord of Dai (d. 168 B.C.), more than twenty texts written on silk, including by far the earliest manuscript copy of the *Yijing* or *Classic of Changes* and two copies of the *Laozi* or *Classic of the Way and Its Virtue*. The early publication of the scrolls containing the *Laozi* made Mawangdui a name known to people everywhere interested in early China, and prompted a tremendous outpouring of scholarship that continues unabated today.[1]

Unfortunately, the complete text of the *Yijing,* including especially the commentaries appended to it in the manuscript, has only recently, about twenty years after its discovery, been made public, and even at that not "formally."[2] Somewhat like the case of the Dead Sea Scrolls controversy in the West, after languishing for years in the hands of the team of scholars officially charged with preparing it for publication, the Mawangdui *Yijing* manuscript was finally made public in transcribed form by other scholars who had access only to photographs of the text. The appearance of these informal transcriptions immediately sparked dozens of scholarly articles and major debates over the nature of the manuscript and even that of the *Yijing* itself.[3] In this section I will give a brief description of the manuscript, a preliminary account of its contents, and some indication of these scholarly debates, still in their incipient stages. I will not offer any (or, at least, many) conclusions of my own, preferring to keep the focus on the translation that follows.[4]

The Mawangdui *Yijing* manuscript was written on two pieces of silk, both about 48 cm wide. The first piece, about 85 cm long, contains the text of the classic itself, i.e., the hexagram and line statements often referred to as the *Zhouyi* 周易 (written in 93 columns of text with between 64 and 81 graphs per column), and a second, commentarial text, in 36 columns of about 72 graphs each (a total of about 2,600 graphs). Although this commentary is apparently untitled, scholars working with the manuscript generally refer to it as *Ersanzi wen* 二三子問 or *The Several Disciples Asked,* the first words of the text. Before being placed into the lacquer hamper, this piece of silk was first folded in half lengthwise three times and then once again from top to bottom. When excavated, it had frayed along most of the creases and had separated into sixteen different pieces. The second piece of silk, dimensions of which seem not yet to have been reported, contains about 180 columns of text divided into four or five discrete commentaries: the *Xici* 繫辭 or *Appended Statements,* the only one of these commentaries of which there is a received version; *Yi zhi yi* 易之義 or *The Properties of the* Changes; *Yao* 要 or *Essentials;* and *Mu He* 繆和 and *Zhao Li* 昭力, both names of interlocutors.

Except along the creases where the silk was folded and whole columns of graphs were obliterated, the manuscript is reasonably legible (and the photographs of it published to date are admirably clear). All of the texts were evidently copied by the same hand in a handwriting very similar to that on the "B" version of the *Laozi* manuscript. Since these texts, like that copy of the *Laozi,* regularly write the word *guo* 國 in places where one would expect *bang* 邦, "country," thus avoiding the tabooed name of Liu Bang, the first Han emperor (r. 202–195 B.C.), but do not avoid the word *ying* 盈, the name of Emperor Hui, Liu Ying (r. 194–188 B.C.), it would seem that the manuscript must have been copied about 190 B.C.

As do the manuscript copies of the *Laozi,* comparison with the received texts of the *Zhouyi* and of the *Appended Statements (Xici)* reveals that the manuscript contains many phonetic loan characters and forms of characters more or less unorthodox; some of these variora may signal significant syntactic differences. Also as in the case of the *Laozi* manuscripts, the general organization of the manuscript versions of both the *Zhouyi* and the *Appended Statements* differs appreciably from those of the received versions. I will try to introduce most of the significant differences in the following discussions of the various individual texts.

THE *ZHOUYI*

The manuscript version of the *Zhouyi* was initially published in transcription in 1984, although complete photographs of the text were not published until 1992. The text, and especially its different organization from that of the received text of the *Zhouyi,* has been much discussed in *Yijing* scholarship over the last ten years. This text of the 64 hexagram statements and associated line statements includes 93 columns of text, with each column having between 64 and 81 characters. The reason for this varying number of characters per column, which is anomalous within the manuscript as a whole, is that each hexagram starts on a new line. The hexagram picture (i.e., the six-lined graphs comprising solid and broken lines) is given at the head of the line, followed by the hexagram name, the hexagram statement, and then each of the six line statements, the hexagram and line statements being separated from each other by round dots.

Except for numerous phonetic loan characters and other unorthodox character forms, there are relatively few substantive variora at the level of the sentence. The most common variora involve the presence or absence of technical divination terminology, such as *ji* 吉, "auspicious," *xiong* 凶, "inauspicious," *hui wang* 悔亡, "regret is gone," and *wu jiu* 无咎, "there is no harm." The apparent instability of these technical divination terms is consistent with a note attributed to Liu Xiang (79–8 B.C.) that the three *jinwen* "New Text" textual traditions of the Western Han occasionally did not contain the terms *wu jiu* and *hui wang,* whereas the *guwen* "Old Text" tradition did.[5]

There are other variora of greater syntactic significance, some of which are discussed below in the "Principles of Translation" section. There are also numerous variora among the names of the hexagrams (fully thirty-three of the sixty-four differing in some degree from the names in the received text). While many of these would seem to be merely cases of graphic variation, some may have important implications for the history of Chinese thought. I have recently suggested elsewhere that the manuscript's readings of *Jian* 鍵, "The Key," and *Chuan* 川, "The Flow," for the pure yang (☰) and pure yin (☷) hexagrams known in the received texts as *Qian* 乾 (usually understood as "The Heavenly Principle") and *Kun* 坤 (usually understood as "The Earthly Principle") seem to derive from characterizations of the male and female genitalia, and thus are probably ancestral to the more abstract meanings of the received names.[6] However, these differences have not yet attracted much notice in China, where it seems to be too often assumed that the received text represents the definitive text, and that variora in the manuscript are due merely to scribal error.

Certainly the most immediately notable difference between the manuscript text and the received text lies in the sequence of hexagrams. Whereas there is no discernible logic to their sequence in the received text, except that hexagrams are grouped by pairs sharing a hexagram picture (either by inversion of the picture or by conversion of all of its lines to their opposites), the sequence of hexagrams given in the manuscript is based on a systematic combination of the hexagrams' constituent trigrams: the top trigram of a hexagram is the basis of its position in the manuscript's sequence; it is then combined in turn in a prescribed sequence with each of the other trigrams serving as its bottom trigram. Each of the eight trigrams forms a set of eight hexagrams sharing that top trigram. These sets are in the following sequence (referring to the trigrams by their names in the manuscript):

Jian	*Gen*	*Kan*	*Chen*	*Chuan*	*Duo*	*Luo*	*Suan*
☰	☶	☵	☳	☷	☱	☲	☴

They combine in turn with trigrams of the bottom trigram in the following sequence (except that each of the top trigrams of a set first combines with itself):

Jian	*Chuan*	*Gen*	*Duo*	*Kan*	*Luo*	*Chen*	*Suan*
☰	☷	☶	☱	☵	☲	☳	☴

This system can be seen clearly in the table on page 28 giving the manuscript sequence.

This is not the place to discuss in detail the relative merits and priority of the manuscript sequence versus the received sequence. Let me just note that all of the following points suggest that the received sequence was in existence before, and probably well before, the time that this manuscript was copied:

a) The sequence of the received text is in pairs of hexagrams sharing one hexagram picture (i.e., when the picture of the first hexagram is inverted, it becomes that of the next hexagram). Many of these pairs are linked both formally (i.e., by the use of similar terms) and conceptually. To give just one example, the fifth lines of both hexagram Sun ䷨, "Decrease," number 12 in the manuscript but 41 in the received sequence (indicated hereafter in this section as M12/R41), and Yi ䷩, "Increase" (M64/R42), the names of which are doubtless related, contain the following identical line statement:

> Someone gives him a turtle worth ten strands (of cowries); (he) cannot disobey it.

Since the manuscript sequence disrupts these pairs, it would seem not to be original to the text.

b) In A.D. 279, an even earlier manuscript text of the *Yijing* was discovered in the tomb of King Xiang of Wei, who died in 296 B.C. According to reports in the *Jinshu* or *History of the Jin Dynasty*, this text was identical to the then known text of the *Yijing*, which is to say, the received text.[7]

c) As we will see below, the various commentaries of the Mawangdui manuscript cite the hexagram and line statements of the *Zhouyi* in an order which is generally that of the received text.

By contrast, I know of no evidence that supports the sequence of the manuscript at any date earlier than that of the manuscript itself.[8]

Finally, the way in which the hexagram pictures are drawn in the manuscript version of the text has also been regarded as significant. In place of the familiar solid (—) and broken (--) lines of the received text, the manuscript has — and ⊥L. The similarity of ⊥L to the early form of the character for *ba* 八, "eight," has led some to see the picture as a numerical formulation (— similarly representing *yi* —, "one"), perhaps similar to the numerical divinatory symbols of the Western Zhou mentioned in the preceding chapter, rather than an imagistic representation of yin and yang or some other such complementary pair.[9]

Following the *Zhouyi* on the same piece of silk is another text in 36 columns of about 72 characters per column for a total of about 2,600 characters. Although the text seems not to have a final tag giving its title and number of characters, as several of the other commentaries do, it does begin with a black, rectangular mark indicative of a new text and it has a coherent structure. It is now generally referred to as *Ersanzi wen* 二三子問 or *The Several Disciples Asked,* since it begins with those words. At the end of column 16 there are three blank spaces, with column 17 beginning a new sentence. Because of this, early reports— still supported by some—suggested that the text is divided into two chapters.[10] However, throughout the text there are several breaks of one or two character spaces, apparently indicating section breaks; it may be that this three-character space is but another section break.

The text is in the form of numerous quotations of Confucius (referred to as "Kongzi") regarding the *Yijing,* prompted occasionally by questions from unidentified disciples. It is divided into thirty-two sections. The first section constitutes a fairly long discourse on the virtue of dragons. The first paragraph of this discourse reads:

> The two or three disciples asked, saying: "The *Changes* often mentions dragons; what is the virtue of the dragon like?" Confucius said: "The dragon is great indeed. The dragon's form shifts. When it approaches the Lord in audience, it manifests the virtue of a spiritual sage; when it rises on high and moves among the stars and planets, the sun and moon, that it is not visible is because it is able to be yang; when it descends through the depths, that it does not drown is because it is able to be yin. Above, the wind and rain carry it; below, there is heaven's . . . Diving into the depths, the fishes and reptiles move before and after it, and of those things that move in the currents, there are none that do not follow it. In the high places, the god of thunder nourishes it, the wind and rain avoid facing it, and the birds and beasts do not disturb it."

Sections two through four and nine through seventeen discuss the line statements of *Jian,* "The Key," and *Chuan,* "The Flow," hexagrams in a way quite similar to the *Wenyan* or *Words on the Text* commentary of

19

the received classic. I will give here just one example, that commenting upon the Elevated Six line of *Jian*.

> The *Changes* says: "The haughty dragon has regrets." Confucius said: "This speaks of being above and treating those below arrogantly; there has never been a case of one who treats those below arrogantly not being in danger. As for the sage's establishment of government, it is like climbing a tree: the higher one gets, the more one fears what is below. Therefore, it says, 'The haughty dragon has regrets.'"

Sections five to eight discuss various line statements in *Jian*, "Afoot" (M20/R39), *Ding,* "The Cauldron" (M56/R50), and *Jin*, "Aquas" (M51/R35), while sections eighteen to thirty-two discuss line statements in *Zhun*, "Hoarding" (M23/R3), *Tongren*, "Gathering Men" (M6/R13), *Dayou,* "The Great Possession" (M50/R14), *Qian*, "Modesty" (M35/R15), *Yu,* "Excess" (M27/R16), *Zhongfu,* "Central Return" (M61/R61), *Shaoguo,* "Small Surpassing" (M28/R62), *Heng,* "Constancy" (M32/R32), *Jie,* "Untangled" (M30/R40), *Gen,* "Stilling" (M9/R52), *Feng,* "Abundance" (M31/R55), and *Weiji,* "Not Yet Completed" (M54/R64), hexagrams. These discussions are generally similar in length and nature to that quoted above for the top line of *Jian*. It is worth noting that the sequence in which these hexagrams are discussed is, with the exception of *Zhongfu* and *Shaoguo,* that of the received classic.

APPENDED STATEMENTS

The second piece of silk begins with the *Xici* 繫辭 or *Appended Statements,* the only one of the manuscript commentary texts that is also found in the received text of the *Yijing*. Initial reports shortly after the manuscript's excavation that it included a text of the *Appended Statements* nearly twice as long as that of the received *Appended Statements* generated even more anticipation than might have been expected for the discovery of the earliest version of perhaps the seminal text in the Chinese philosophical tradition.[11] The initial reports proved to be unfounded, the result of conflating the text of the *Appended Statements* with the following text on the same piece of silk: *Yi zhi yi* or *The Properties of the* Changes. Although there is no title or character count given at the end of the *Appended Statements* text, and although the last column of *The Properties of the* Changes is defective, the first columns of both texts are headed with very clear black, rectangular markers, indicative in the manuscript of a new text.[12] It is now just about universally accepted that the manuscript text of the *Appended Statements* ends in the forty-seventh column of text. The most precise count of characters in the text suggests that the original manuscript included 3,344 characters, of which 2,908 are now legible.[13] Unlike the received version of the *Appended Statements,* which is divided into two parts of twelve chapters each (according to the arrangement of Zhu Xi [A.D. 1130–1200], in which the text is most often encountered in the West), the manuscript shows no evidence of either sections or chapters.

There are three or four fairly extended passages, including some entire chapters, that are not found in the manuscript version of the *Appended Statements.* These are as follows:

a) Chapter A9, the so-called "Dayan" or "Great Elaboration" chapter, which expostulates an elaborate method of divination. Unlike the other passages missing from the manuscript *Appended Statements,* this passage is not found in any of the other manuscript commentaries.

b) Passages in Chapter B5, from "The Master said, 'He who is in danger secures his position'" to "The pivot is the incipience of action and the preview of auspiciousness" (133 characters in all) and from "The Master said, 'Mr. Yan's son is just about there'" until the end of the chapter (149 characters in all), are not found in the manuscript *Appended Statements* but are found in the commentary *Essentials* instead.

c) All of B6, B7, B8, most of B9 (except for "As for the miscellaneous things and manifest virtues, in distinguishing right and wrong, then the lower and middle lines [*sic*] are not complete. The first is greatly important; presence and absence, auspiciousness and inauspiciousness will then be knowable"), and all of B10 and B11 (again, according to Zhu Xi's arrangement) are found not in the manuscript *Appended Statements,* but rather in the following text, *The Properties of the* Changes.

There are also other textual differences, less structural but no less important, between the manuscript text and the received text. These differences have led already to an important debate over the original nature of the *Appended Statements,* involving two related issues: the

21

priority of the two textual traditions, and the original nature of the *Appended Statements.* This debate seems to have been opened in 1989 by Chen Guying, now editor-in-chief of a new journal entitled *Researches on Daoist Culture.*[14] Chen and his followers argue that the *Appended Statements* originally derived from Daoist circles, though it was subsequently added to by Confucians. Indeed, one of these followers, Wang Baoxuan, apparently the only one of them to have seen the complete Mawangdui manuscript at the time of writing, has gone one step further to argue that the manuscript text preserves this Daoist orientation, the subsequent Confucian accretions being found instead in the manuscript's *The Properties of the* Changes commentary.[15] On the other hand, this "Daoist" view has been rebutted, most vigorously by Liao Mingchun, another of those who seem to have had greatest access to the manuscript.[16] Since this debate is part and parcel of an ongoing reexamination, taking place in both China and the West, of the general nature of Warring States, Qin, and Han intellectual history, it seems prudent here just to note its existence and to look forward to future developments in this regard.[17]

THE PROPERTIES OF THE CHANGES

Following the *Appended Statements,* the next column begins with a black, rectangular mark indicative of the beginning of a text, and then the words: "The Master said: 'The propriety of the *Changes* lies only in the yin and yang.'" Although the final column of this text is almost completely illegible, all but obliterating the title and character count, there is now a growing consensus that it is an independent text which is best referred to as *Yi zhi yi* 易之義. The text is at least 45 columns long, though due to a break in the silk in the middle of the text it is possible that there were originally two or three columns more than this. A rough approximation of the number of characters in the text would be about 3,100. The final quarter or more of the text consists of sections B6 through B11 of the received *Appended Statements,* sections that, as already noted, are missing in the manuscript *Appended Statements*; this is one of the main reasons that scholars initially believed that this text was a continuation of the *Appended Statements.* Also included in this commentary (at about lines 13–15) are the first three sections of the received *Shuo gua* or *Discussion of the Hexagrams* commentary.

In contrast to the debate about the nature of the manuscript *Appended*

Statements, all scholars agree that the *The Properties of the* Changes commentary presents a very strong Confucian bias. After a brief introductory passage discussing the interplay of yin and yang, the text goes through a sequential discussion of many of the 64 hexagrams of the *Zhouyi*. These discussions, which are reminiscent of those in the *Shuo gua* commentary, focus almost entirely on the names of the hexagrams. It is again worth noting that the sequence in which they are presented is generally that of the received text, rather than that of the manuscript *Zhouyi*. Because the text is badly preserved here, I will quote just a few of the hexagram discussions by way of illustrating its nature.

> *Song,* "Lawsuit," derives from suspicion. *Shi,* "The Troops," derives from carting. *Bi,* "Alliance," derives from fewness of number. . . . [*Yi,* "Increase":] *Tai,* "Greatness," is the intercourse between the top and bottom. *Fu,* "The Wife," is the perversion of [yin] and yang.

After then quoting the first three sections of the received *Discussion of the Hexagrams* commentary (cols. 13–15), *The Properties of the* Changes turns to a detailed discussion of the first two hexagrams: *Jian,* "The Key," and *Chuan,* "The Flow." This discussion begins with a categorization of *Jian* as representing martial virtues and *Chuan* as representing civil virtues, which, though by no means incongruous with the standard interpretations of these two hexagrams, is nonetheless rather unique.

> This is why the appropriateness of heaven is hard and vigorous, moving without cease; its auspiciousness is to protect merit. Without softness to rescue them, (even) those that do not die necessarily perish. What sets yang in motion perishes, which is why fire is not auspicious. The appropriateness of earth is soft and weak, submerged and not moving; its auspiciousness is to [protect calm. Without] hardness to . . . it, it would be exhausted and lost. What sets yin in motion is submersion, which is why water is not auspicious. Therefore, the propriety of the martial is to protect merit and constantly to die; the propriety of the civil is to protect calm and constantly to be exhausted. This is why only after the soft is not warped is the civil able to be victorious, and why only after the hard is not broken is the martial able to be calm. The *Changes* says: "Straight, square and great, not [repeated, auspicious]" . . . is lodged in the civil and

martial; this is the commendation of the *Changes*. The Master said: "That the six hard lines of *Jian* are able to be square is due to the virtue of (kings) Tang and Wu. . . . That the six soft lines of *Chuan* are able to comply with each other is due to the perfection of (king) Wen."

After this detailed discussion of *Jian* and *Chuan* hexagrams, the commentary ends with the several passages found in sections B6 through B11 of the received *Appended Statements*. While the borrowed passages generally correspond reasonably well to their counterparts in the received text, they include a number of interpolations, perhaps suggesting that the editor of *The Properties of the* Changes was quoting a preexisting text of the *Appended Statements*.[18]

THE ESSENTIALS

Although neither the last column of *The Properties of the* Changes nor the next several columns of text are preserved well, a black, rectangular marker is apparently clearly visible marking a new text. Some 20 columns later, the text ends in the middle of a column, followed by a space and then the word *yao* 要, "essentials," evidently the title of the commentary following *The Properties of the* Changes, and then, after another space, the number "1,648." Based on the average of slightly more than seventy characters per column seen throughout the Mawangdui *Yijing* manuscript, Liao Mingchun estimates that there were probably 24 columns of text in the original manuscript. Of the total of 1,648 characters, only about 1,040 are still legible.

The text is divided into several sections by black dots. The first third or so of the text is too fragmentary to attempt a description. Columns 9–12 are essentially the latter half of section B5 of the received text of the *Appended Statements*. Columns 12–18 record a conversation between an aged Confucius and his disciple Zi Gong concerning the *Changes* and especially the role of divination in its use. The last section, from the bottom of column 18 through column 24, concerns the hexagrams *Sun*, "Decrease," and *Yi*, "Increase," which Confucius is here made to regard as the culmination of wisdom in the *Zhouyi*.

The conversation between Confucius and Zi Gong, and especially Zi Gong's apparent misunderstanding of Confucius's interest in the text, has already attracted considerable scholarly interest.[19] Zi Gong criticizes Confucius for changing his teaching about the importance of the *Yijing* and for performing divinations. Confucius responds that while he does indeed perform divinations, there is a major difference between his use of the text and that of others: he regards the *Yijing* as a repository of ancient wisdom. This would seem to signal recognition of a dramatic change in the function and status of the text.

> Zi Gong said: "Does the Master also believe in milfoil divination?" The Master said: "I am right in only seventy out of one hundred prognostications. Even with the prognostications of Liangshan of Zhou one necessarily follows it most of the time and no more." The Master said: "As for the *Changes,* I do indeed put its prayers and divinations last, only observing its virtue and propriety. Intuiting the commendations to reach the number, and understanding the number to reach virtue, is to have humaneness and to put it into motion properly. If the commendations do not lead to the number, then one merely acts as a magician; if the number does not lead to virtue, then one merely acts as a scribe. The divinations of scribes and magicians tend toward it but are not yet there; delight in it but are not correct. Perhaps it will be because of the *Changes* that sires of later generations will doubt me. I seek its virtue and nothing more. I am on the same road as the scribes and magicians but end up differently. The conduct of the gentleman's virtue is to seek blessings; that is why he sacrifices, but little; the righteousness of his humaneness is to seek auspiciousness; that is why he divines, but rarely. Do not the divinations of priests and magicians come last!"

MU HE, ZHAO LI

The Mawangdui *Yijing* manuscript ends with a very lengthy text that was first published in transcription only in June of 1995, and has thus not yet been the subject of any research. The column immediately after the last column of *Essentials* begins with a black, rectangular mark, followed with the words: "Mu He asked of his teacher, saying." After about seventy columns of text, there is a blank space followed by the two characters "Mu He" 繆和, but no character count. The next column of text begins, without a black, rectangular mark, with the words: "Zhao

Li asked saying." The text continues for another 14 columns, in the middle of the last of which are the two characters "Zhao Li" 昭力 followed, after a space, by the number "6,000." It is clear that this number 6,000 represents the total character count of both texts *Mu He* and *Zhao Li*; it would seem that they should be regarded as two chapters of a single text.

The first chapter includes questions asked of an unnamed teacher by Mu He and four others: Lü Chang, Wu Meng, Zhang She, and Li Ping. No identifications of any of these figures, or of Zhao Li, seem to have been suggested. Both texts are generally interrogatory in nature, and their content is also fairly similar, though *Mu He* tends to treat more specific questions while *Zhao Li* attempts to draw more general conclusions. They include 27 different sections, divided in the text with black dots. Of these sections, 24 are in *Mu He*. The first 12 sections are initiated by questions regarding individual line statements. Beginning with Section 13 and continuing until Section 24, the form changes; now instead of questions and answers, there are quotations of "the Master," presumably referring to Confucius. In sections 13–18, the Master discusses one line statement per section. Sections 19–24, on the other hand, begin with a historical story and then conclude with the citation of a line statement from the *Zhouyi* as demonstration of the moral of the story, similar to the way that the *Han Shi waizhuan* uses quotations from the *Shijing* or *Classic of Poetry* to prove its points. These historical stories concern events from the reigns of King Zhuang of Chu (613 B.C.), King Goujian of Yue (496 B.C.), King Fucha of Wu (495 B.C.), and Lord Wen of Wei (446 B.C.).

Zhao Li consists of three sections, in all of which Zhao Li asks his teacher questions. Whereas *Mu He* discusses one hexagram or line statement at a time, *Zhao Li* groups several of them together and then draws a general conclusion. For instance, its first section discusses the Six in the Fourth line of *Shi*, "The Troops" (M37/R7), and the Nine in the Third and Six in the Fifth lines of *Taixu*, "Great Storage" (M10/R26), by way of illustrating relations between a ruler and his ministers.

Neither *Mu He* nor *Zhao Li* employs any of the numerological exegetical techniques that would become popular later in the Han dynasty to explain the significance of the various hexagram and line statements that they discuss. Indeed, in only one place does *Mu He* even employ a trigram "image" to explain a statement. Instead, *Mu He* focuses on the virtue and righteousness to be gained from the text, while *Zhao Li* is devoted entirely to discussing its political significance.

26

CONCLUSIONS

The scholarly world has had a long wait to get to see the manuscript text of the *Yijing* discovered at Mawangdui in 1973. Now that it is available, it is not surprising that attention should center to a great extent on the relative similarities and differences between the manuscript and the received text. Other scholars intrigued by the heretofore unknown are beginning to produce studies of the other Mawangdui commentaries: *The Several Disciples Asked, The Properties of the* Changes, *Essentials,* and *Mu He, Zhao Li.* All of these studies will certainly contribute to our understanding of that most crucial period in the development of the *Yijing* tradition—the half-century or so on either side of the Qin–Han transition. It is my hope that the English translation of this manuscript presented in this volume will encourage Western students of the *Yijing* to join in the reevaluation of that tradition.

1	2	3	4	5	6	7	8
Jian	*Fu*	*Yuan*	*Li*	*Song*	*Tongren*	*Wumeng*	*Gou*
鍵	婦	掾	禮	訟	同人	无孟	狗
䷀	䷋	䷠	䷉	䷅	䷌	䷘	䷫
乾	否	遯	履	訟	同人	无妄	姤
Qian	*Pi*	*Dun*	*Lü*	*Song*	*Tongren*	*Wuwang*	*Gou*
1	12	33	10	6	13	25	44

9	10	11	12	13	14	15	16
Gen	*Taixu*	*Bo*	*Sun*	*Meng*	*Fan*	*Yi*	*Gu*
根	泰畜	剝	損	蒙	繁	頤	箇
䷳	䷙	䷖	䷨	䷃	䷕	䷚	䷑
艮	大畜	剝	損	蒙	賁	頤	蠱
Gen	*Daxu*	*Bo*	*Sun*	*Meng*	*Ben*	*Yi*	*Gu*
52	26	23	41	4	22	27	18

17	18	19	20	21	22	23	24
Gan	*Ru*	*Bi*	*Jian*	*Jie*	*Jiji*	*Zhun*	*Jing*
贛	繻	比	蹇	節	既濟	屯	井
䷜	䷄	䷇	䷦	䷻	䷾	䷂	䷯
坎	濡	比	蹇	節	既濟	屯	井
Kan	*Xu*	*Bi*	*Jian*	*Jie*	*Jiji*	*Zhun*	*Jing*
29	5	8	39	60	63	3	48

25	26	27	28	29	30	31	32
Chen	*Taizhuang*	*Yu*	*Shaoguo*	*Guimei*	*Jie*	*Feng*	*Heng*
辰	泰壯	余	少過	歸妹	解	豐	恆
䷲	䷡	䷏	䷽	䷵	䷧	䷶	䷟
震	大壯	豫	小過	歸妹	解	豐	恆
Zhen	*Dazhuang*	*Yu*	*Xiaoguo*	*Guimei*	*Jie*	*Feng*	*Heng*
51	34	16	62	54	40	55	32

33	34	35	36	37	38	39	40
Chuan	*Tai*	*Qian*	*Lin*	*Shi*	*Mingyi*	*Fu*	*Deng*
川	泰	嗛	林	師	明夷	復	登
䷁	䷊	䷎	䷒	䷆	䷣	䷗	䷭
坤	泰	謙	臨	師	明夷	復	升
Kun	*Tai*	*Qian*	*Lin*	*Shi*	*Mingyi*	*Fu*	*Sheng*
2	11	15	19	7	36	24	46

41	42	43	44	45	46	47	48
Duo	*Guai*	*Zu*	*Qin*	*Kun*	*Le*	*Sui*	*Taiguo*
奪	訣	卒	欽	困	勒	隋	泰過
䷹	䷪	䷬	䷞	䷮	䷰	䷐	䷛
兌	夬	萃	咸	困	革	隨	大過
Dui	*Guai*	*Cui*	*Xian*	*Kun*	*Ge*	*Sui*	*Daguo*
58	43	45	31	47	49	17	28

49	50	51	52	53	54	55	56
Luo	*Dayou*	*Jin*	*Lü*	*Guai*	*Weiji*	*Shi Ke*	*Ding*
羅	大有	溍	旅	乖	未濟	筮嗑	鼎
䷝	䷍	䷢	䷷	䷥	䷿	䷔	䷱
離	大有	晉	旅	睽	未濟	噬嗑	鼎
Li	*Dayou*	*Jin*	*Lü*	*Kui*	*Weiji*	*Shi Ke*	*Ding*
30	14	35	56	38	64	21	50

57	58	59	60	61	62	63	64
Suan	*Shaoshu*	*Guan*	*Jian*	*Zhongfu*	*Huan*	*Jiaren*	*Yi*
筭	少藝	觀	漸	中復	渙	家人	益
䷸	䷈	䷓	䷴	䷼	䷺	䷤	䷩
巽	小畜	觀	漸	中孚	渙	家人	益
Xun	*Xiaoxu*	*Guan*	*Jian*	*Zhongfu*	*Huan*	*Jiaren*	*Yi*
57	9	20	53	61	59	37	42

The sequence number and name above each hexagram picture refer to the Mawangdui manuscript, while those below refer to the received text.

PRINCIPLES OF TRANSLATION

In the following translations, I endeavor to translate the Mawangdui *Yijing* manuscript. This is not as straightforward a proposition as it may sound. Anyone who has worked with early manuscript materials is aware that they are filled with graphs the standard meanings of which are palpably nonsensical in the context but are homophonous or nearly homophonous with words that would be sensible; these are so-called phonetic loans. A translator who insisted on translating a manuscript "just as it is written," taking every graph as standing for the word with which it is conventionally associated in the standardized writing system, would surely not do justice to the text. On the other hand, the possibility of phonetic loans does not give the translator license to change the text at will. To the extent that the translator can reach a "doctrine of the mean" between these two courses, he will probably best represent the text as it was intended by its copyist.

In the case of a manuscript with a received counterpart, such as the hexagram and line statements and the *Xici* commentary of the *Yijing,* the problems of interpretation and translation are both lessened and heightened at the same time.[1] Since there is a stable text against which to compare readings of the manuscript, one can tell immediately whether the graph the manuscript's copyist used to write a word is the same graph used by others, especially the great Han dynasty scholars to whom we trace the textual tradition of the extant *Yijing*. When the graphs match, we have a strong presumption, though not certainty, that the graph represents the word (or words) with which it is usually associated. When the graphs do not match, however, the translator must choose

30

between one or the other, or perhaps even a third reading. There has been a strong tendency among the few studies of the Mawangdui *Yijing* that have appeared to date to assume that the received text is more or less definitive, and that when the Mawangdui manuscript varies from it the manuscript ought to be "corrected." This is often obviously the case; for example, when the Nine in the Fifth line of *Jian* 鍵, "The Key" (hexagram 1 in the manuscript and also in the received text, in which the hexagram is called *Qian* 乾, usually understood as "The Heavenly Principle"), reads in the manuscript *fei long zai tian* 翡龍在天, instead of the received text's *fei long zai tian* 飛龍在天, there can be no doubt that *fei* 翡, "red-feathered sparrow," has been used to write the homophonous *fei* 飛, "to fly," and that the manuscript should be translated "flying dragon in the sky," identical to the received text. On the other hand, particularly in the case of a text such as the *Yijing,* the enigmatic images of which have often inspired wildly different interpretations, the discovery of an early manuscript (in this case, one 350 years older than the next-earliest version of the text[2]) provides a wonderful opportunity to consider afresh other possible readings. For instance, when the manuscript writes the independent formulas *zheng ji* 征吉, "to campaign is auspicious," or *zheng xiong* 征凶, "to campaign is inauspicious," or *you fu* 有孚, variously understood as "there is a captive" or "there is sincerity," as *zheng ji* 正吉, "to be upright is auspicious," *zheng xiong* 正凶, "to be upright is inauspicious," and *you fu* 有復, "there is a return," there seems to me to be no good basis on which to decide between the readings, and thus I have preferred to maintain the "literal" sense of the manuscript.

Fortunately, in other cases of variora between the manuscript and the received text, there is other evidence besides the "divining" of the translator to help us choose between the alternatives. Put in broadest terms this evidence can be either internal to the text, primarily grammatical and contextual in nature, or external, primarily other variora within the received textual tradition. Allow me to illustrate the role of these sorts of evidence with two examples each, one in which the received text seems to be the best reading, two in which the manuscript text is either the best reading or at least a viable alternative, and one where neither the received text nor the manuscript seems to be the best reading but rather the variation between them points to yet a third reading.

In the Nine in the Fifth line of *Fu* 婦, "The Wife" (hexagram 2, or in the received text *Pi* 否, "Negation," hexagram 12), for the manuscript's *qi wang qi wang, ji yu fu sang* 其亡其亡, 繫于枹桑, which literally

31

means "it is gone, it is gone, hit on a drum-stick mulberry," the received text reads *qi wang qi wang, xi yu bao sang* 其亡其亡, 繫于苞桑, literally, "it is gone, it is gone, tied to a bushy mulberry." I think it goes without saying that the *fu* (archaic *b'iog) 枹, "drum-stick," of the manuscript is a phonetic loan for *bao* (archaic *pog) 苞, "bushy," as written in the received text. The variation between *ji* 擊, "to hit," and *xi* 繫, "to tie" (which, it should probably be pointed out, is systematic throughout the manuscript), while not quite so obvious, can probably also be decided in favor of the received text's reading given the presence of the preposition *yu* 于, which is standard with *xi*, "to tie," but would be hard to explain coming after *ji*, "to hit." Thus, in my translation I assume that the copyist intended to write *qi wang qi wang, xi yu bao sang*, "it is gone, it is gone, tied to a bushy mulberry," despite the graphs that he used to write it.

An example in which context seems to support several of the manuscript's readings in place of those of the received text is the Nine in the Second line of *Jing* 井, "The Well" (hexagram 24, or 48 in the received text). In the manuscript, the line reads *jing du she fu, wei bi ju* 井瀆射付, 唯敝句, as opposed to the received text's *jing gu she fu, weng bi lou* 井谷射鮒, 甕敝漏, which the Wilhelm/Baynes translation gives as "At the wellhole one shoots fishes. The jug is broken and leaks."[3] Of the four variora in this single line, one represents simple classifier variation, with the received text's reading "filling out" the unelaborated form seen in the manuscript: the *fu* 付 (literally, "to attach to") of the manuscript is surely the protograph of the received text's *fu* 鮒, a small silver fish such as smelt. Almost as unproblematic, it seems to me, is the preferability of the manuscript's *du* 瀆, "ditch; murky" over the received text's *gu* 谷, "valley; mouth of a stream," especially when this line is compared to other lines of the same hexagram, such as the Initial Six line, which reads *jing ni bu shi* 井泥不食, "If the well is muddy do not (eat:) drink"; thus, this first clause of the Nine in the Second line is probably best translated as "If the well is murky shoot the smelt." The two variora in the second clause, *wei* 唯, "only; to be" for *weng* 甕 "earthenware jug," and (*ju* 句:) *gou* 苟, "fish-trap" for *lou* 漏, "to leak," are interdependent. The writing of *ju* 句 for *gou* 苟 is common throughout the Mawangdui manuscripts,[4] and can be assumed here, in which case the association between fishing by fish-trap and by shooting, as in the first clause, would seem to recommend it over the reading *lou*, "to leak," of the received text. Once this emendation is made, then it is necessary also to accept the copular *wei* 唯 of the manuscript in place of the *weng* 甕, "earthenware jug," the graph of which includes the 隹 component of *wei*. In the absence of any evidence other than just the two texts, the inter-clausal consistency perhaps recommends the reading of the manuscript: "If the well is murky shoot the smelt; it is only (because of) the worn-out fish-trap."

Sometimes there is other evidence that can be helpful in deciding between two alternative readings. The Six in the Third line of *Guimei* 歸妹, "Returning Maiden" (M29/R54), reads in the manuscript *gui mei yi ru* 歸妹以嬬, "The returning maiden with consorts," whereas in the received text it reads *gui mei yi xu* 歸妹以須, which is so unclear that it has given rise to such opposite interpretations as "The marrying maiden as a slave,"[5] and "The Marrying Maiden should take a waiting approach to marriage."[6] Comparison with the parallel Initial Nine line, *gui mei yi di* 歸妹以娣, "The returning maiden with younger sisters,"[7] would doubtless suffice for us to decide in favor of the manuscript's *ru* 嬬, "weak; secondary wife," as against the *xu* 須, "beard; to wait; to need" of the received text. The case is all but clinched when we find evidence that at least five other texts from the Han period also read *ru* 嬬[8]; since there is no chance of cross-influence between these other texts and the manuscript, which after all was underground from 168 B.C. on, we can only conclude that they all derive from a common earlier text.

Finally, there are also cases in which neither the manuscript nor the received text seems to be the best reading; rather, the comparison of their readings may point to yet a third reading. In one case that I might cite as an example, we are fortunate that the third reading is attested in other Han-period texts, and thus is almost certainly the best reading. The Six in the Fourth line of *Yi* 頤, "Jaws" (M15/R27), reads in the manuscript: *dian yi; ji; hu shi chenchen, qi rong didi; wu jiu* 顛頤, 吉, 虎視沈沈, 其容笛笛, 无咎, the superficial translation of which might read something like: "Upside-down jaws; auspicious. The tiger looks in such a submerged way, his appearance is so flute-like; there is no trouble." In the received text, the line reads: *dian yi; ji; hu shi dandan, qi yu zhuzhu; wu jiu* 顛頤, 吉, 虎視眈眈, 其欲逐逐, 无咎, for which a literal translation might be: "Upside-down jaws; auspicious. The tiger looks with eyes downcast, his desires are so pursuing; there is no trouble." Of the variora in this line, *chen* 沈, "to submerge," as opposed to *dan* 眈, "eyes downcast," is simple classifier variation, both graphs being used to write the word *dan*, "eyes downcast." In the case of the second variorum, the manuscript's *rong* 容, "appearance," as opposed to the

33

received text's *yu* 欲, "to desire," the choice is not so simple, if indeed a choice can even be made. The two words are related both graphically (both sharing the 谷 component) and phonetically (the archaic pronunciations being *jiwong vs. *jiwok), and both seem to be sensible in the context, even if the context is not immediately sensible. The modifier describing the "appearance" or "desires" is, in the manuscript, *di* 笛, a type of flute, or *zhu* 逐, "to pursue," in the received text. Since *di*, "flute," seems not to be sensible here, and its archaic pronunciation is very close to that of the received text's *zhu* (*diekw vs. *drjekw), it might be reasonable to consider it as a simple phonetic loan and accept the reading of the received text: "so pursuing." However, there are at least three other Han-period texts cited as reading *you* 攸, 悠, or 筃, "far; distant; sad, pensive."[9] Since in the Han period *you* (*regw) was a virtual homophone of *di* and *zhu*, it is also a viable alternative here. Indeed, since the reduplicative *youyou* 悠悠 was a common modifier in Western Zhou times (occurring twelve times in the *Shijing* or *Classic of Poetry*), whereas *zhuzhu* does not occur in any early source other than this line statement, and since the downcast eyes of the tiger, mentioned in the preceding clause, might give him the appearance of being "sad" rather than "pursuing," all of this seems to me to suggest that *you* 悠, "sad," is the best reading here. Thus, combining all of the available evidence, we come to the following reading: *hu shi dandan, qi rong youyou* 虎視眈眈, 其容悠悠, which might best be translated: "The tiger looks with eyes downcast, his appearance is so sad."

It is not my intention, either here or in the notes to the translation, to provide this amount of discussion for all of the variora between the manuscript and the received text of the *Yijing*. While I will endeavor to point out, in notes, all but the most inconsequential variora, I will generally restrict my comments to just the different meanings of the readings, content that the translation will reflect my choice between them. I hope that this level of annotation will hit a happy medium, providing general readers with the range of variations available without burdening the text unduly, while at the same time providing just enough information so that the careful scholar will be able to intuit the reasons behind my choices but still leaving plenty of work for her in the future. For essentially the same reasons, I have also not attempted to substantiate or explain my translations. This is very much a first effort to make available to a wider reading audience, both general and scholarly, the earliest, yet newest, text of one of the greatest books of world literature, the *Yijing*. I look forward to the corrections that others will certainly make.

CONVENTIONS OF PRESENTATION

a) For the *Zhouyi,* i.e., the hexagram and line statements, the sequence of hexagrams follows that of the manuscript; I provide in a note to the hexagram name the hexagram's number in the received sequence. I also indicate there if the hexagram name differs in the two texts.

b) For each hexagram, I provide on the left-hand side of facing pages the original Chinese text of both the manuscript (at the top of the page) and the received text (at the bottom of the page); the translation is given on the right-hand side, with end notes describing the variora between the readings of the manuscript and the received text. At places where the manuscript is defective, I base the translation on the received text, enclosing it in square brackets [ ].

c) The translation of the line statements is designed to differentiate what I view as the three constituent parts of a line statement: the Image (single indentation), Injunction (double indentation), and Prognostication/Verification (triple indentation). For discussion of these terms, see Shaughnessy, "The Composition of the *Zhouyi,*" 139–58.

d) For the various commentaries, I provide the Chinese text of only the manuscript. For passages where there is a received counterpart, I again note variora between the reading of the manuscript and the received text. Passages of *The Several Disciples Asked* and *The Essentials* that have received counterparts are indicated by italics in the translation. At places where the manuscript is defective and there is a received text, I base the translation on the received text, enclosing it in square brackets [ ]. Where there is no received text, I use two dots .. to indicate a single missing character, and three dots . . . to indicate an indeterminate number of missing characters.

e) I indicate in parentheses ( ) the end of columns of text within each commentary. Paragraph breaks are those of the transcriptions by Chen Songchang and/or Liao Mingchun.

f) For the commentaries, I identify in notes quotations of the *Zhouyi* hexagram and line statements, providing the number of the hexagram in both the manuscript and the received text's sequence.

THE *ZHOUYI*

☰ 鍵 1

鍵元亨利貞

初九浸龍勿用

九二見龍在田利見大人

九三君子終日鍵〻夕泥若厲无咎

九四或鰝在淵无咎

九五翟龍在天利見大人

尙九抗龍有悔

迵九見群龍無首吉

☰ 乾 1

乾元亨利貞

初九潛龍勿用

九二見龍在田利見大人

九三君子終日乾乾夕惕若厲无咎

九四或躍在淵无咎

九五飛龍在天利見大人

上九亢龍有悔

用九見群龍無首吉

38

1. *JIAN*, "THE KEY"[1] ☰

The Key: Primary reception[2]; beneficial to determine.

Initial Nine:
>   Submersed[3] dragon;
>>   do not use.

Nine in the Second:
>   Appearing dragon in the fields;
>>   beneficial to see the great man.

Nine in the Third:
>   The gentleman throughout the day is so initiating;
>   at night he is ashen[4] as if in danger;
>>   there is no trouble.

Nine in the Fourth:
>   And now jumping[5] in the depths;
>>   there is no trouble.

Nine in the Fifth:
>   Flying[6] dragon in the heavens;
>>   beneficial to see the great man.

Elevated[7] Nine:
>   Resisting[8] dragon;
>>   there is regret.

Unified[9] Nine:
>   See the flock of dragons without heads;
>>   auspicious.

䷁婦 2

婦之非人不利君子貞大往小來

初六犮茅茹以其蓍貞吉亨

六二枹承小人吉大人不亨

六三枹憂

九四有命无咎檮羅齒

九五休婦大人吉其〻亡〻擊于枹桑

尙九頉婦先不後喜

䷋否 12

否之匪人不利君子貞大往小來

初六拔茅茹以其彙貞吉亨

六二包承小人吉大人否亨

六三包羞

九四有命无咎疇離祉

九五休否大人吉其亡其亡繫于苞桑

上九傾否先否後喜

2. *FU*, "THE WIFE"[1] ䷋

The wife's non-persons; not beneficial for the gentleman to determine;
the great go, the little come.

Initial Six:
    Plucking[2] the cogongrass stem with its roots[3];
        determination is auspicious;
           receipt.

Six in the Second:
    Wrapping[4] the steamed offering:
           for the little man auspicious,
           for the great man negative;
           receipt.

Six in the Third:
    (Wrapping:) Enfolding sadness.[5]

Nine in the Fourth:
    There is a command;
           there is no trouble;
    blessings fastened to the split-log.[6]

Nine in the Fifth:
    Beneficent wife;
           for the great man auspicious;
    it is lost, it is lost,
    tied[7] to a bushy[8] mulberry.

Elevated Nine:
    Momentary[9] wife;
           at first negative,[10] later happy.

☶ 掾 3

掾亨小利貞

初六掾尾厲勿用有攸往

六二共之用黃牛之勒莫之勝奪

九三爲掾有疾厲畜僕妾吉

九四好掾君子吉小人不

九五嘉掾貞吉

尙九肥掾先不利

☶ 遯 33

遯亨小利貞

初六遯尾厲勿用有攸往

六二執之用黃牛之革莫之勝說

九三係遯有疾厲畜臣妾吉

九四好遯君子吉小人否

九五嘉遯貞吉

上九肥遯无不利

3. YUAN, "WIELDING"[1] ☰

Wielding: Receipt; little beneficial to determine.

Initial Six:
> Wield the tail;
>> danger;
>> do not herewith have any place to go.

Six in the Second:
> Uphold[2] it using a yellow ox's bridle[3];
>> no one will succeed in overturning[4] it.

Nine in the Third:
> Do[5] the wielding;
>> there is sickness;
>> danger;
>> keeping servants[6] and consorts is auspicious.

Nine in the Fourth:
> Good wielding;
>> for the gentleman auspicious,
>> for the little man negative.[7]

Nine in the Fifth:
> Enjoyable wielding;
>> determination is auspicious.

Elevated Nine:
> Fattened wielding;
>> there is nothing[8] not beneficial.

☰ 禮 4

禮虎尾不眞人亨

初九錯禮往无咎

九二禮道亶ゝ幽人貞吉

六三眇能視跛能利禮虎尾眞人兇武人迴于大君

九四禮虎尾朔ゝ終吉

九五夬禮貞厲

尙九視禮巧翟其震元吉

☰ 履 10

履虎尾不咥人亨

初九素履往无咎

九二履道坦坦幽人貞吉

六三眇能視跛能履履虎尾咥人凶武人爲于大君

九四履虎尾愬愬終吉

九五夬履貞厲

上九視履考祥其旋元吉

4. *LI*, "TREADING"[1] ☰

Treading on a tiger's tail; not a real[2] man; receipt.

Initial Nine:
> Counter[3] treading;
>> in going there is no trouble.

Nine in the Second:
> Treading the road so sincerely[4];
>> the dark man's determination is auspicious.

Six in the Third:
> The blind are able to see,
> the lame are able to tread.[5]
> Treading on a tiger's tail;
>> for a real man inauspicious.
> A military man is united[6] with the great lord.

Nine in the Fourth:
> Treading on a tiger's tail so panicky[7];
>> in the end auspicious.

Nine in the Fifth:
> Resolute[8] treading;
>> determination is dangerous.

Elevated Nine:
> Looking and treading, crafty[9] and soaring[10] its revolving[11];
>> prime auspiciousness.

䷅ 訟 5

訟有復洫寧克吉冬兒利用見大人不利涉大川

初六不永所事少有言冬吉

九二不克訟歸而逋其邑人三百戶无省

六三食舊德貞厲或從王事无成

九四不克訟復即命俞安貞吉

九五訟元吉

尚九或賜之服帶終朝三搋之

䷅ 訟 6

訟有孚窒惕中吉終凶利見大人不利涉大川

初六不永所事小有言終吉

九二不克訟歸而逋其邑人三百戶无眚

六三食舊德貞厲終吉或從王事无成

九四不克訟復即命渝安貞吉

九五訟元吉

上九或錫之鞶帶終朝三褫之

5 . *SONG, "LAWSUIT"*[1] ☰

Lawsuit: There is a return[2]; pitying[3] and tranquil[4], it succeeds to be[5] auspicious, but in the end[6] is inauspicious; beneficial herewith[7] to see the great man; not beneficial to ford the great river.

Initial Six:
>   Not perpetuating where it serves;
>>   there are a few[8] words;
>>   in the end auspicious.

Nine in the Second:
>   Not succeeding at the lawsuit;
>   returning and fleeing, three hundred households
>   of his city people are without inspection.[9]

Six in the Third:
>   Eating old virtue;
>>   determination is dangerous.[10]
>   Someone follows the king's service, without completion.

Nine in the Fourth:
>   Not succeeding at the lawsuit;
>   returning and attending to the command,
>   it changes[11] to peace;
>>   determination is auspicious.

Nine in the Fifth:
>   Lawsuit;
>>   prime auspiciousness.

Elevated Nine:
>   Someone awards[12] him a leather[13] belt,
>   by the end of the morning thrice strips[14] it.

☲ 同人 6

同人于野亨利涉大川利君子貞

初九同人于門无咎

六二同人于宗闔

九三服容□莽登其高□三歲不興

□□□□庸弗克攻吉

九五同人先號桃後芙大師克相遇

尙九同人于茭无悔

☲ 同人 13

同人于野亨利涉大川利君子貞

初九同人于門无咎

六二同人于宗吝

九三伏戎于莽升其高陵三歲不興

九四乘其墉弗克攻吉

九五同人先號咷而後笑大師克相遇

上九同人于郊无悔

48

6. TONGREN, "GATHERING MEN"[1] ☰

Gathering men in the wilds; receipt; beneficial to ford the great river; beneficial for the gentleman to determine.

Initial Nine:
>   Gathering men at the gate;
>>   there is no trouble.

Six in the Second:
>   Gathering men at the ancestral temple;
>>   distress.[2]

Nine in the Third:
>   Surrendered[3] appearance[4] [in] tall grass:
>   Climbing[5] its high [peak],
>   for three years it does not arise.

[Nine in the Fourth:
>   Riding astride its] wall;
>>   you will not succeed in attacking it;
>>   auspicious.

Nine in the Fifth:
>   Gathering men at first weeping and wailing,
>   but later[6] laughing;
>   the great captains succeed in meeting each other.

Elevated Nine:
>   Gathering men in the pasture[7];
>>   there is no regret.

☶ 无孟 7

无孟元亨利貞非正有省不利有攸往

初九无孟往吉

六二不耕穫不菑餘利□□往

六三无□□□或擊□□□□之得邑人之茲

九四可貞无咎

九五无孟之疾勿樂有喜

尙九无孟之行有省无攸利

☶ 无妄 25

无妄元亨利貞其匪正有眚不利有攸往

初九无妄往吉

六二不耕穫不菑畬則利有攸往

六三无妄之災或繫之牛行人之得邑人之災

九四可貞无咎

九五无妄之疾勿藥有喜

上九无妄行有眚无攸利

Pestilence: Prime receipt; beneficial to determine. If it is not[2] upright there will be an inspection[3]; not beneficial to have someplace to go.

Initial Nine:
> The pestilence goes;
>> auspicious.

Six in the Second:
> Not sowing or reaping,
> not breaking new fields nor working old fields[4];
>> beneficial [to have someplace] to go.[5]

Six in the Third:
> The pestilence's disaster:
> someone ties[6] [it to an ox.
> The traveling man]'s gain,
> is this[7] of the city man.

Nine in the Fourth:
>> Able to be determined;
>>> there is no trouble.

Nine in the Fifth:
> The pestilence's illness:
> there is no medicine but there is happiness.

Elevated Nine:
> The pestilence's motion[8];
> there is an inspection;
>> there is no place to benefit.

☷ 狗 8

狗女壯勿用取女

初六擊于金梯貞吉有攸往見兇贏豨復適屬

九二枹有魚无咎不利賓

九三□□□□□□□□□咎

九四枹无魚正兇

五五以忌枹苬含章或損自天

尙九狗其角閽无咎

☴ 姤 44

姤女壯勿用取女

初六繫于金柅貞吉有攸往見凶贏豕孚蹢躅

九二包有魚无咎不利賓

九三臀无膚其行次且厲无大咎

九四包无魚起凶

九五以杞包瓜含章有隕自天

上九姤其角吝无咎

52

8. GOU, "MEETING"[1] ☰

[Meeting]: The maiden matures; do not herewith take a maiden.

Initial Six:
   Tied[2] to a metal ladder[3];
      determination is auspicious.
      If you have someplace to go,
      you will see inauspiciousness;
   the emaciated piglet[4] returns[5] helter-skelter.

Nine in the Second:
   The wrapper[6] has fish;
         there is no trouble;
      not beneficial to have audience.

Nine in the Third:
   [The buttocks has no skin;
   his movements are hither and thither;
         danger;
         there is no great] trouble.

Nine in the Fourth:
   The wrapper has no fish;
      to be upright[7] is inauspicious.

(Five:) Nine[8] in the Fifth:
   With jealousy[9] wrap the gourd;
   it contains a pattern;
   something[10] drops[11] from the heavens.

Elevated Nine:
   Meeting its horns;
         distress;
         there is no trouble.

䷳ 根 9

根其北不濩其身行其廷不見其人无咎

初六根其止无咎利永貞

六二根其肥不登其隋其心不快

九□□□□戻其胂屬薰心

六四根其貊

六五根其胶言有序悔亡

佲九敦根吉

䷳ 艮 52

艮其背不獲其身行其庭不見其人无咎

初六艮其趾无咎利永貞

六二艮其腓不拯其隨其心不快

九三艮其限列其夤屬薰心

六四艮其身无咎

六五艮其輔言有序悔亡

上九敦艮吉

Stilling his back, but not getting his body: Walking into his courtyard, but not seeing his person; there is no trouble.

Initial Six:
    Stilling his foot:
        there is no trouble;
      beneficial for permanent determination.

Six in the Second:
    Stilling his calves[2]:
    Not raising aloft[3] his rent flesh,
    his heart is not glad.

Nine [in the Third:
    Stilling his midsection]:
    Scratching[4] his spine[5];
        danger;
      smoke the heart.

Six in the Fourth:
    Stilling his torso.[6]

Six in the Fifth:
    Stilling his cheeks:
    words have sequence;
        regret is gone.

Elevated Nine:
    Thick roots;
        auspicious.

☰ 泰畜 10

泰蓄利貞不家食吉利涉大川

初九有厲利巳

九二車說緮

九三良馬逐利根貞曰闌車□利有攸往

六四童牛之鞫元吉

六五哭豨之牙吉

佝九何天之瞿亨

☰ 大畜 26

大畜利貞不家食吉利涉大川

初九有厲利巳

九二輿說輹

九三良馬逐利艱貞曰閑輿衛利有攸往

六四童牛之牿元吉

六五豶豕之牙吉

上九何天之衢亨

56

Great Storage: Beneficial to determine; not eating at home is auspicious; beneficial to ford the great river.

Initial Nine:
> There is danger;
> beneficial to stop.

Nine in the Second:
> The cart[2] throws off an axle-strut.[3]

Nine in the Third:
> A fine horse follows[4];
>> beneficial for determination about difficulty.[5]
> It is called a barrier-cart [defense].[6]
>> Beneficial to have someplace to go.

Six in the Fourth:
> The young ox's restraint[7];
>> prime auspiciousness.

Six in the Fifth:
> The crying[8] pig's[9] teeth;
>> auspicious.

Elevated Six:
> How wary[10] is heaven;
>> receipt.

☷ 剝 11

剝不利有攸往

初六剝臧以足戕貞兇

六二剝臧以辯戕貞兇

六三剝无咎

六四剝臧以膚兇

六五貫魚食宮人籠无不利

尙九石果不食君子得車小人剝蘆

☶ 剝 23

剝不利有攸往

初六剝牀以足蔑貞凶

六二剝牀以辨蔑貞凶

六三剝之无咎

六四剝牀以膚凶

六五貫魚以宮人籠无不利

上九碩果不食君子得輿小人剝蘆

58

11. BO, "FLAYING"[1] ䷖

Flaying: Not beneficial to have someplace to go.

Initial Six:
    Flaying the good[2] together with the legs;
        determination about the military is inauspicious.

Six in the Second:
    Flaying the good together with the dividers[3];
        determination about the military is inauspicious.

Six in the Third:
    Flaying[4];
        there is no trouble.

Six in the Fourth:
    Flaying the good together with the skin;
        inauspicious.

Six in the Fifth:
    Strung fish;
    eating[5] the palace men's steamer[6];
        there is nothing not beneficial.

Elevated Nine:
    The stone[7] fruit is not eaten:
    The gentleman obtains a chariot,[8]
    the little man flays a gourd.[9]

☶ 損 12

損有復元吉無咎可貞□有攸往禽之用二巧可用芳
初九已事端往无咎酌損之
九二利貞正兇弗損益之
六三ゝ人行則損一ゝ人ゝ行則得其友
六四損其疾事端有喜无咎
六五益之十偶之龜弗克回元吉
尚九弗損益之无□貞吉有攸往得僕无家

☶ 損 41

損有孚元吉无咎可貞利有攸往曷之用二簋可用享
初九已事遄往无咎酌損之
九二利貞征凶弗損益之
六三三人行則損一人一人行則得其友
六四損其疾使遄有喜无咎
六五或益之十朋之龜弗克違元吉
上九弗損益之无咎貞吉利有攸往得臣无家

12. *SUN*, "DECREASE"[1] ䷨

Decrease: There is a return[2]; prime auspiciousness; there is no trouble.
It can be determined. [Beneficial] to have someplace to go. Why[3] use
two tureens[4]; you can use aromatic grass.[5]

Initial Nine:
>   Already[6] serving the ends[7] in going;
>   there is no trouble;
>   toasting decreases it.

Nine in the Second:
>   Beneficial to determine;
>   to be upright[8] is inauspicious.
>   Not decreasing it, but increasing it.

Six in the Third:
>   If three men move then they will decrease by one man;
>   If one man moves then he will obtain his friend.

Six in the Fourth:
>   Decreasing his illness;
>   serving[9] ends has happiness;
>   there is no trouble.

Six in the Fifth:
>   Increasing[10] it by ten double-strands of turtles;
>   you cannot deflect[11] it;
>   prime auspiciousness.

Elevated Nine:
>   Not decreasing it, but increasing it;
>   there is no [trouble];
>   determination is auspicious;
>   there is someplace to go[12];
>   obtain a servant[13] without family.

☶ 蒙 13

□□□□求童ぃ蒙ぃ求我初筮吉再參擩ぃ即不吉利貞

初六廢蒙利用刑人用說桎梏已往閵

九二枹蒙吉入婦吉子克家

六三勿用取□□□夫不有躬无攸利

□□□蒙閵

六五童蒙□

□□□□□□□利所寇

☶ 蒙 4

蒙亨匪我求童蒙童蒙求我初筮告再三瀆瀆則不告利貞

初六發蒙利用刑人用說桎梏以往吝

九二包蒙吉納婦吉子克家

六三勿用取女見金夫不有躬无攸利

六四困蒙吝

六五童蒙吉

上九擊蒙不利爲寇利禦寇

[Folly: Receipt; it is not we] who seek youthful folly; youthful folly seeks us. The initial milfoil divination is auspicious,[2] but if two or three times drawn out,[3] being drawn out then[4] it is not auspicious; beneficial to determine.

Initial Six:
> Discarding[5] folly;
>> beneficial to use a punished man,
>> and herewith to remove shackles and manacles.
>> What has already[6] gone is distressful.

Nine in the Second:
> Wrapping[7] folly;
>> auspicious.
> Sending in[8] the wife;
>> auspicious.
> The son can marry.

Six in the Third:
> Do not use to take [a woman;
> see the metal] fellow who does not have a torso;
>> there is no place beneficial.

[Six in the Fourth]:
> Bound folly;
>> distress.

Six in the Fifth:
> Youthful folly;
>> [auspicious].

[Elevated Nine:
> Hitting the folly;
>> not beneficial to be a robber],
>> beneficial to have that which[9] robs.

䷕ 繁 14

□□□□有攸往

□□□□□舍車而徒

六二繫其□

六三繫茹濡茹永貞吉

六四繫茹蕃茹白馬翰茹非寇闒詬

六五繫于□□□白戔〻闈終□

□□□□□□

䷕ 賁 22

賁亨小利有攸往

初九賁其趾舍車而徒

六二賁其須

九三賁如濡如永貞吉

六四賁如皤如白馬翰如匪寇婚媾

六五賁于丘園束帛戔戔吝終吉

上九白賁无咎

1 4 . *F A N ,* " L U X U R I A N C E "[1] ䷒

[Luxuriance: Receipt; a little beneficial] to have someplace to go.

[Initial Nine:
    Making luxurious his feet];
    discarding the chariot and going on foot.

Six in the Second:
    Making luxurious his [beard].

Nine in the Third:
    Luxuriantly,[2] glossily;
        permanent determination is auspicious.

Six in the Fourth:
    Luxuriantly, lushly,[3]
    the white horse is lofty-like;
        it is not the robbers who confusedly[4] slander.[5]

Six in the Fifth:
    Luxuriant in [the mound garden;
    the bolt] of silk[6] is so fragmentary;
            distress;
        in the end [auspicious].

[Elevated Nine:
    White luxury;
            there is no trouble.]

䷚ 頤 15

□□□□□□□□口實

初九舍爾靈龜□我短頤凶

六二曰顚頤梻經于北頤正凶

六三梻頤貞凶十年勿用无攸利

六四顚頤吉虎視沈ヽ其容笛ヽ无咎

六五□□□□□□□□□□川

□□□□□□□涉大川

䷚ 頤 27

頤貞吉觀頤自求口實

初九舍爾靈龜觀我朵頤凶

六二顚頤拂經于丘頤征凶

六三拂頤貞凶十年勿用无攸利

六四顚頤吉虎視耽耽其欲逐逐无咎

六五拂經居貞吉不可涉大川

上九由頤厲吉利涉大川

[Jaws: Determination is auspicious. View the jaw; oneself seeking] the mouth's fullness.

Initial Nine:
    Dispensing with your numinous turtle,
    and [viewing] our shortened[2] jaw;
        inauspicious.

Six in the Second:
    Say[3] upside-down jaw;
    threshing[4] the warp at the northern[5] jaw;
        to be upright[6] is inauspicious.

Six in the Third:
    Threshing the jaw;
        determination is inauspicious;
        for ten years do not use it;
        there is no place beneficial.

Six in the Fourth:
    Upside-down jaw;
        auspicious.
    The tiger looks with eyes downcast,[7]
    his appearance[8] is so sad[9];
        there is no trouble.

Six in the Fifth:
    [Threshing the warp;
        determination about dwelling is auspicious;
        one may not ford the great] river.

[Elevated Nine:
    From the jaw;
        danger;
        auspicious;
        beneficial] to ford the great river.

☶ 箇 16

箇□吉亨利涉大川先甲三日後甲三日

初六榦父之箇有子巧无咎厲終吉

□□榦母之箇不可貞

九三榦父之箇少有悔无大咎

六四浴父之箇往見閵

六五榦父之箇用輿

尙九不事王矦高尙其德兇

☶ 蠱 12

蠱元亨利涉大川先甲三日後甲三日

初六幹父之蠱有子考无咎厲終吉

九二幹母之蠱不可貞

九三幹父之蠱小有悔无大咎

六四裕父之蠱往見吝

六五幹父之蠱用譽

上九不事王侯高尙其事

68

16. GU, "BRANCH"[1] ䷑

Branch: [Prime] auspiciousness[2]; receipt. Beneficial to ford the great river; preceding *jia* by three days, following *jia* by three days.

Initial Six:
> The stem father's branch;
> there is a son crafty[3];
>> there is no trouble;
>> danger;
>> in the end auspicious.

[Nine in the Second]:
> The stem mother's branch;
>> one may not determine.

Nine in the Third:
> The stem father's branch;
>> there is a little regret;
>> there is no great trouble.

Six in the Fourth:
> The bathed[4] father's branch;
>> going to see is distressful.

Six in the Fifth:
> The stem father's branch;
>> use a cart.[5]

Elevated Nine:
> Not serving king or lord,
> but highly elevating his virtue[6];
>> inauspicious.[7]

≡ 贛 17

習贛有復寫心亨行有尚

初六習贛人贛閻凶

九二贛有訨求少得

六三來之贛、喩且訨人□贛閻□□

六四奠酒巧詠用缶人茢自牖終无咎

九五贛不盈塭既平无咎

尙六系用讘繆親之于蘈勒三歲弗得兇

≡ 坎 29

習坎有孚維心亨行有尚

初六習坎入于坎窨凶

九二坎有險求小得

六三來之坎坎險且枕入于坎窨勿用

六四樽酒簋貳用缶納約自牖終无咎

九五坎不盈祗既平无咎

上六係用徽纆寘于叢棘三歲不得凶

70

1 7 . *X I G A N ,*
" R E P E A T E D E N T R A P M E N T " [1] ䷜

Repeated[2] Entrapment: There is a return[3]; the appended[4] heart; receipt;
in motion there will be elevation.

Initial Six:
    Repeated entrapment;
    entering[5] the trap pit;
        inauspicious.

Nine in the Second:
    The trap has depth[6];
        in seeking there is a little gain.

Six in the Third:
    Bringing it so entrappedly,
    both steep[7] and deep[8];
    entering the trap pit;
        [do not use it].

Six in the Fourth:
    Offering[9] wine and tureens[10] in pairs[11];
        use earthenware.
    Take in[12] the angelica[13] from the window;
        in the end there is no trouble.

Nine in the Fifth:
    The trap is not filled,
    but the sandbar[14] has been flattened;
        there is no trouble.

Elevated Six:
    The attachment uses braids[15] and cords:
    Place[16] him in the clumped[17] thornbushes,[18]
    for three years not getting him;
        inauspicious.

☰☰ 襦 18

襦有復光亨貞吉利涉大川

初九襦于茭利用恒无咎

九二襦于沙少有言多吉

□三□于泥致寇至

六四襦于血出自穴

六五襦于酒食貞吉

尙六人于穴有不楚客三人來敬之終吉

☰☰ 濡 5

需有孚光亨貞吉利涉大川

初九需于郊利用恒无咎

九二需于沙小有言終吉

九三需于泥致寇至

六四需于血出自穴

九五需于酒食貞吉

上六入于穴有不速之客三人來敬之終吉

18. *RU* (SHORT COAT:), "MOISTENED"[1] ䷄

Moistened: There is a return[2]; radiant receipt; determination is auspicious; beneficial to ford the great river.

Initial Nine:
    Moistened in the pasture[3];
        beneficial to use constancy;
           there is no trouble.

Nine in the Second:
    Moistened in the sand;
        there are a few words;
        in the end auspicious.

[Nine] in the Third:
    [Moistened] in the mud;
        it causes robbers to arrive.

Six in the Fourth:
    Moistened in the blood;
    it comes out from the cavity.

(Six:) Nine[4] in the Fifth:
    Moistened in the wine and food;
        determination is auspicious.

Elevated Six:
    Entering into the cavity;
    there are unbidden[5] guests,
    three men, who come;
        respect them;
           in the end auspicious.

䷇ 比 19

比吉原筮元永貞无咎不寧方來後夫兌

初六有復比之无咎有復盈缶多來或池吉

六二□□□□貞吉

六三比之非人

六四外比之貞吉

九五顯比王用三驅失前禽邑人不戒吉

尙六比无首凶

䷇ 比 8

比吉原筮元永貞无咎不寧方來後夫凶

初六有孚比之无咎有孚盈缶終來有它吉

六二比之自內貞吉

六三比之匪人

六四外比之貞吉

九五顯比王用三驅失前禽邑人不誠吉

上六比之无首凶

Alliance: Auspicious. The original milfoil divination: prime; permanent determination is no trouble. The untranquil land comes; for the latter fellow inauspicious.

Initial Six:
>   There is a return.[2]
>   Ally with him;
>>   there is no trouble.
>   There is a return;
>>   fill the earthenware;
>>>   when winter[3] comes perhaps it will be harmful[4];
>>>   auspicious.

Six in the Second:
>   [Ally with him from within];
>>   determination is auspicious.

Six in the Third:
>   Ally with him the non-human.

Six in the Fourth:
>   From outside ally with him;
>>   determination is auspicious.

Nine in the Fifth:
>   Lustrously ally.
>   The king herewith thrice drives (the hunt),
>   losing the front catch;
>   the city men are not warned[5];
>>   auspicious.

Elevated Six:
>   The ally[6] does not have a head:
>>   inauspicious.

☷ 蹇 20

蹇利西南不利東北利見大人貞吉

初六往蹇來輿

六二王僕蹇ゞ非□之故

□□□□□□

□□往蹇來連

九五大蹇侚來

尚六往蹇來石吉利見大人

☶ 蹇 39

蹇利西南不利東北利見大人貞吉

初六往蹇來譽

六二王臣蹇蹇匪躬之故

九三往蹇來反

六四往蹇來連

九五大蹇朋來

上六往蹇來碩吉利見大人

76

Afoot: Beneficial to the southwest, not beneficial to the northeast; beneficial to see the great man; determination is auspicious.

Initial Six:
Going afoot, coming in a cart.[2]

Six in the Second:
The king's servant[3] is so afoot;
it is not [the body[4]]'s reason.

[Nine in the Third:
Going afoot,[5] coming in return.

Six in the Fourth]:
Going afoot, coming connected.

Nine in the Fifth:
Greatly afoot, the friend[6] comes.

Elevated Six:
Going afoot, coming with swelled head[7];
auspicious;
beneficial to see the great man.

☱ 節 21

節亨枯節不可貞

初九不出戶牖无咎

九二不出門廷凶

六三不節若則□□□咎

六四□□□

□□□□吉往得尙

尙六枯節貞凶悔亡

☴ 節 60

節亨苦節不可貞

初九不出戶庭无咎

九二不出門庭凶

六三不節若則嗟若无咎

六四安節亨

九五甘節吉往有尙

上六苦節貞凶悔亡

21. *JIE*, "MODERATION"[1] ䷻

Moderation: Receipt. Withered[2] moderation; one may not determine.

Initial Nine:
    Not going out of door or window[3];
        there is no trouble.

Nine in the Second:
    Not going out of gate or courtyard;
        inauspicious.

Six in the Third:
    If one is not moderate-like,
    then [one will be sighing-like;
        there is no] trouble.

Six in the Fourth:
    [Placid moderation;
        receipt].

[Nine in the Fifth:
    Sweet moderation];
        auspicious;
    in going there will be elevation.

Elevated Six:
    Withered moderation;
        determination is inauspicious;
        regret is gone.

䷾ 既濟 22

既濟亨小利貞初吉冬乳

初六拽其綸濡其尾无咎

六二婦亡其發勿逐七日得

□□高宗伐鬼□□年克之小人勿用

六四繻有衣茹冬日戒

九五東鄰殺牛以祭不若西鄰之濯祭實受其福吉

尙六濡其首厲

䷾ 既濟 63

既濟亨小利貞初吉終亂

初九曳其輪濡其尾无咎

六二婦喪其茀勿逐七日得

九三高宗伐鬼方三年克之小人勿用

六四繻有衣袽終日戒

九五東鄰殺牛不如西鄰之禴祭實受其福

上六濡其首厲

22. *JIJI*, "ALREADY COMPLETED"[1] ䷾

Already Completed: Receipt; slightly beneficial to determine; initially auspicious, in the end[2] disordered.[3]

Initial (Six:) Nine[4]:
>Dragging[5] his ribbon,[6] wetting his tail;
>>there is no trouble.

Six in the Second:
>The wife loses[7] her hair[8];
>>do not follow,[9]
>>in seven days you will get it.

[Nine in the Third]:
>The High Ancestor attacks the Devil-[land,
>in three years] conquering it;
>>the little man should not use it.

Six in the Fourth:
>The short coat[10] has jacket wadding[11];
>>in winter[12] days be warned.

Nine in the Fifth:
>The eastern neighbor kills an ox in order to sacrifice[13];
>it is not as good as[14] the western neighbor's spring
>sacrifice[15] in really receiving its blessing;
>>auspicious.[16]

Elevated Six:
>Wetting his head;
>>danger.

☳ 屯 23

屯元亨利貞勿用有攸往利律侯

初九半遠利居貞利建侯

六二屯如壇如乘馬煩如非寇闓厚□子貞不字十年乃字

六三即鹿毋莘唯人于林中君子幾不如舍往哭

六四乘馬□如求闓厚往吉无不利

九五屯其膏小貞吉大貞凶

尚六乘馬煩如汲血連如

☳ 屯 3

屯元亨利貞勿用有攸往利建侯

初九磐桓利居貞利建侯

六二屯如邅如乘馬班如匪寇婚媾女子貞不字十年乃字

六三即鹿无虞惟入于林中君子幾不如舍往吝

六四乘馬班如求婚媾往吉无不利

九五屯其膏小貞吉大貞凶

上六乘馬班如泣血漣如

Hoarding: Prime receipt; beneficial to determine. Do not herewith have someplace to go; beneficial to establish[2] a lord.

Initial Nine:
> To and fro[3];
>> beneficial to determine about a dwelling;
>> beneficial to establish a lord.

Six in the Second:
> Hoardingly, earth-moundlike,[4]
> a team of horses vexatious-like[5];
>> it is not robbers who confusedly[6] enrich.[7]
>> The [female] child's determination
>> is not to get pregnant;
>> in ten years then she gets pregnant.

Six in the Third:
> Approaching the deer without ornamentation,[8]
> it is only to enter into the forest.
>> For the gentleman it is just about as good
>> as dispensing with it;
>> to go is distressful.

Six in the Fourth:
> A team of horses [vexatious]-like,
> seeking confused enrichment;
>> to go is auspicious;
>> there is nothing not beneficial.

Nine in the Fifth:
> Hoarding its fat;
>> little determination is auspicious,
>> great determination is inauspicious.

Elevated Six:
> A team of horses vexatious-like,
> dipping[9] blood streamingly.[10]

三 井 24

井莒邑不莒井无亡无得往來井ゝ颭至亦未汲井羆其刑垬凶

初六井泥不食舊井无禽

九二井瀆射付唯敝句

九三井蛙不食爲我心塞可用汲王明並受其福

六四井柝无咎

九五井戾寒潦食

尙六井收勿幕有復元吉

三 井 48

井改邑不改井无喪无得往來井井汔至亦未繘井羸其瓶凶

初六井泥不食舊井无禽

九二井谷射鮒甕敝漏

九三井渫不食爲我心惻可用汲王明並受其福

六四井甃无咎

九五井洌寒泉食

上六井收勿幕有孚元吉

24. *JING*, "THE WELL"[1] ䷯

The Well: Changing[2] the city but not changing the well; there is no loss,[3] there is no gain. Going and coming so orderly; when the drying up[4] arrives one also has not yet drawn[5] from the well; burdening[6] its formed[7] earthenware jug; inauspicious.

Initial Six:
   If the well is muddy do not drink;
   the old well does not have game.

Nine in the Second:
   If the well is murky[8] shoot the smelt;
   it is only the worn-out fish-trap.[9]

Nine in the Third:
   If the well is seeping do not drink;
   it makes my heart blocked[10];
   it can be used to draw water;
   the king's brightness together receives its blessing.

Six in the Fourth:
   The well is walled[11];
               there is no trouble.

Nine in the Fifth:
   If the well is crisscrossed[12] with cold springs, drink.

Elevated Six:
   If the well is arrested, do not cover it;
      there is a return[13];
            prime auspiciousness.

☶ 辰 25

辰亨辰來玥、芙言亞、辰敬百里不亡鈚觴

初九辰來玥、後芙□亞、吉

六二辰來厲意亡貝齎于九陵勿逐七日得

六三辰疏、辰行無省

九四辰逐泥

六五辰往來厲意无亡有事

尙六辰昔、視懼、正凶辰不于其躬于其鄰往无咎閵詬有言

☳ 震 51

震亨震來虩虩笑言啞啞震驚百里不喪匕鬯

初九震來虩虩後笑言啞啞吉

六二震來厲億喪貝躋于九陵勿逐七日得

六三震蘇蘇震行无眚

九四震逐泥

六五震往來厲意无喪有事

上六震索索視矍矍征凶震不于其躬于其鄰无咎婚媾有言

86

Thunder: Receipt; thunder comes so renewingly[2]; laughter[3] and talk *yaya*; thunder alarms[4] one hundred miles; not losing[5] the ladle or goblet.[6]

Initial Nine:
> Thunder comes so renewingly;
> afterwards laughter and talk *yaya*;
>> auspicious.

Six in the Second:
> Thunder comes so dangerously;
> one loses cowries;
> sacrificing[7] to the nine peaks;
>> do not follow,[8]
>> in seven days you will get it.

Six in the Third:
> Thunder is so slow[9];
> thunder moves without inspection.[10]

Nine in the Fourth:
> Thunder is followed by mud.

Six in the Fifth:
> Thunder goes and comes so dangerously;
>> there is no loss,
>> there is service.

Elevated Six:
> Thunder is so clapping[11];
> looking so scared[12];
>> to be upright[13] is inauspicious.
> Thunder is not in his body, but in his neighbor;
>> in going[14] there is no trouble.
>> In confused slander[15] there is talk.

䷲泰壯 26

泰壯利貞

初九壯于止正凶有復

九二貞吉

九三小人用壯君子用亡貞厲羝羊觸藩羸其角

九四貞吉悔亡藩块不羸壯于泰車之緮

六五亡羊于易无悔

尙六羝羊觸藩不能退不能遂无攸利根則吉

䷡大壯 34

大壯利貞

初九壯于趾征凶有孚

九二貞吉

九三小人用壯君子用罔貞厲羝羊觸藩羸其角

九四貞吉悔亡藩決不羸壯于大輿之輹

六五喪羊于易无悔

上六羝羊觸藩不能退不能遂无攸利艱則吉

26. *TAIZHUANG*, "GREAT MATURITY"[1] ䷡

Great Maturity: Beneficial to determine.

Initial Nine:
>   Mature in the foot;
>>   to be upright[2] is inauspicious;
>>   there is a return.[3]

Nine in the Second:
>   Determination is auspicious.

Nine in the Third:
>   The little man uses maturity,
>   the gentleman uses loss[4];
>>   determination is dangerous.
>   A ram butts a fence, and weakens its horns.

Nine in the Fourth:
>>   Determination is auspicious;
>>   regret is gone.
>   The fence[5] block[6] is not weakened,
>   but is matured by the great cart's[7] axle-strut.[8]

Six in the Fifth:
>   Losing[9] sheep at Yi;
>>   there is no regret.

Elevated Six:
>   A ram butts a fence,
>   is not able to retreat and is not able to follow;
>>   there is no place beneficial;
>>   difficult[10] but then auspicious.

䷏ 余 27

餘利建疾行師

初六鳴餘凶

六二疥于石不終日貞吉

六三杆餘悔遲有悔

九四允餘大有得勿疑儚甲讒

六五貞疾恒不死

尙六冥餘成或諭无咎

䷏ 豫 16

豫利建侯行師

初六鳴豫凶

六二介于石不終日貞吉

六三盱豫悔遲有悔

九四由豫大有得勿疑朋盍簪

六五貞疾恒不死

上六冥豫成有渝无咎

Excess: Beneficial to establish a lord and to move troops.

Initial Nine:
    Calling out in excess;
        inauspicious.

Six in the Second:
    Scratched[2] on a rock;
    not to the end of the day;
        determination is auspicious.

Six in the Third:
    A bowl's[3] excess;
        regret; being slow there is regret.

Nine in the Fourth:
    Really[4] excess;
        if one greatly has gain, do not doubt;
    cowries and shells[5] slander.[6]

Six in the Fifth:
        Determination is illness;
        if constant you will not die.

Elevated Six:
    Dark excess;
        if complete perhaps[7] you will be informed[8];
        there is no trouble.

☳ 少過 28

少過亨利貞可小事不可大事翡鳥遺之音不宜上宜下泰吉

初六羿鳥以凶

六二過其祖愚其比不及其君愚其僕无咎

九三弗過仿之從或臧之凶

九四无咎弗過愚之往厲必革勿用永貞

六五密雲不雨自我西茭公射取皮在穴

尙六弗愚過之羿鳥羅之凶是謂茲省

☳ 小過 62

小過亨利貞可小事不可大事飛鳥遺之音不宜上宜下大吉

初六飛鳥以凶

六二過其祖遇其妣不及其君遇其臣无咎

九三弗過防之從或戕之凶

九四无咎弗過遇之往厲必戒勿用永貞

六五密雲不雨自我西郊公弋取彼在穴

上六弗遇過之飛鳥離之凶是謂災眚

28. *SHAOGUO,*
"SMALL SURPASSING"[1] ䷽

Small Surpassing: Receipt; beneficial to determine; possible for little service, but not possible for great service. The sound left by the flying bird is not proper for ascent but is proper for descent; greatly[2] auspicious.

Initial Six:
>The flying bird brings inauspiciousness.

Six in the Second:
>Surpassing his grandfather, meeting[3] his grandmother[4]:
>Not reaching his lord, meeting his servant[5];
>>there is no trouble.

Nine in the Third:
>Not surpassing him, but repelling[6] him,
>following which someone injures him[7];
>>inauspicious.

Nine in the Fourth:
>>There is no trouble.
>Not surpassing him, but meeting him;
>>to go is dangerous, there necessarily being a revolt.[8]
>Do not herewith determine permanently.

Six in the Fifth:
>The dense clouds do not rain from our western pasture[9];
>the duke shoots[10] and takes the skin[11] in the cavern.

Elevated Six:
>Not meeting him, but surpassing him;
>the flying bird is netted[12] in it;
>>inauspicious.
>>This is called calamitous[13] imperfection.[14]

䷵歸妹 29

歸妹正凶无攸利

初九歸妹以弟跛能利正吉

九二眇能視利幽人貞

六三歸妹以嬬□歸以弟

九四歸妹衍期遲歸有時

六五帝乙歸妹其君之袂不如其弟之快良日月既望吉

尚六女承筐无實士刲羊无血无攸利

䷵歸妹 54

歸妹征凶无攸利

初九歸妹以娣跛能履征吉

九二眇能視利幽人之貞

六三歸妹以須反歸以娣

九四歸妹愆期遲歸有時

六五帝乙歸妹其君之袂不如其娣之袂良月幾望吉

上六女承筐无實士刲羊无血无攸利

29. *GUIMEI,*
"RETURNING MAIDEN"[1] ䷵

Returning maiden: To be upright[2] is inauspicious; there is no place beneficial.

Initial Nine:
>   The returning maiden with younger sisters[3];
>   the lame are able to walk[4];
>>   to be upright is auspicious.

Nine in the Second:
>   The blind are able to see;
>>   beneficial for a dark man to determine.[5]

Six in the Third:
>   The returning maiden with consorts[6] [turns around]
>   and returns with younger sisters.[7]

Six in the Fourth:
>   The returning maiden exceeds[8] the appointed time,
>   and tardily returns having time.

Six in the Fifth:
>   Di Yi marries off the maiden:
>   The primary wife's sleeves are not as fine
>   as her younger sisters' sleeves;
>   the day's[9] moon is past[10] full;
>>   auspicious.

Elevated Six:
>   The woman holds up the basket, there is no fruit,
>   The man stabs the sheep, there is no blood;
>>   there is no place beneficial.

☷ 解 30

解利西南无所往其來復吉有攸往宿吉

初六无咎

九二田獲三狐得□□□□

□□□且乘致寇至貞閵

九四解其栂偭至此復

六五君子唯有解吉有復于小人

尙六公用射敻于高庸之上獲之无不利

☷ 解 40

解利西南无所往其來復吉有攸往夙吉

初六无咎

九二田獲三狐得黃矢貞吉

六三負且乘致寇至貞吝

九四解而拇朋至斯孚

六五君子維有解吉有孚于小人

上六公用射隼于高墉之上獲之无不利

Untangled: Beneficial to the southwest; there is nowhere to go; his coming in return is auspicious; there is someplace to go to spend the night[2]; auspicious.

Initial Six:
>   There is no trouble.

Nine in the Second:
>   In the fields bagging three foxes,
>   and getting [a yellow arrowhead;
>   >   determination is auspicious].

[Six in the Third:
>   Carrying on the back] and riding in a cart
>   brings robbers to arrive;
>   >   determination is distressful.

Nine in the Fourth:
>   Untangling his[3] hemlock[4];
>   a friend arrives and returns[5] this.[6]

Six in the Fifth:
>   The gentleman only[7] is untangled;
>   >   auspicious;
>   there is a return[8] among the little men.

Elevated Six:
>   The duke herewith shoots a hawk[9] on the top of a high wall, bagging it;
>   >   there is nothing not beneficial.

䷶豐 31

豐亨王叚之勿憂宜日中

初九禺其肥主唯旬无咎往有尙

六二豐其剖日中見斗往得疑□有復洫若

九三豐其蔮日中見茉折其右弓无咎

九四豐其剖日中見斗禺其夷主吉

六五來章有慶舉吉

尙六豐其屋剖其家闚其戶毘其无人三歲不逤兒

䷶豐 55

豐亨王假之勿憂宜日中

初九遇其配主雖旬无咎往有尙

六二豐其蔀日中見斗往得疑疾有孚發若吉

九三豐其沛日中見沬折其右肱无咎

九四豐其蔀日中見斗遇其夷主吉

六五來章有慶譽吉

上六豐其屋蔀其家闚其戶闃其无人三歲不覿凶

Abundance: Receipt; the king approaches it; do not be sad. It is proper for the middle of the day.

Initial Nine:
> Meeting[2] his consort's[3] ruler;
> it is only[4] the ten-day week;
> > there is no trouble;
> > in going there will be elevation.

Six in the Second:
> Making abundant his curtain[5];
> in the middle of the day one sees the Dipper;
> > in going one gets a suspicious [illness];
> > there is a return[6] leaking-like.[7]

Nine in the Third:
> Making abundant his screen[8];
> in the middle of the day one sees small stars[9];
> breaking his right bow[10];
> > there is no trouble.

Nine in the Fourth:
> Making abundant his curtain;
> in the middle of the day one sees the Dipper;
> meeting his placid ruler;
> > auspicious.

Six in the Fifth:
> There comes a pattern, celebratory and uplifting[11];
> > auspicious.

Elevated Six:
> Making abundant his room,
> screening his house, and arching his window[12];
> he is alarmed[13] at his having no people;
> > for three years he does not follow[14];
> > > inauspicious.

䷟恆 32

恒亨无咎利貞利有攸往
初六㚆恒貞凶无攸利
九二悔亡
九三不恒其德或承之羞貞閵
九四田无禽
六五恒其德貞婦人□夫子凶
尚六㚆恒兇

䷟恆 32

恒亨无咎利貞利有攸往
初六浚恒貞凶无攸利
九二悔亡
九三不恒其德或承之羞貞吝
九四田无禽
六五恒其德貞婦人吉夫子凶
上六振恒凶

100

Constancy: Receipt; there is no trouble; beneficial to determine; beneficial to have someplace to go.

Initial Six:
>Distant[2] constancy;
>>determination is inauspicious;
>>there is no place beneficial.

Nine in the Second:
>>Regret is gone.

Nine in the Third:
>Not making constant his virtue,
>he perhaps receives its disgrace;
>>determination is distressful.

Nine in the Fourth:
>In the fields there is no game.

Six in the Fifth:
>Making constant his virtue;
>>determination is [auspicious] for the wife,
>>inauspicious for the husband.

Elevated Six:
>Distant[3] constancy;
>>inauspicious.

䷁ 川 33

川元亨利牝馬之貞君子有攸往先迷後得主利西南得朋東北亡朋
安貞吉

初六禮霜堅冰至

六二直方大不習无不利

六三合章可貞或從王事无□有終

□□□□□□□□

六五黃常元吉

尙六龍戰于野其血玄黃

迵六利永貞

䷁ 坤 2

坤元亨利牝馬之貞君子有攸往先迷後得主利西南得朋東北喪朋
安貞吉

初六履霜堅冰至

六二直方大不習无不利

六三含章可貞或從王事无成有終

六四括囊无咎无譽

六五黃裳元吉

上六龍戰于野其血玄黃

用六利永貞

The Flow: Prime receipt; beneficial for the determination of a mare; the gentleman has someplace to go, is first lost but later gains his ruler; beneficial to the southwest to gain a friend, to the northeast to lose[2] a friend; contented determination is auspicious.

Initial Six:
>Treading[3] on frost:
>the firm ice will arrive.

Six in the Second:
>Straight, square, and great;
>>not repeated;
>>there is nothing not beneficial.

Six in the Third:
>Enclosing[4] a pattern;
>>it is permissible to determine.
>Someone follows the king's service;
>>there is no [completion], there is an end.

[Six in the Fourth:
>Tying the sack;
>>there is no trouble, there is no praise.]

Six in the Fifth:
>Yellow skirts[5];
>>prime auspiciousness.

Elevated Six:
>The dragon fights in the wilds:
>its blood is black and yellow.

Unified[6] Six:
>Beneficial to determine permanently.

䷊ 泰 34

□□□□□□□□

□九戊茅茹以其胃□吉

九二枹妄用馮河不騢遺弗忘得尙于中行

九三无平不波无往不復根□□□□□其復于食□□

□□□□□□□□□□□□□

□□帝乙歸妹以齒□□

尙六城復于湟□用師自邑告命貞闐

䷊ 泰 11

泰小往大來吉亨

初九拔茅茹以其彙征吉

九二包荒用馮河不遐遺朋亡得尙于中行

九三无平不陂无往不復艱貞无咎勿恤其孚于食有福

六四翩翩不富以其鄰不戒以孚

六五帝乙歸妹以祉元吉

上六城復于隍勿用師自邑告命貞吝

[Greatness: The little go and the great come; auspicious; receipt.]

[Initial] Nine:
    Plucking[2] the cogongrass stem with its roots[3];
        [to be upright[4]] is auspicious.

Nine in the Second:
    Wrapped[5] recklessness[6];
        herewith ford the river;
        not distantly[7] leaving it behind and not forgetting
        it,[8] gains elevation in the central ranks.

Nine in the Third:
    There is no flat that does not slope,[9]
    there is no going that does not return;
            in [determination] about difficulty,[10]
            [there is no trouble;
        do not pity] his return[11];
        in eating [there is good fortune].

Six in the Fourth:
    So fluttering, not wealthy together with [his neighbors;
        not warned about his return[12]].

[Six in the Fifth]:
    Di Yi marries off the maiden by age[13];
        [prime auspiciousness].

Elevated Six:
    The city wall falls into the moat;
        [do not] use troops;
        from the city announce the mandate;
        determination is distressful.

☲ 嗛 35

□□□子有終

初六嗛ゝ君子用涉大川吉

六二鳴嗛貞吉

九三勞嗛君子有終吉

六四无不利譌嗛

六五不富以其鄰□□□□□不利

尙六鳴嗛□□□□□□□

☶ 謙 15

謙亨君子有終

初六謙謙君子用涉大川吉

六二鳴謙貞吉

九三勞謙君子有終吉

六四无不利撝謙

六五不富以其鄰利用侵伐无不利

上六鳴謙利用行師征邑國

[Modesty: Receipt; the gentle]man has an end.

Initial Six:
　So modest is the gentleman;
　　herewith ford the great river;
　　　auspicious.

Six in the Second:
　Calling modesty;
　　determination is auspicious.

Nine in the Third:
　Toiling modesty;
　　　the gentleman has an end;
　　　auspicious.

Six in the Fourth:
　　There is nothing not beneficial.
　False[2] modesty.

Six in the Fifth:
　Not wealthy together with his neighbors;
　　[beneficial herewith to invade and attack;
　　there is nothing] not beneficial.

Elevated Six:
　Calling modesty;
　　[beneficial herewith to move troops to campaign
　　against city and state].

䷒ 林 36

□□□利貞至于八月有□

初九禁林貞吉

九二禁林吉无不利

六三甘林无攸利旣憂之无咎

六四至林无咎

□五知林大□□□□

□□敦林吉无咎

䷒ 臨 19

臨元亨利貞至于八月有凶

初九咸臨貞吉

九二咸臨吉无不利

六三甘臨无攸利旣憂之无咎

六四至臨无咎

六五知臨大君之宜吉

上六敦臨吉无咎

[The Forest: Prime receipt]; beneficial to determine; arriving at the eighth month there is [inauspiciousness].

Initial Nine:
> Prohibited[2] forest;
>> determination is auspicious.

Nine in the Second:
> Prohibited forest;
>> auspicious;
> there is nothing not beneficial.

Six in the Third:
> Sweet forest;
>> there is no place beneficial;
>>> having been saddened by it, there is no trouble.

Six in the Fourth:
> Arriving at the forest;
>> there is no trouble.

[Six] in the Fifth:
> Knowing the forest;
>> the great [lord's propriety is auspicious].

[Elevated Six]:
> Thick forest;
>> auspicious;
>> there is no trouble.

䷆ 師 37

□□□人吉无咎

初六師□以律不臧兇

九二在師中吉无咎王三湯命

六三師或輿屍兇

六四師左次无咎

六五田有禽利執言无咎長子率師弟子輿屍貞凶

尚六大人君有命啓國承家小人勿□

䷆ 師 7

師貞丈人吉无咎

初六師出以律否臧凶

九二在師中吉无咎王三錫命

六三師或輿尸凶

六四師左次无咎

六五田有禽利執言无咎長子帥師弟子輿尸貞凶

上六大君有命開國承家小人勿用

[The Troops: Determination for the senior] man is auspicious; there is no trouble.

Initial Six:
> Troops [go out] in ranks;
>> it is not[2] good;
>>> inauspicious.

Nine in the Second:
> In the troops' midst;
>> auspicious;
>>> there is no trouble;
> the king thrice awards[3] the command.

Six in the Third:
> Of the troops some join with[4] the corpses[5];
>> inauspicious.

Six in the Fourth:
> The troops camp on the left;
>> there is no trouble.

Six in the Fifth:
> In the fields there is game;
>> beneficial to shackle prisoners;
>>> there is no trouble.
> The eldest son leads the troops,
> the younger son carts corpses;
>> determination is inauspicious.

Elevated Six:
> The great man's lord[6] has a mandate,
> to open[7] the state and uphold the families;
>> the little man should not [use it].

䷣明夷 38

明夷利根貞

初九明夷于蜚垂其左翼君子于行三日不食有攸往主人有言

六二明夷ゝ于左股用撜馬牀吉

九三明夷ゝ于南守得其大首不可疾貞

六四明夷ゝ于左腹獲明夷之心于出門廷

六五箕子之明夷利貞

佔六不明海初登于天後人于地

䷣明夷 36

明夷利艱貞

初九明夷于飛垂其翼君子于行三日不食有攸往主人有言

六二明夷夷于左股用拯馬壯吉

九三明夷于南狩得其大首不可疾貞

六四入于左腹獲明夷之心于出門庭

六五箕子之明夷利貞

上六不明晦初登于天後入于地

38. *MINGYI*,
"CALLING PHEASANT"[1] ䷣

Calling pheasant: Beneficial to determine about difficulty.[2]

Initial Nine:
>The calling pheasant in flight,
>drops its left[3] wing:
>The gentleman on the move,
>for three days does not eat;
>>there is someplace to go;
>>the ruler has words.

Six in the Second:
>The calling pheasant is wounded in the left thigh;
>>herewith hold aloft[4] the horse's vitality[5];
>>>auspicious.

Nine in the Third:
>The calling pheasant is wounded in the southern hunt,[6]
>getting its great head;
>>it is not permissible to determine about illness.

Six in the Fourth:
>The calling pheasant is wounded[7] in the left belly:
>Bagging the calling pheasant's heart,
>in going out of the gate and courtyard.

Six in the Fifth:
>Jizi's calling pheasant;
>>beneficial to determine.

Elevated Six:
>Not bright or dark[8]:
>initially it rises into the heavens,
>afterwards it enters into the ground.

䷗ 復 39

復亨出人无疾堋來无咎反復其道七日來復利有攸往

初九不遠復无提悔元吉

六二休復□

六三編復厲无咎

六四中行獨復

六五敦復无悔

尙六迷復兇有茲省用行師終有大敗以其國君凶至十年弗克正

䷗ 復 24

復亨出入无疾朋來无咎反復其道七日來復利有攸往

初九不遠復无祇悔元吉

六二休復吉

六三頻復厲无咎

六四中行獨復

六五敦復无悔

上六迷復凶有災眚用行師終有大敗以其國君凶至于十年不克征

Returning: Receipt; in exiting and entering there is no illness; when the burying[2] comes there is no trouble; turning around and returning to its way, in seven days it comes in return; beneficial to have someplace to go.

Initial Nine:
> Not returning from afar;
>> there is no mention[3] of regret;
>> prime auspiciousness.

Six in the Second:
> Beneficent return;
>> [auspicious].

Six in the Third:
> Sequenced[4] return;
>> danger; there is no trouble.

Six in the Fourth:
> In the ranks there is solitary return.

Six in the Fifth:
> Thick return;
>> there is no regret.

Elevated Six:
> Lost return;
>> inauspicious.
> There being this inspection,[5] herewith move troops;
> in the end there will be a great defeat,
> together with its state lord;
>> inauspicious;
> until the tenth year you cannot make it upright.[6]

䷲登 40

登元亨利見大人勿血南正吉

初六允登大吉

九二復乃利用禴无咎

□□登虛邑

六四□□□□□□□无咎

六五貞吉登階

尙六冥登利于不息之貞

䷭升 46

升元亨用見大人勿恤南征吉

初六允升大吉

九二孚乃利用禴无咎

九三升虛邑

六四王用亨于岐山吉无咎

六五貞吉升階

上六冥升利于不息之貞

116

40. *DENG*, "ASCENDING"[1] ䷭

Ascending: Prime receipt; beneficial to see the great man. Do not pity.[2]
For the southern campaign,[3] auspicious.

Initial Six:
>Really ascending;
>>greatly auspicious.

Nine in the Second:
>Returning[4] then beneficial to use the spring sacrifice[5];
>>there is no trouble.

[Nine in the Third]:
>Ascending the empty city.

Six in the Fourth:
>[The king herewith makes offering on Mount Qi;
>>auspicious];
>>there is no trouble.

Six in the Fifth:
>>Determination is auspicious.
>Ascending the stairs.

Elevated Six:
>Dark ascent;
>>beneficial for unceasing determination.

䷲ 奪 41

奪亨小利貞

初九休奪吉

九二澥吉悔亡

六三來奪兇

九四章奪未寧□疾有喜

九□□于□□□

尙六景奪

䷹ 兑 58

兑亨利貞

初九和兑吉

九二孚兑吉悔亡

六三來兑凶

九四商兑未寧介疾有喜

九五孚于剝有厲

上六引兑

41. *DUO*, "USURPATION" [1] ䷨

Usurpation: Receipt; a little[2] beneficial to determine.

Initial Nine:
    Beneficent[3] usurpation;
        auspicious.

Nine in the Second:
    Sincere[4] (usurpation);
        auspicious; regret is gone.

(Nine:) Six[5] in the Third:
    Coming usurpation;
        inauspicious.

Nine in the Fourth:
    Patterned[6] usurpation;
        not yet at peace;
        a transitional illness has happiness.

Nine [in the Fifth:
    Sincerity] in [flaying;
        there is danger.]

Elevated Six:
    Shadowy[7] usurpation.

☰ 訣 42

夬陽于王廷復號有厲告自邑不利節戎利有攸往

初九牀于前止往不勝爲咎

九二傷號暮夜有戎勿血

□三牀于頯有凶君子缺ゝ獨行愚雨如濡有慍无咎

九四脈无膚其行鄒胥牽羊悔亡聞言不信

九五莧勲缺ゝ中行无咎

尙六无號冬有凶

☰ 夬 43

夬揚于王庭孚號有厲告自邑不利即戎利有攸往

初九壯于前趾往不勝爲咎

九二惕號莫夜有戎勿恤

九三壯于頄有凶君子夬夬獨行遇雨若濡有慍无咎

九四臀无膚其行次且牽羊悔亡聞言不信

九五莧陸夬夬中行无咎

上六无號終有凶

120

42. GUAI, "RESOLUTION"[1] ䷪

Resolution: Raised up[2] at the royal court, returning[3] crying out; there is danger. Announcing from the city; not beneficial to regulate[4] the belligerents; beneficial to have someplace to go.

Initial Nine:
    Mature[5] in the front foot[6];
        to go will not be victorious, but will be trouble.

Nine in the Second:
    Softly[7] crying out;
    at dusk and at night there are belligerents;
        do not pity[8] (them).

[Nine] in the Third:
    Mature in the cheekbones[9];
            there is inauspiciousness.
    The gentleman so broken-up[10] moves alone,
    meeting[11] rain that is like[12] moistening;
        there are hot-springs[13];
        there is no trouble.

Nine in the Fourth:
    The lips[14] do not have skin;
    his movement is herky-jerky,[15] pulling sheep;
        regret is gone;
        you will hear words that are not trustworthy.

Nine in the Fifth:
    The amaranth burns[16] so broken-up,
    in the middle of the ranks;
        there is no trouble.

Elevated Six:
    There is no crying out;
        in the winter[17] there is inauspiciousness.

䷬ 卒 43

卒王叚于廟利見大人亨利貞用大生吉利有攸往
初六有復不終乃乳乃卒若其號一屋于芺勿血往无咎
六二引吉无咎復乃利用濯
六三卒若嗟若无攸利往无咎少闔
九四大吉无咎
九五卒有立无咎非復元永貞悔亡
尙六粢欤涕洎无咎

䷬ 卒 45

萃亨王假有廟利見大人亨利貞用大牲吉利有攸往
初六有孚不終乃亂乃萃若號一握爲笑勿恤往无咎
六二引吉无咎孚乃利用禴
六三萃如嗟如无攸利往无咎小吝
九四大吉无咎
九五萃有位无咎匪孚元永貞悔亡
上六齎咨涕洟无咎

Finished: The king enters into the temple; beneficial to see the great man; receipt; beneficial to determine. Using the great animal offering[2] is auspicious; beneficial to have someplace to go.

Initial Six:
> There is a return[3] that does not end,
> but then is disordered[4] and then finished.
> It is as if he[5] cries out,
> one room[6] in[7] laughter;
>> do not pity[8] (them);
>>> in going there is no trouble.

Six in the Second:
>>> Extended auspiciousness;
>>> there is no trouble.
>> Returning then beneficial to use
>> the spring sacrifice.[9]

Six in the Third:
> Finished-like, sighing-like[10];
>> there is no place beneficial;
>>> in going there is no trouble;
>>> small[11] distress.

Nine in the Fourth:
>>> Great auspiciousness;
>>> there is no trouble.

Nine in the Fifth:
> In finishing there is position[12];
>> there is no trouble.
> It is not a return;
>> prime permanent determination;
>> regret is gone.

Elevated Six:
> Snuffling[13] tears and snivel[14];
>> there is no trouble.

☷☶ 欽 44

欽亨利貞取女吉

初六欽其栂

六二欽其躄凶居吉

九三欽其躄執其隨闔

九四貞吉悔亡童丶往來儦從璽思

九五欽其股无悔

尙六欽其胶陜舌

☷☶ 咸 31

咸亨利貞取女吉

初六咸其拇

六二咸其腓凶居吉

九三咸其股執其隨往吝

九四貞吉悔亡憧憧往來朋從爾思

九五咸其脢无悔

上六咸其輔頰舌

Feelings: Receipt; beneficial to determine; to take to wife a woman is auspicious.

Initial Six:
    Feeling his big toe.[2]

Six in the Second:
    Feeling his calf[3];
           inauspicious;
      to dwell is auspicious.

Nine in the Third:
    Feeling his (calf:) thigh[4]:
    holding to his follower;
        distress.[5]

Nine in the Fourth:
        Determination is auspicious;
          regret is gone.
    So undecided[6] going and coming,
    a friend follows you[7] in thought.

Nine in the Fifth:
    Feeling his (thigh:) spine[8];
        there is no regret.

Elevated Six:
    Feeling his cheeks,[9] jowls,[10] and tongue.

䷮ 困 45

困亨貞大人吉无咎有言不信

初六辰困于株木人于要浴三歲不擩凶

九二困于酒食絑發方來利用芳祀正凶无咎

六三困于石號于疾莉人于其宮不見其妻凶

九四來徐困于□□閽有終

九五貳椽困于赤發乃徐有說利用芳祀

尙六困于褐纍于貳椽曰悔夷有悔貞吉

䷮ 困 47

困亨貞大人吉无咎有言不信

初六臀困于株木入于幽谷三歲不覿

九二困于酒食朱紱方來利用享祀征凶无咎

六三困于石據于蒺藜入于其宮不見其妻凶

九四來徐徐困于金車吝有終

九五劓刖困于赤紱乃徐有說利用祭祀

上六困于葛藟于臲卼曰動悔有悔征吉

126

Entangled: Receipt; determination for the great man is auspicious; there is no trouble. There are words that are not trustworthy.

Initial Six:
> The lips[2] are entangled in a columnar tree:
> Entering into a dark[3] valley,[4]
> for three years he is not drawn out[5];
>> inauspicious.[6]

Nine in the Second:
> Entangled in wine and food:
>> the scarlet[7] kneepads[8] having just arrived,
>> it is beneficial to use an aromatic grass[9] sacrifice;
>> to be upright[10] is inauspicious;
>>> there is no trouble.

Six in the Third:
> Entangled in stone, and crying out[11] in the thistles[12]:
> Entering into his palace, and not seeing his wife;
>> inauspicious.

Nine in the Fourth:
> Coming slowly,[13]
> entangled in [the metal chariot];
>> distress; there is an end.

Nine in the Fifth:
> Doubled[14] rafters[15];
> entangled in crimson kneepads,
> then slowly having extrication;
>> beneficial to use an aromatic grass sacrifice.

Elevated Six:
> Entangled in the creeping vines[16] in the doubled rafters.
>> Say "regretting the level"[17];
>>> there is regret;
>>> determination[18] is auspicious.

☲ 勒 46

□□□□復元亨利貞悔亡

初九共用黃牛之勒

六二□□乃勒之正吉□□

□□□□貞□□言三□□復

九四悔□有復茝命吉

九五大人虎便未占有復

尙六君子豹便小人勒□□□居貞吉

☲ 革 49

革巳日乃孚元亨利貞悔亡

初九鞏用黃牛之革

六二巳日乃革之征吉无咎

九三征凶貞厲革言三就有孚

九四悔亡有孚改命吉

九五大人虎變未占有孚

上六君子豹變小人革面征凶居貞吉

128

[The Bridle: On the *si* day then] return[2]; prime receipt; beneficial to determine; regret is gone.

Initial Nine:
Together[3] use the yellow ox's bridle.

Six in the Second:
[On the *si* day] then bridle it;
to be upright[4] is auspicious;
there is no trouble.

[Nine in the Third:
To be upright[5] is inauspicious];
determination is [dangerous].
When bridling words thrice [approach,
there is] a return.

Nine in the Fourth:
Regret [is gone];
there is a return that changes[6] the mandate;
auspicious.

Nine in the Fifth:
The great man's tiger whip[7];
not yet having prognosticated, there is a return.

Elevated Six:
The gentleman's leopard whip;
the little man bridles [the face;
to be upright is inauspicious];
determination about dwelling is auspicious.

䷐ 隋 47

隋元亨利貞无咎
初九官或諭貞吉出門交有功
六二係小子失丈夫
六三係丈夫失小子隋有求得利居貞
九四隋有獲貞凶有復在道已明何咎
九五復于嘉吉
尙九枸係之乃從蘲之王用芳于西山

䷐ 隨 17

隨元亨利貞无咎
初九官有渝貞吉出門交有功
六二係小子失丈夫
六三係丈夫失小子隨有求得利居貞
九四隨有獲貞凶有孚在道以明何咎
九五孚于嘉吉
上六拘係之乃從維之王用亨于西山

47. SUI, "FOLLOWING"[1] ䷐

Following: Prime receipt; beneficial to determine; there is no trouble.

Initial Nine:
>The office perhaps[2] notifies[3];
>>determination is auspicious;
>>going out of the gate to interact has results.

Six in the Second:
>Tying the little son, losing the senior fellow.

Six in the Third:
>Tying the senior fellow, losing the little son;
>>in following there is the seeking to get;
>>beneficial to determine about dwelling.

Nine in the Fourth:
>In following there is a catch;
>>determination is inauspicious.
>There is a return[4] on the way;
>at the end[5] of brightness, what trouble is there?

Nine in the Fifth:
>Returning in joy[6];
>>auspicious.

Elevated (Nine:) Six[7]:
>Grabbing[8] and tying him,
>and thereafter binding[9] him;
>the king uses aromatic grass[10] on the western mountain.

䷋泰過 48

泰過棟䷞利有攸往亨

初六籍用白茅无咎

九二楛楊生黃老夫得其女妻无不利

九三棟橈凶

九四棟䷞吉有它闔

六五楛楊生華老婦得其士夫无咎无譽

尙九過涉滅釘凶无咎

䷛大過 28

大過棟橈利有攸往亨

初六藉用白茅无咎

九二枯楊生稊老夫得其女妻无不利

九三棟橈凶

九四棟隆吉有它吝

九五枯楊生華老婦得其士夫无咎无譽

上六過涉滅頂凶无咎

132

48. *TAIGUO,*
"GREAT SURPASSING"[1] ䷛

Great Surpassing: The ridgepole bows upward[2]; beneficial to have someplace to go; receipt.

Initial Six:
> For the mat use white cogongrass;
>> there is no trouble.

Nine in the Second:
> The bitter[3] poplar gives life to sprouts[4]:
> The old fellow gets his maiden consort;
>> there is nothing not beneficial.

Nine in the Third:
> The ridgepole sags;
>> inauspicious.

Nine in the Fourth:
> The ridgepole bows upward[5];
>> auspicious;
>> there is harm; distress.

(Six:) Nine[6] in the Fifth:
> The bitter poplar gives life to flowers:
> The old wife gets her siring husband;
>> there is no trouble, there is no praise.

Elevated (Nine:) Six[7]:
> Surpassing and fording causes the top of the head[8]
> to vanish;
>> inauspicious;
>> there is no trouble.

☲ 羅 49

羅利貞亨畜牝牛吉

初九禮昔然敬之无咎

六二黃羅元吉

九三日稷之羅不鼓埴而歌即大經之跘凶

九四出如來如紛如死如棄如

六五出涕沱若□跘若吉

尙九王出正有嘉折首獲不戲无咎

☲ 離 30

離利貞亨畜牝牛吉

初九履錯然敬之无咎

六二黃離元吉

九三日昃之離不鼓缶而歌則大耋之嗟凶

九四突如其來如焚如死如棄如

六五出涕沱若戚嗟若吉

上九王用出征有嘉折首獲匪其醜无咎

134

49. *LUO*, "THE NET"[1] ䷝

The Net: Beneficial to determine; receipt; raising a cow is auspicious.

Initial Nine:
>   Treading[2] counter-wise[3];
>>   respect it;
>>>   there is no trouble.

Six in the Second:
>   Yellow net;
>>   prime auspiciousness.

Nine in the Third:
>   The net of the sun's decline[4]:
>   not drumming the earthenware jar and yet singing,
>   then[5] the sighing[6] of the great mourning kerchief[7];
>>   inauspicious.

Nine in the Fourth:
>   As if going out,[8] as if coming,[9]
>   as if confused,[10] as if dying, as if dismissing.

Six in the Fifth:
>   Going out with tears as if streaming
>   and [grief] as if sighing;
>>   auspicious.

Elevated Nine:
>   The king goes out on campaign[11];
>   there is the joy of cutting off heads
>   and bagging the non-masses[12];
>>   there is no trouble.

☰ 大有 50

大有元亨

初九无交禽非咎根則无咎

九二泰車以載有攸往无咎

九三公用芳于天子小人弗克

九四□□彭无咎

六五闕復交如委如終吉

尙九自天右之吉无不利

☰ 大有 14

大有元亨

初九无交害匪咎艱則无咎

九二大車以載有攸往无咎

九三公用亨于天子小人弗克

九四匪其彭无咎

六五厥孚交如威如吉

上九自天祐之吉无不利

50. *DAYOU,*
"THE GREAT POSSESSION"[1] ䷍

The Great Possession: Prime receipt.

Initial Nine:
> There is no exchanging of harm[2] that is not trouble;
>> if in difficulty[3] then there will be no trouble.

Nine in the Second:
> The great cart is used to carry;
>> there is someplace to go;
>>> there is no trouble.

Nine in the Third:
> The duke uses aromatic grass[4] to the Son of Heaven;
>> the little man is not capable of it.

Nine in the Fourth:
> [It is not his] fullness;
>> there is no trouble.

Six in the Fifth:
> His[5] return[6] is crossed-like, stooped-like[7];
>> in the end it is auspicious.

Elevated Nine:
> From heaven blessing[8] it;
>> auspicious;
> there is nothing not beneficial.

☷ 溍 51

溍康矦用賜馬蕃庶晝日三綏
初九溍如浚如貞吉悔亡復浴无咎
六二溍如□如貞吉受□□□□其王母
六三衆允悔亡
九四溍如炙鼠貞厲
六五悔亡矢得勿血往吉无不利
尚九溍其角唯用伐邑厲吉无咎貞閵

☷ 晉 35

晉康侯用錫馬蕃庶晝日三接
初六晉如摧如貞吉罔孚裕无咎
六二晉如愁如貞吉受茲介福于其王母
六三衆允悔亡
九四晉如鼫鼠貞厲
六五悔亡失得勿恤往吉无不利
上九晉其角維用伐邑厲吉无咎貞吝

138

5 1 . *JIN*, "A Q U A S" [1] ䷢

Aquas: The Lord of Kang is herewith awarded[2] horses in luxuriant number, during daylight thrice connecting.[3]

Initial (Nine:) Six[4]:
Aquatically, deeply[5];
determination is auspicious;
regret is gone.[6]
Returning[7] to the bath[8];
there is no trouble.

Six in the Second:
Aquatically, [gloom]-ily;
determination is auspicious.
Receiving [this strong good fortune from] his royal mother.

Six in the Third:
The masses are real;
regret is gone.

Nine in the Fourth:
Aquatically the mole cricket[9];
determination is dangerous.

Six in the Fifth:
Regret is gone.
The arrow[10] is gotten;
do not pity[11];
going is auspicious;
there is nothing not beneficial.

Elevated Nine:
Aquatic his horns;
it is only[12] to be used to attack the city;
danger;
auspicious;
there is no trouble;
determination is distressful.

☰☴ 旅 52

旅少亨旅貞吉
初六旅瑣、此其所取火
六二旅旣次壞其茨得童剝貞
九三□□□□□□□□□
□□□□□□其潛斧□心不快
六五射雉一矢亡終以舉命
尙九鳥夢其巢旅人先芺後摅桃亡牛于易兌

☰☶ 旅 56

旅小亨旅貞吉
初六旅瑣瑣斯其所取災
六二旅即次懷其資得童僕貞
九三旅焚其次喪其童僕貞厲
九四旅于處得其資斧我心不快
六五射雉一矢亡終以譽命
上九鳥焚其巢旅人先笑後號咷喪牛于易凶

52. LÜ, "TRAVELING"[1] ䷛

Traveling: Small[2] receipt. Traveling; determination is auspicious.

Initial Six:
    Traveling so trivially;
    this[3] is the fire[4] that he has taken.

Six in the Second:
    In traveling having just[5] lodged,
    he cherishes[6] his belongings,[7]
    getting the young servant's[8] determination.

Nine in the Third:
    [In traveling burning his lodging,
    and losing his young servant;
        determination is dangerous.]

[Nine in the Fourth:
    In traveling, staying put,
    he gets] his goods[9] and ax;
    [my] heart is not happy.

Six in the Fifth:
    Shooting the pheasant,
    one arrow is gone;
    in the winter[10] he is thereby presented[11] a command.

Elevated Nine:
    A crow[12] disorders[13] its nest;
    the traveler first laughs and later weeps[14] and wails,[15]
    losing an ox at Yi;
        inauspicious.

☲乖 53

乖小事吉

初九悔亡、馬勿逐自復見亞人无咎

九二无咎九二愚主于巷无咎

六三見車恝其牛誙其□□□□无初有終

九四乖苽愚元夫交復厲无咎

六五悔亡登宗筮膚往何咎

尙九乖苽見豨負塗載鬼一車先張之柧後說之壼非寇闞厚往愚雨
即吉

☲睽 38

睽小事吉

初九悔亡喪馬勿逐自復見惡人无咎

九二遇主于巷无咎

六三見輿曳其牛掣其人天且劓无初有終

九四睽孤遇元夫交孚厲无咎

六五悔亡厥宗噬膚往何咎

上九睽孤見豕負塗載鬼一車先張之弧後說之弧匪寇婚媾往遇雨
則吉

142

53. GUAI, "PERVERSION"[1] ☰

Perversion: Little affairs are auspicious.

Initial Nine:

       Regret is gone;

Losing[2] a horse, do not pursue[3];

it will of itself return.

Seeing an ugly[4] man;

         there is no trouble.

Nine in the Second:

       There is no trouble.

Nine in the Second[5]:

Meeting[6] the ruler in an alley;

        there is no trouble.

Six in the Third:

Seeing the cart[7] with one horn upturned,

its cow dragging (*sic*),[8]

its [man branded on the forehead and with his nose cut off];

       there is no beginning, there is an end.

Nine in the Fourth:

Perverse solitude[9];

meeting the prime fellow and interacting returning[10];

       danger; there is no trouble.

Six in the Fifth:

       Regret is gone.

Climbing up[11] the ancestral temple and biting[12] flesh;

     in going what trouble is there?

Elevated Nine:

Perverse solitude;

seeing a pig[13] with mud on its back

and one cart carrying ghosts;

the first drawn bow[14] is later released into the jar[15];

it is not robbers who in the evening[16] have intercourse[17];

     going and meeting rain then it will be[18] auspicious.

☲ 末濟 54

未濟亨小狐气涉濡其尾无攸利

初六濡其尾閵

九二抴其綸貞

六三未濟正凶利涉大川

九四貞吉悔亡□□□□方三年有商于大國

□五貞吉悔亡君子之光有復吉

尙九有復于飲酒无咎濡其首有復失是

☲ 末濟 64

未濟亨小狐汔濟濡其尾无攸利

初六濡其尾吝

九二曳其輪貞吉

六三未濟征凶利涉大川

九四貞吉悔亡震用伐鬼方三年有賞于大國

六五貞吉无悔君子之光有孚吉

上九有孚于飲酒无咎濡其首有孚失是

144

54. WEIJI, "NOT YET COMPLETED"[1] ䷿

Not Yet Completed: Receipt; the little fox at the point of[2] fording,[3] wets his tail; there is no place beneficial.

Initial Six:
> Wetting his tail;
>> distress.

Nine in the Second:
> Dragging[4] his sash[5];
>> determination.[6]

Six in the Third:
> Not yet completed;
>> to be upright[7] is inauspicious;
>> beneficial to ford the great river.

Nine in the Fourth:
>> Determination is auspicious;
>>> regret is gone.
> [Zhen herewith attacks the Devil]-land,
> in three years having a reward[8] from the great state.

[Six] in the Fifth:
>> Determination is auspicious;
>>> regret is gone.[9]
> The gentleman's radiance has a return[10];
>> auspicious.

Elevated Nine:
> There is a return in drinking wine;
>> there is no trouble.
> Wetting his head;
> there is a return, losing this.

☶ 筮嗑 55

□□□利用獄

初九 句□□止无咎

六二 筮膚滅鼻无咎

六三 筮腊肉愚毒少閵无咎

九四 筮乾瓊得金矢根貞吉

六五 筮乾肉愚毒貞厲无咎

尙九 荷校滅耳兇

☲ 噬嗑 21

噬嗑亨利用獄

初九 屨校滅趾无咎

六二 噬膚滅鼻无咎

六三 噬腊肉遇毒小吝无咎

九四 噬乾胏得金矢利艱貞吉

六五 噬乾肉得黃金貞厲无咎

上九 何校滅耳凶

55. *SHI KE*, "BITING AND CHEWING"[1] ䷔

Biting and Chewing: Receipt; beneficial to use a court case.

Initial Nine:
> Wearing [stocks] on the feet[2] and with [cut off] feet[3];
>> there is no trouble.

Six in the Second:
> Biting flesh and cutting off the nose;
>> there is no trouble.

Six in the Third:
> Biting dried meat and meeting with[4] poison;
>> small[5] distress;
>> there is no trouble.

Nine in the Fourth:
> Biting dry preserved meat,[6]
> and getting a metal arrow(head);
>> determination about difficulty[7] is auspicious.

Six in the Fifth:
> Biting dry meat and meeting with poison[8];
>> determination is dangerous;
>> there is no trouble.

Elevated Nine:
> Carrying[9] a cangue on the shoulders and with a cut-off ear;
>> inauspicious.

☲ 鼎 56

□□□□□

初六鼎塤止利□不得妾以其子无咎

九二鼎有實我戕有疾不我能節吉

九三鼎耳勒其行塞雉膏不食方雨□□□□

□□□□□復公莹其刑屋□

六五鼎黃□□□□□

□□□□□□□无不利

☲ 鼎 50

鼎元吉亨

初六鼎顛趾利出否得妾以其子无咎

九二鼎有實我仇有疾不我能即吉

九三鼎耳革其行塞雉膏不食方雨虧悔終吉

九四鼎折足覆公餗其形渥凶

六五鼎黃耳金鉉利貞

上九鼎玉鉉大吉无不利

The Cauldron: Prime auspiciousness; receipt.

Initial Six:
 The cauldron's upturned[2] legs[3];
  beneficial [to expel] the bad[4];
 getting a consort together with her son;
   there is no trouble.

Nine in the Second:
 The cauldron has substance:
 My enemy[5] has an illness;
 it is not able to approach[6] me;
   auspicious.

Nine in the Third:
 The cauldron's ears are bridled[7]:
 his motion is blocked;
 the pheasant fat is not edible;
 the countryside rain [diminishes;
   regret, in the end auspicious].

[Nine in the Fourth:
 The cauldron's broken leg]:
 Overturns[8] the duke's stew[9];
 his punishment[10] is execution-in-chamber[11];
   [inauspicious].

Six in the Fifth:
 The cauldron's yellow [ears and metal bar;
  beneficial to determine].

[Elevated Nine:
 The cauldron's jade bar;
   greatly auspicious];
  there is nothing not beneficial.

䷸ 筭 57

□□亨利有攸往利見大□

初六進內利武人之貞

九二筭在牀下用使巫忿若吉无咎

九三編筭閵

六四悔亡田獲三品

九五貞吉悔亡无不利无□有終先庚三□後庚三日吉

尙九筭在牀下亡其潜斧貞凶

䷸ 巽 57

巽小亨利有攸往利見大人

初六進退利武人之貞

九二巽在牀下用史巫紛若吉无咎

九三頻巽吝

六四悔亡田獲三品

九五貞吉悔亡无不利无初有終先庚三日後庚三日吉

上九巽在牀下喪其資斧貞凶

57. *SUAN*, "CALCULATIONS"[1] ䷸

[Calculations: Little] receipt; beneficial to have someplace to go; beneficial to see the great [man].

Initial Six:
>Entering the inside[2];
>>beneficial for a military man's determination.

Nine in the Second:
>Calculations are under the bed,
>herewith causing[3] the magicians to be indignant-like[4];
>>auspicious;
>>there is no trouble.

Nine in the Third:
>Sequenced[5] calculation;
>>distress.

Six in the Fourth:
>>Regret is gone.
>In the fields bagging three types.

Nine in the Fifth:
>>Determination is auspicious;
>>>regret is gone;
>>there is nothing not beneficial;
>>there is no [beginning], there is an end.
>Preceding the *geng* day by three [days],
>following the *geng* day by three days;
>>auspicious.

Elevated Nine:
>Calculations are under the bed;
>losing[6] his goods[7] and ax;
>>determination is inauspicious.

☰ 少穀 58

少穀亨密雲不雨自我西茭

初九復自道何其咎吉

九二堅復吉

九三車說緮夫妻反目

六四有復血去湯□无咎

九五有復孿如富以其鄰

尚九既雨既處尚得載女貞厲月幾望君子正兒

☰ 小畜 9

小畜亨密雲不雨自我西郊

初九復自道何其咎吉

九二牽復吉

九三輿說輻夫妻反目

六四有孚血去惕出无咎

九五有孚攣如富以其鄰

上九既雨既處尚德載婦貞厲月幾望君子征凶

152

58. *SHAOSHU,*
"SMALL HARVEST"[1] ䷈

Small Harvest: Receipt; dense clouds do not rain, from our western pasture.[2]

Initial Nine:
>Returning from the way,
>what could its trouble be?
>>Auspicious.

Nine in the Second:
>A firm[3] return;
>>auspicious.

Nine in the Third:
>The cart[4] throws its axle-strut[5] ;
>the husband and consort cross eyes.

Six in the Fourth:
>There is a return[6];
>blood departs, warily[7] [exiting];
>>there is no trouble.

Nine in the Fifth:
>There is a return linkedly[8];
>wealthy together with his neighbor.

Elevated Nine:
>Having rained and having stopped,
>he still gets[9] to ride;
>>for a maiden[10] to determine is auspicious;
>the moon is almost full;
>>for the gentleman to be upright[11] is inauspicious.

☲ 觀 59

觀盥而不薦有復□若

初六童觀小人无咎君子闇

六二覘觀利女貞

六三觀我生進退

六四觀國之光□用賓于王

九五觀我生君子无咎

尚九觀其生君子无咎

☴ 觀 20

觀盥而不薦有孚顒若

初六童觀小人无咎君子吝

六二闚觀利女貞

六三觀我生進退

六四觀國之光利用賓于王

九五觀我生君子无咎

上九觀其生君子无咎

Looking Up: Washing the hands but not making offering[2]; there is a return[3] with [head held high].

Initial Six:
>   The youth looks up;
>>   for the little man there is no trouble,
>>   for the gentleman distress.

Six in the Second:
>   Peeking[4] a look up;
>>   beneficial for the maiden to determine.

Six in the Third:
>   Looking up at my life advancing and retreating.

Six in the Fourth:
>   Looking up at the state's radiance;
>>   beneficial [herewith] to be entertained
>>   in audience by the king.

Nine in the Fifth:
>   Looking up at my life;
>>   for the gentleman there is no trouble.

Elevated Nine:
>   Looking up at his life;
>>   for the gentleman there is no trouble.

☲ 漸 60

漸女歸吉利貞

初六鳴漸于淵小子癘有言无咎

六二鳴漸于坂酒食衍、吉

九三鳴漸于陸□□□復婦繩不□凶利所寇

六四鳴漸于木或直其寇戩无咎

九五鳴漸于陵婦三歲不繩終莫之勝吉

尚九鳴漸于陸其羽可用爲宜吉

☶ 漸 53

漸女歸吉利貞

初六鴻漸于干小子厲有言无咎

六二鴻漸于磐飲食衍衍吉

九三鴻漸于陸夫征不復婦孕不育凶利禦寇

六四鴻漸于木或得其桷无咎

九五鴻漸于陵婦三歲不孕終莫之勝吉

上九鴻漸于陸其羽可用爲儀吉

156

60. JIAN, "ADVANCING"[1] ䷴

Advancing: For the maiden to return is auspicious; beneficial to determine.

Initial Six:
>The wild goose advances to the depths[2]:
>>for the little son dangerous[3];
>>there are words;
>>there is no trouble.

Six in the Second:
>The wild goose advances to the slope[4]:
>Wine[5] and food so overflowing[6];
>>auspicious.

Nine in the Third:
>The wild goose advances to the land:
>[The husband campaigns but does not] return,
>the wife is pregnant[7] but does not [give birth];
>>inauspicious;
>>beneficial to have that which[8] robs.

Six in the Fourth:
>The wild goose advances to the tree:
>perhaps getting[9] what the robbers rejected[10];
>>there is no trouble.

Nine in the Fifth:
>The wild goose advances to the mound:
>The wife for three years does not get pregnant;
>in the end nothing overcomes it;
>>auspicious.

Elevated Nine:
>The wild goose advances to the land:
>its feathers can be used to be emblems[11];
>>auspicious.

䷼ 中復 61

中復豚魚吉和涉大川利貞

初九杅吉有它不寧

九二鳴鶴在陰其子和之□□□□□□□嬴□

□□□□或鼓或皮或汲或歌

六四月既望馬必亡无咎

九五有復論如无咎

尙九翰音登于天貞凶

䷼ 中孚 61

中孚豚魚吉利涉大川利貞

初九虞吉有它不燕

九二鳴鶴在陰其子和之我有好爵吾與爾靡之

六三得敵或鼓或罷或泣或歌

六四月幾望馬匹亡无咎

九五有孚攣如无咎

上九翰音登于天貞凶

61. *ZHONGFU,* "CENTRAL RETURN" [1] ䷼

Central Return:The piglet and fish are auspicious; (harmonious:) bene-ficial[2] to ford the great river; beneficial to determine.

Initial Nine:
    Self-satisfied[3] auspiciousness;
    there are others not tranquil.[4]

Nine in the Second:
    A calling crane in the shade,
    its young harmonizes with it:
    [We have a good chalice,
    I will] down[5] [it with you].

[Six in the Third:
    Getting an enemy:]
    Now drumming, now weary,[6]
    Now crying,[7] now singing.

Six in the Fourth:
    The moon is past full;
    the horse will necessarily[8] be lost;
        there is no trouble.

Nine in the Fifth:
    There is a return linkedly[9];
        there is no trouble.

Elevated Six:
    The golden pheasant's[10] sound ascends to the heavens;
        determination is inauspicious.

☴ 渙 62

渙亨王叚于廟利涉大川利貞

初六撜馬吉悔亡

九二渙賁其階悔亡

六三渙其躬无咎

九四渙其群元吉渙□□□娣所思

九五渙其肝大號渙王居无咎

尚九渙其血去湯出

☴ 渙 59

渙亨王假有廟利涉大川利貞

初六用拯馬壯吉

九二渙奔其機悔亡

六三渙其躬无悔

六四渙其群元吉渙有丘匪夷所思

九五渙汗其大號渙王居无咎

上九渙其血去逖出无咎

Dispersal: Receipt; the king approaches into[2] the temple; beneficial to ford the great river; beneficial to determine.

Initial Six:
    Holding aloft[3] a horse[4];
        auspicious;
            regret is gone.[5]

Nine in the Second:
    Dispersal rushes[6] its stairs[7];
        regret is gone.

Six in the Third:
    Dispersing his torso;
        there is no trouble.

(Nine:) Six[8] in the Fourth:
    Dispersing his flock;
        prime auspiciousness.
    Dispersal [has a hillock;
    it is not] that about which the younger sister[9] thinks.

Nine in the Fifth:
    Dispersing his liver with a great cry.[10]
    Dispersing the king's residence;
        there is no trouble.

Elevated Nine:
    Dispersing his blood,
    he departs, warily[11] exiting.[12]

☲ 家人 63

家人利女貞

初九門有家悔亡

六二无攸遂在中貴貞吉

九三家人樊〻悔厲吉婦子裏〻終閵

六四富家大吉

九五王叚有家勿血往吉

尚九有復委如終吉

☲ 家人 37

家人利女貞

初九閑有家悔亡

六二无攸遂在中饋貞吉

九三家人嗃嗃悔厲吉婦子嘻嘻終吝

六四富家大吉

九五王假有家勿恤吉

上九有孚威如終吉

63. *JIAREN*,
"FAMILY MEMBERS"[1] ☲

Family Members: Beneficial for the maiden to determine.

Initial Nine:
> The gate[2] has a family;
>> regret is gone.

Six in the Second:
> There is no place to follow,
> in the middle of the food[3];
>> determination is auspicious.

Nine in the Third:
> The family members so excited[4];
>> regret;
>> danger;
>> auspicious.
> The wife and children are so introspective[5];
>> in the end distress.

Six in the Fourth:
> A wealthy family;
>> greatly auspicious.

Nine in the Fifth:
> The king approaches his family;
>> do not pity;
>> going[6] is auspicious.

Elevated Nine:
> There is a return[7] stooped-like[8];
>> in the end auspicious.

䷩ 益 64

益利用攸往利涉大川

初九利用爲大作元吉无咎

九二或益之十倗之龜弗亨回永貞吉王用芳于帝吉

六三益之用工事无咎有復中行告公用圀

六四中行告公從利用爲家遷國

九五有復惠心勿問元吉有復惠我德

尙九莫益之或擊之立心勿恆兇

䷩ 益 42

益利有攸往利涉大川

初九利用爲大作元吉无咎

六二或益之十朋之龜弗克違永貞吉王用享于帝吉

六三益之用凶事无咎有孚中行告公用圭

六四中行告公從利用爲依遷國

九五有孚惠心勿問元吉有孚惠我德

上九莫益之或擊之立心勿恆凶

Increase: Beneficial herewith to have someplace to go; beneficial to ford the great river.

Initial Nine:
> Beneficial herewith to do the great creation;
>> prime auspiciousness;
>> there is no trouble.

(Nine:) Six[2] in the Second:
> Someone increases it by ten double-strands of turtles;
> you cannot[3] deflect[4] it;
>> permanent determination is auspicious.
> The king uses aromatic grass[5] to Di;
>> auspicious.

Six in the Third:
> Increase it, using work[6] service;
>> there is no trouble.
> There is a return[7] in the middle of the ranks,
> reporting to the duke using a tessera.[8]

Six in the Fourth:
> In the middle of the ranks reporting to the duke to follow;
>> beneficial herewith to make a family[9]
>> and to transfer the state.

Nine in the Fifth:
> There is a return with kind heart;
>> do not question it;
>>> prime auspiciousness.
> There is a return that treats kindly my virtue.

Elevated Nine:
> No one increases it, someone hits it;
> establishing the heart, but not making it constant;
>> inauspicious.

THE SEVERAL
DISCIPLES
ASKED

二三字問

二厽 (三) 子問曰: 易屢稱于龍, 龍之德何如? 孔子曰: 龍大矣. 龍刑 (形) 罨 (遷), 叚 (假) 賓於帝, 倪神聖之德也. 高尙行虖 (乎) 星辰日月而不眺, 能陽也; 下綸窮深瀟 (淵) 之瀟 (淵) 而不沫, 能陰也. 上則風雨奉之, 下綸則有天□□□. □ (1) 乎深汄, 則魚蛟先後之, 水流之物莫不隋 (隨) 從; 陵處, 則雷神養之, 風雨辟 (避) 鄉 (嚮), 鳥守 (獸) 弗干. 曰: 龍大矣. 龍既能雲變, 有 (又) 能蛇變, 有 (又) 能魚變. 騖 (飛) 鳥蚰蟲, 唯所欲化, 而不失本刑 (形), 神能之至也. □□□□□ (2) □□□□□□為, 有弗能察也. 知 (智) 者不能察其變, 辯者不能□其美, 至巧不能赢其文(?). □□□鳥□也, 功(?) □為, 化蚰蟲, 神貴之容也, 天下之貴物也.

168

The several disciples asked, saying: "The *Changes* often mentions dragons; what is the virtue of the dragon like?" Confucius said: "The dragon is great indeed. The dragon's form shifts. When it approaches the Lord in audience, it manifests the virtue of a spiritual sage. That on high it rises and moves among the stars and planets, sun and moon, and yet does not look far away is because it is able to be *yang*; that below it moves throughout the depths of the deep, and yet does not drown is because it is able to be *yin*. Above, the wind and rain hold it aloft; below there is heaven .. .. (1) into the deep currents, the fishes and reptiles surround it and of those beings of the watery currents there is none that does not follow it; perched up high, the god of thunder nourishes it, the wind and rain avoid facing it, and the birds and beasts do not disturb it."

(He) said: "The dragon is great indeed. While the dragon is able to change into a cloud, it is also able to change into a reptile, and also able to change into a fish, a flying bird, or a slithery reptile. No matter how it wants to transform, that it does not lose its basic form is because it is the epitome of spiritual ability. .. .. (2) .. .. in it, there is that which you cannot examine. The wise one cannot examine its changes, the disputant cannot .. its beauty, and even the most clever cannot outdo its markings. .. .. .. birds .., achievement .. in it, transforms into a slithery reptile is because it has the capacity of spiritual honor and is the most honored being under heaven."

169

曰: 龍大矣. 龍之□德也, 曰□□□□□ (3) 易□□□□, 爵之曰
君子; 戒事敬合, 精白柔和, 而不諱賢, 爵之曰夫子. 或大或小,
其方一也. 至用□也, 而名之曰君子, 兼, "黃常 (裳)" 近之矣; 尊
威精白堅强, 行之不可撓也, "不習" 近之矣. ・易曰: "[寢] 龍勿
(4) 用." 孔子曰: 龍寢矣而不陽, 時至矣而不出, 可謂寢矣. 大人
安失 (佚) 矣而不朝, 諂獻在廷, 亦猶龍之寢也. 其行減而不可用
也, 故曰 "寢龍勿用". ・易曰: "杬 (亢) 龍有悔." 孔子曰: 此言爲
上而驕下, 驕下而不殆者, 未 (5) 之有也. 聖人之立正 (政) 也. 若
遁 (循) 木, 俞 (愈) 高俞 (愈) 畏下, 故曰 "杬 (亢) 龍有悔". ・易
曰: "龍戰于野, 其血玄黃." 孔子曰: 此言大人之寶德而施教於民
也. 夫文之孝, 釆物暴存者, 其唯龍乎? 德義廣大, 法物備具者,
(6) [其唯] 聖人乎? "龍戰于野" 者, 言大人之廣德而下綏 (接) 民
也; "其血玄黃" 者, 見文也. 聖人出法教以道 (導) 民, 亦猶龍之
文也, 可謂 "玄黃" 矣, 故曰 "龍". 見龍而稱莫大焉. ・易曰: "王
臣蹇蹇, 非今之故." 孔子 (7) 曰: "王臣蹇蹇" 者, 言其難也. 夫唯
智 (知) 其難也,

(He) said: "The dragon is great indeed. As for the dragon's .. virtue, it is called .. .. (3) *Changes* .. .. ennobling it one calls it a 'gentleman'; that it is careful of affairs and comes together respectfully, in seminal purity and tender harmony and yet does not conceal its worthiness, one ennobles it calling it 'master.' Now great, now little, its direction is as one. It is most useful .., and one names it 'gentleman,' for which 'Yellow skirts' approximates it.[1] Venerably awe-inspiring, seminally pure and firmly strong, when in motion it cannot be deflected, for which 'not repeated' approximates it."[2]

The *Changes* says: "The [sleeping] dragon; do not use."[3] Confucius said: "That the dragon sleeps and is not *yang* is because when the time arrives but it does not come out, it can be called sleeping. That the great man is content with (loss:) idleness and does not go to court, being on guard and restrained at home, is also just like the sleeping of the dragon. Because its motion is muddled and it cannot be used, therefore it says, 'The sleeping dragon; do not use.'"

The *Changes* says: "The rafting (*sic*) dragon; there is regret."[4] Confucius said: "This speaks of being above and treating those below arrogantly; there has never been a case (5)[5] of one who treats those below arrogantly not being in danger. As for the sage's establishment of government, it is like climbing a tree: the higher one gets, the more one fears what is below. Therefore it says: 'The rafting dragon; there is regret.'"

The *Changes* says: "The dragon fights in the wilds; its blood is black and yellow."[6] Confucius said: "This speaks of the great man's treasuring virtue and effecting education among the people. As for the filiality of culture, is it only the dragon whose gathering of beings includes even those who have survived violence? [Is it only] the sage whose virtue and propriety are broad and great and whose modeling of beings is complete? (6) 'The dragon battles in the wilds' speaks of the great man's broad virtue connecting with the people below. 'Its blood is black and yellow' manifests (markings:) culture. That the sage issues laws and teachings in order to lead the people is also like the dragon's markings, which can indeed be called 'black and yellow.' Therefore, it is called 'dragon.' When you have seen a dragon, there is no mention greater than it."

The *Changes* says: "The king's retainer is hobbled, hobbled; it is not the present's reason."[7] Confucius said: (7) " 'The king's retainer is hobbled, hobbled' speaks of his difficulty. It is only because he knows of the

171

故重言之, 以戒今也. 君子智 (知) 難而備 [之, 則] 不難矣; 見幾而務之, □有功矣, 故備難□易. 務幾者, 成存其人, 不言吉凶焉. "非今之故" 者, 非言獨今也, 古以狀也. ·易曰: "鼎折 (8) 足, 復 (覆) 公葲 (餗), 其刑屋 (渥), 凶." 孔子曰: 此言下不勝任也. 非其任而任之, 能毋折虖 (乎)? 下不用則城不守, 師不戰, 內亂□上, 謂 "折足"; 路其國, [無 (蕪) 其] 地, 五種不收, 謂 "復 (覆) 公葲 (餗)"; □養不至, 饑餓不得食, 謂 "形屋 (渥)". 二厽 (三) 子問曰: 人君至于饑 (9) 乎? 孔子曰: 昔者晉厲公路其國, 無 (蕪) 其地, 出田七月不歸, 民反諸雲夢, 無車而獨行, □□□□□□公□□□□□□□□□饑(?) 不得食亓 (六) 月, 此 "其刑屋 (渥)" 也. 故曰德義無小, 失宗無大, 此之謂也. ·易曰: "鼎玉鉉 (鉉), [大] 吉, (10) 無不利." 孔子曰: 鼎大矣. 鼎之遷也, 不自往, 必入 (人) 舉之, 大人之貞也. 鼎之舉也, 不以其止, 以□□□□□□□□□□□□□□□賢以舉忌也. 明君立正 (政), 賢輔強 (弼) 之, 將何爲而不利? 故曰 "大吉".

172

difficulty that it therefore reiterates it to warn the present age. If the gentleman knows of the difficulty and prepares for [it, then] it will not be at all difficult. When he sees the pivot and acts on it, .. there will be achievement. Therefore, by preparing for difficulty, .. easy; by acting on the pivot, he completes and maintains his person, and there is no mention of auspiciousness or inauspiciousness in it. 'It is not the present's reason' is not to speak only of the present, but that things are shaped in the past."

The *Changes* says: "The cauldron's broken (8) leg: Overturns the duke's stew; his punishment is execution-in-chamber; inauspicious."[8] Confucius said: "This speaks of the lower not being capable of fulfilling its responsibility. If it is not its responsibility yet it assumes it, can it not be broken? If the lower is not used, then the city wall will not be guarded and the troops will not fight; internal disorder .. the higher is what is meant by 'broken leg.' To bring defeat to his state, [to make waste of his] land, and not to harvest the five crops is what is meant by 'overturning the duke's stew.' Food not being available and the hungry not getting to eat is what is meant by the 'punishment is execution-in-chamber.'" The several disciples asked, saying: "Does the lord of men arrive at being hungry (9)?" Confucius said: "Of old, Duke Li of Jin (r. 580–573 b.c.) brought defeat to his state and made waste of his land. He went out to hunt in the seventh month but did not return, the people turning against him at Yunmeng (in present day Baocheng county, Shaanxi); without a chariot he had to walk by himself, ... duke .. .. hungry and did not get to eat for six months; this is 'his punishment is execution-in-chamber.' Therefore, it is said 'Of virtue and propriety there is nothing small, and in losing the ancestral temple there is nothing great,' which is what is meant by this."

The *Changes* says: "The cauldron's jade bar; [greatly] auspicious; (10) there is nothing not beneficial."[9] Confucius said: "The cauldron is great indeed. As for the shifting of the cauldron, it does not go of its own accord, but there must be a man to lift it; this is the determination of a great man. The lifting of the cauldron is not done by its legs, but by .. .. the worthy man uses it to lift up jealousy. When an enlightened lord establishes government, and worthy men support and help him, what could be done that would not be beneficial? Therefore, it says: 'Greatly auspicious.'"

・易曰: "康侯用錫馬番 (蕃) (11) 庶, 晝日三接." 孔子曰: 此言聖王之安世者也. 聖之正 (政), 牛參弗服, 馬恒弗駕, 不憂 (擾) 乘牝馬□□□□□□□□□粜 (糧?) 時至, 芻稾不重, 故曰 "錫馬". 聖人之立正 (政) 也, 必尊天而敬衆, 理順五行, 天地無困, 民□不 (12) 滲(?), 甘露時雨聚降, 剽 (飄) 風苦雨不至, 民心相酌以壽, 故曰 "番 (蕃) 庶". 聖王各有厽 (三) 公, 厽 (三) 卿, "晝日三 [接]" □□□□□者也. ・易曰: "聒 (括) 囊, 無咎無譽". 孔子曰: 此言箴小人之口也. 小人多言多過, 多事多患. □□ (13) □以衍矣. 而不可以言箴之. 其猶 "聒 (括) 囊" 也, 莫出莫入, 故曰 "無咎無譽". 二厽 (三) 子問曰: 獨無箴于聖□□□□□□聖人之言也, 德之首也. 聖人之有口也, 猶地之有川浴 (谷) 也, 財用所劖出也; 猶山林陵澤也, 衣食□ (14) □ [所] 劖生也. 聖人壹言, 萬世用之. 唯恐其不言也, 有何箴焉? ・卦曰: "見龍在田, 利見大人." 孔子曰: □□□□□□□□嗛 (謙) 易告也, 就民易遇也, 聖人君子之貞也. 度 (庶?) 民宜之, 故曰 "利以見大人". ・

174

The *Changes* says: "The vigorous lord is herewith awarded horses in luxuriant (11) number; during daylight thrice connecting."[10] Confucius said: "This speaks of the sage king's pacifying the world. With a sage's government, oxen work together without being hitched and horses persevere without being driven. One need not worry about harnessing mares .. .. meal arrives in a timely manner while forage and hay is not duplicated; therefore, it says 'is awarded horses.' As for the sage's establishment of government, he necessarily venerates heaven and respects the masses; his organization complies with the five phases, so that heaven and earth have no troubles and the people .. are not (12) stained, the sweet dew and timely rain fall in abundance, the fierce winds and bitter rains do not arrive, and the people's sentiments toast each other to long life; therefore, it says 'in luxuriant numbers.' The sage kings each had three dukes and three ministers: 'during daylight thrice [connecting]' .. .. [is what is meant by] this."

The *Changes* says: "Tying the sack; there is no trouble, there is no praise."[11] Confucius said: "This speaks of shutting the small man's mouth. When the small man talks a lot he makes a lot of mistakes, and when he has many activities he has many anxieties. .. .. (13) .. through superfluousness. And yet, you cannot shut him up through words. It is just like 'tying a pouch': nothing comes out but nothing goes in. Therefore, it says 'there is no trouble, there is no praise.'" The several disciples asked, saying: "Is it only in the case of the sage that there is no shutting .. .. ..?" [Confucius said]: "As for the sayings of the sages, they are the head of virtue. The sage's having a mouth is just like the earth's having a river valley: it is that from which goods and services are transported out; it is just like the mountain forests' peaks and ponds: it is that from which clothing and food .. (14) .. are brought to life. A sage's single word will be used by ten-thousand generations. One fears only that he will not speak. How could there be any shutting him up?"

The hexagram says: "Appearing dragon in the fields; beneficial to see the great man."[12] Confucius said: .. .. modesty it is easy to report and according with the people it is easy to meet, is the determination of the sage and gentleman. The masses of people regard it as appropriate; therefore it says 'beneficial in order (*sic*[13]) to see the great man.'"

卦曰: "君子終日鍵 (乾) 鍵 (乾), (15) [夕沂 (惕) 若] 厲, 無咎." 孔子曰: 此言君子務時, 時至而動□□□□□□屈力以成功, 亦日中而不止, 時年至而不淹. 君子之務時, 猶馳驅也, 故曰 "君子終日鍵 (乾) 鍵 (乾)". 時盡而止之以置身, 置身而靜, 故曰 "夕沂 (惕)若厲, 無咎". (16)

易 [曰: "蜚 (飛) 龍在] 天, 利見大人." [孔子曰: 此] 言□□□□□□□□□君子在上, [則] 民被其利, 賢者不離, 故曰: "蜚 (飛) 龍在天, 利見大人". ·卦曰: "見群龍 [無首], 吉." 孔子曰: 龍神威而精處□□□□□□□□□□ (17) 用□□□□□首者□□□□□□□□□□□□見君子□吉也. ·卦曰: "履霜, 堅冰至." 孔子曰: 此言天時譖(?), 戒葆常也. 歲□田產(?) 濕, 以□㝮 (乎) 始於□ (18) 之□□□□□守之□□□□□□□□□□□德與天道始, 必順五行, 其孫貴而宗不偈(? 滅). ·卦曰: "直方大, 不習, 無不利." 孔子曰: □□也, 方者□ (19) 大者言其直或之容□□□□□□□□□□□□□□□□□□□無不□, 故曰 "無不利". ·卦曰: "含章可貞." □□□□□□□□□□□□□□□□□□□□□□□□ (20) 含亦美, 貞之可也, 亦□□□□□□□□. [·]

176

The hexagram says: "The gentleman to the end of the day is so initiating; (15) [at night he is wary as if] there is danger; there is no trouble."[14] Confucius said: "This speaks of the gentleman striving to be timely; when the time arrives he moves .... bending his strength in order to complete his accomplishments, also not stopping in the middle of the day and not slowing up when getting on in years. The gentleman's striving to be timely also stirs others; therefore it says 'The gentleman to the end of the day is so initiating.' Settling oneself such that you stop when the time is past is to relax and be calm; therefore it says 'at night he is wary as if there is danger; there is no trouble.' " (16)

The *Changes* [says: "Flying dragon in the] heavens; beneficial to see the great man."[15] [Confucius said: "This] speaks .... the gentleman is on high, [then] the people will be covered by his beneficence and the worthy will not depart; therefore it says 'Flying dragon in the heavens; beneficial to see the great man.'"

The hexagram says: "See the flock of dragons [without heads]; auspicious."[16] Confucius said: "The dragon is awe-inspiring in spirit but settled in essence .. .. (17) use .. .. head .. .. to see the gentleman .. auspicious."

The hexagram says: "Treading on frost; the firm ice will arrive."[17] Confucius said: "This speaks of heaven's timely warning to protect the long-lasting. The year . . . southwest warm,[18] in order . . . with respect to the beginning . . . (18) it .. .. maintain it .. .. virtue begins together with the heavenly Way, and necessarily complies with the Five Phases; his descendants will be honored and the ancestral temple will not be destroyed."

The hexagram says: "Straight, square, and great; not repeated; there is nothing not beneficial." Confucius said: ". . . , as for 'square,' . . . (19) 'great' speaks of the appearance of his being 'straight' .. .. there is nothing not .. , therefore it says 'there is nothing not beneficial.'"

The hexagram says: "Containing a pattern; it is permissible to determine."[19] .. .. (20) contained is also beautiful, the permissibility of determination, also .. ..

卦曰: □□□□□□□□□□□□□□□□□□□□之事矣. □□
□□□□□□□□□□□□□□□□□□□□□□□□□□□□
□□□ (21) □者也. 元, 善之始也. □□□□□□□□□色之徒
嗛□□□□□□. [·卦曰: "屯其膏, 小貞吉], 大貞凶." 孔子曰:
屯☒而上通其德, 無□☒ (22) 小民家息以緓衣□□□□□□
□□□□屯輪之, 其吉亦宜矣. 大貞□□□□□□□川流下而
貨(?) 留□年敎十□□□□□□□□□□□□□□□□□□□□
□□□□□□□□ (23) 賫□財弗施則□. [·卦曰: "同人于野,
亨, 利] 涉大川." 孔子曰: 此言大德之好遠也. □□□□□□□
悳(? 德), 和同者衆, 以濟大事, 故曰 ["利涉大川". ·] 卦曰: "同
人於門, 无咎." [孔子曰:] □□□□□□□□□□ (24) 而已矣. 小
德□□□. [·卦曰: "同人于] 宗, 貞藺 (吝)." 孔子曰: 此言其所同
唯其室人而 [已], 其所同☒, 故曰 "貞藺 (吝)". ·卦曰: "絞如委
如, 吉". 孔 [子] 曰: 絞, 日也; 委, 老也. 老曰之□□□, 故曰 "吉".
·卦曰: "嗛 (謙), 亨, 君子有 (25) 夂 (終), 吉." 孔子曰: □□□□
□□□□□上川 (坤) 而下根 (艮), 川 (坤) (此處疑有脫文) 也; 根
(艮), 精質也, 君子之行也. □□□□□□□□吉焉. 吉, 嗛 (謙)
也; 凶, 橋 (驕) 也.

178

The hexagram says: ".. .. .. affair.
.. .. (21) .. .
'Prime' is the beginning of goodness. .. .. disciples of sex
modestly .. .."

[The hexagram says: "Hoarding its fat; little determination is aus-
picious], great determination is inauspicious."[20] Confucius said: " 'To
hoard' . . . and making its virtue penetrate above, there is nothing . . .
(22) the little people's families rest in order to sew clothing .. ..
.. .. hoarding and circulating it, its auspiciousness is also appropriate indeed. 'Great determination' .. .. the river flows down
and wares remain .. years burst ten .. ..
.. .. (23) hire .. resources and not to put them into
circulation then .. ."

[The hexagram says: "Gathering men in the wilds; receipt; benefi-
cial] to ford the great river."[21] Confucius said: "This speaks of the great
virtue's fondness for the distant. .. .. virtue, those who come
together harmoniously are the masses, in order to complete great affairs;
therefore it says ['beneficial to ford the great river']."

The hexagram says: "Gathering men at the gate; there is no trouble."[22]
[Confucius said]: ".. .. .. (24) and that is all. The little
virtue .. .."

[The hexagram says: "Gathering men at] the ancestral temple; determination is distressful."[23] Confucius said: "This speaks of those who
are gathered together being only men of the house and that is all; those
that are gathered together . . . ; therefore it says 'determination is distressful.' "

The hexagram says: "Crossed-like, stooped-like; auspicious."[24]
Confucius said: " 'Crossed' is the sun; 'stooped' is an elder. An elder says
it .. .. ..; therefore it says 'auspicious.' "

The hexagram says: "Modesty; receipt; the gentleman has (25) an
end; auspicious."[25] Confucius said: ".. .. .. the top (trigram)
is *Chuan* and the bottom (trigram) is *Gen Chuan*.[26] *Gen* is pure substance,
the action of the gentleman. .. .. auspiciousness in it. Auspiciousness is modesty; inauspiciousness is arrogance. Heaven disorders

天亂驕而成嗛 (謙), 地僻(?) 驕而實嗛 (謙), 鬼神禍福嗛 (謙), 人亞 (惡) 驕而好嗛 (謙). □□□□ (26) □□□□□□□□□□好, 美不伐也. 夫不伐德者, 君子也. 其盈如□□□□□□□□□而再說, 其有終也宜矣. ·卦曰: "盱予 (豫), 悔." 孔子曰: 此言鼓樂而不忘亞 (德) 也. 夫忘□□□□□□ (27) □□□□□□□□□□□□□□□□至者, 其病亦至, 不可辟 (避), 禍福成(?) □□□□□□□□□□□□□□□行, 禍福畢至, 知 (智) 者知之, 故廏客恐懼, 日慢(?) 一日, 猶有過行. 卒焉之(?) □□□□□ (28) □□□□□□□ [·卦曰: "鳴鶴在陰, 其子和之, 我] 有好爵, 與璽 (爾) 羸 (靡) [之." 孔子曰:] □□□□□□□□□□□□□□□其子隨之, 通也; 昌 (倡) 而和之, 和也. 曰和同至矣. "好爵" 者, 言耆 (旨) 酒也. 弗□□□□□ (29) 曰□□□□□□□□□□□□□□□□之德. 唯飲與食, 絕甘分□. [·卦曰: "密雲不雨, 自我西郊, 公射取皮 (彼) 在穴." 孔] 子曰: 此言聲 (聖) 君之下舉乎山林, 拔取之中也, 故曰: "公射取皮 (彼) 在穴". □□□□□, (30) 故曰 "自我 [西郊]". □□□□□□□□□□□□□美(?), 故曰 "利貞". 其占曰: 豐□□□□□□□□□□□ [·卦] 曰: "不 [恒其德, 或] 承之憂 (羞), 貞藺 (吝)." 孔子曰: 此言小人知善而弗爲, 攻(?) 維而無止, □□□□, [故曰: "不] (31) 恒其德". □□□□□□□□□□□□□□□□□也. 劭 (飭) 行

180

the arrogant and completes the modest, while earth avoids the arrogant and makes real the modest; ghosts and spirits give ill fortune (to the arrogant and) good fortune to the modest, while men hate the arrogant and like [the modest]. .. .. (26) .. .. good, beauty is not boastful. He who does not boast of virtue is a gentleman. His repletion is like .. .. and said again, his having an end is also appropriate."

The hexagram says: "Wide-eyed comfort; regret."[27] Confucius said: "This speaks of drumming the music but not forgetting virtue. The forgetting .. .. (27) .. .. arrival, its illness also arrives and cannot be avoided, ill and good fortune complete .. .. motion, ill and good fortune both arrive; the knowledgeable know it, and therefore the stable guests tremble with trepidation, day by day fearing (?) and yet still having excess motion. Finishing in it .. .. (28) .. .."

[The hexagram says: "A calling crane in the shade, its young harmonizes with it: We] have a fine chalice, I will down [it] with you."[28] Confucius said]: ".. .. .. that its young follows it is connection; that it leads and it harmonizes with it is harmony. It says that harmony arrives together. 'A fine chalice' speaks of drawing wine; it is not to .. .. (29) to say .. .. virtue. Only drinking and eating break off the sweetness and divide .. ."

[The hexagram says: "The dense clouds do not rain from our western pasture; the duke shoots and takes the skin in the cavern."][29] Confucius said: "This speaks of those beneath the sagely lord being raised up in the mountain forests, and being taken from their midsts; therefore it says 'The duke shoots and takes the skin in the cavern.' .. .., (30) therefore it says 'From our [western pasture].' .. .. beauty, therefore it says 'beneficial to determine.' Its prognostication says: 'Abundance .. .."

[The hexagram] says: "Not [making constant his virtue, he perhaps] receives its sadness; determination is distressful."[30] Confucius said: "This speaks of the little man's knowing goodness but not doing it, attacking the secure and not stopping, ... ; [therefore it says 'Not] (31) making constant his virtue.' .. .. Acting

以後民者謂大寨(?), 遠人倡至謂□□. [·] 卦曰: "公用射雕於 [高墉之上], 無不利." 孔子曰: 此言人君高志求賢, 賢者在上, 則 因☒用之, 故曰☒ (32) □□□□□. [·] 卦曰: ["根 (艮) 其北 (背), 不獲其身; 行其庭, 不見其人. 孔子] 曰: "根 (艮) 其北 (背)" 者, 言□事也; "不獲其身" 者, 精□□□也. 敬官任事, 身□□者 鮮矣. 其占曰: 能精能白, 必爲上客; 能白能精, 必爲□以精白踝 □□ (33) "[行] 其庭, 不見其 [人". ·] 卦曰: ["艮其輔,] 言有序." 孔子曰: □言也, 吉凶之至也. 必皆於言語擇善□□□□擇利而 言害, 塞人之美, 陽人之亞 (惡), 可謂无德, 其凶亦宜矣. 君子慮 之內, 發之□□□□□□□ (34) □不言害, 塞人之亞 (惡), 陽 [人 之] 美, 可謂 "有序" 矣. ·卦曰: "豐, 亨, 王叚 (假) [之], 勿自(?) 憂, 宜日中." 孔子曰: □□□也. "勿憂", 用賢弗害也. 日中而盛, 用賢弗害, 其亨亦宜矣. 黃帝四輔, 堯立三卿, 帝□□□□□□□ (35) □□□□曰□其肝□□□□魚大羹也, 肝言其內, 內其大美, 其外必有大聲問. ·

severely in order to put the people last is called great obstruction (?); distant people happily arriving is called .. .. ."

The hexagram says: "The duke herewith shoots a hawk [on the top of a high wall]; there is nothing not beneficial."[31] Confucius said: "This speaks of the lord of men's high ambition to seek worthies. Since the worthies are on top, then he accords . . . to use them; therefore it says . . . (32) .. .."

The hexagram says: ["Stilling his back, but not getting his body: Walking into his courtyard, but not seeing his person."[32] Confucius] said: " 'Stilling his back' speaks of .. affairs. 'Not getting his body' is essentially .. .. To be respectful of office and responsible for affairs, rare indeed is it that the person .. .. . Its prognostication says: 'Able to be pure, able to be white, one will necessarily be a high guest; able to be white, able to be pure, one will necessarily be .. through purity and whiteness to grow the masses[33] .. .. (33). '[Walking] into his courtyard, but not seeing his [person].' "

The hexagram says: "[Stilling his cheeks: words] have sequence."[34] Confucius said: "As for .. 'words,' they are the epitome of auspiciousness and inauspiciousness. In the case of speech, one must always choose good .. .. to choose benefit and speak of harm obstructs man's beauty and brightens man's ugliness; this can be said to be without virtue and its inauspiciousness also being appropriate. The gentleman ponders it within and expresses it .. .. (34) .. does not speak of harm. To obstruct man's ugliness and to brighten [man's] beauty can be said to 'have sequence.' "

The hexagram says: "Abundance: Receipt; the king approaches [it]; do not be self (sic) sad; it is proper for the middle of the day."[35] Confucius said: ".. .. .. . 'Do not be sad' is to use the worthy and not to harm them. To be full in the middle of the day and to use the worthy and not to harm them, its 'receipt' is also appropriate. The Yellow Emperor had four assistants, Yao established the three ministers, and Emperor .. .. (35) .. .."

[The hexagram] says: "[Dispersing] its liver .. .. fish great broth. 'Liver' speaks of its interior. Its interior being greatly beautiful, its exterior will necessarily have a great sound to be heard."

卦曰: "未濟, 亨, [小狐] 涉川幾濟, 濡其尾, 无逌 (逌) 利." 孔子
曰: 此言始易而終難也, 小人之貞也. (36)

The hexagram says: "Not yet completed: Receipt; [the little fox] fording the river and almost completed, wets his tail; there is no place beneficial."[36] Confucius said: "This speaks of the beginning being easy and the end being difficult, the determination of the little man." (36)

A P P E N D E D

S T A T E M E N T S

天奠 (尊) 地庳 (卑), 鍵 (乾) 川 (坤) 定矣. 庳 (卑) 高已陳, 貴賤立 (位) 矣. 動靜有常, 剛柔斷矣. 方以類宊 (聚), 物以群 [分, 吉凶生矣. 在天成象], 在地成刑 (形), [變] 化見矣. 見 [故] 剛柔相摩, 八卦 [相蕩, 鼓之雷霆, 潤之以風雨, 日月運行, 一寒一暑.] (1) 鍵 (乾) 道成男, 川 (坤) 道成女, 鍵 (乾) 知大始, 川 (坤) 作成物. 鍵 (乾) 以易 〈知〉, 川 (坤) 以閒 (簡) 能. 易則傷 (易) 知, 閒 (簡) 則易從. 傷 (易) 知則有親, 傷 (易) 從則有功. 有親則可久, 有功則可大也. 可久則賢人之德, [可大則賢人之業. 易閒 (簡) 而天下之] (2) 理得, 理得而成立 (位) 乎其中.

耴 (聖) 人設卦觀馬 (象), 毄 (繫) 辭焉而明吉凶,

Heaven being venerable and earth base, *Jian*, "The Key,"[1] and *Chuan*, "The Flow,"[2] are settled. The base and high already being arrayed, the noble and mean are established. Motion and rest having constancy, the hard and soft are divided. The directions being gathered according to category, and beings being [divided] according to groups, [auspiciousness and in-auspiciousness come to life. In the heavens completing images] and on earth completing forms, [changes] and transformations become apparent. This is [why] the hard and soft rub against each other, and the eight trigrams [wash across each other, drumming them with thunder and lightning, moistening them with wind and rain, the sun and moon moving in cycles, one cold and one hot.] (1) The way of "The Key" completes the male; the way of "The Flow" completes the female. "The Key" knows the great beginning; "The Flow" performs the completing of beings. "The Key" through change <knows>[3]; "The Flow" through the crack[4] is capable. With change, then it is easy to know[5]; through the crack then it is easy to follow. Being easy to know, then there is closeness; being easy to follow, then there is accomplishment. There being closeness, then it can be long-lived; there being accomplishment, then it can be great. Being long-lived, then (it is) the virtue of the worthy man; [being great, then (it is) the enterprise of the worthy man. With change and the crack, (2) the pattern of all under heaven] is gotten, and the pattern being gotten it completes the positions in its midst.

The sage constructed the hexagrams by observing the images.[6] Appending statements to them, he illuminated the auspicious and

剛柔相逐而生變化, 是故吉凶也者, 得失之馬 (象) 也. 悬 (悔) 闇 (吝) 也者, 憂虞之馬 (象) 也. 通變化也者, 進退之馬 (象) 也. 剛柔也者, 晝夜之馬 (象) 也. 六爻 [之] (3) 動, 三亟 (極) 之道也. 是故君子之所居而安者, 易之序(?) 也. 所樂而妧 (玩), 敎 (爻) 之始也. 君子居則觀其馬 (象) 而妧 (玩) 其辭, 動則觀其變而妧 (玩) 其占, 是以自天右 (祐) 之, 吉, 無不利也.

緣 (彖) 者, 言如馬 (象) 者也. 肴 (爻) 者, 言如 (4) 變者也. 吉凶也者, 言其失得也. 悬 (悔) 闇 (吝) 也者, 言如小疵也. 無咎也者, 言補過也. 是故列貴賤 [者] 存乎立 (位), 極大小者存乎卦. 辯吉凶者存乎辭, 憂悬 (悔) 闇 (吝) 者存乎分, 振無咎存乎謀. 是故卦有大 (5) 小, 辭有險易. 辭者, 各指其所之也.

《易》與天地順, 故能彌論天下之道, 卬 (仰) 以觀于天文, 頫 (頫) 以觀于地理, 是故知幽明之故, 觀始反 (返) 冬 (終), 故知死生之說. 精氣爲物, 斿 (游) 魂爲變, 故知鬼神之精 (情) 狀. 與天 (6) [地] 相校, 故不回. 知周乎萬物, 道齊乎天下, 故不過. 方行不遺, 樂天知命, 故不憂. 安地厚乎仁, 故能睰 (愛). 犯(範) 回 (圍)

inauspicious. The hard and the soft following[7] each other gives life to the alternations and transformations. This is why "auspicious" and "inauspicious" are the images of gain and loss. "Regret" and "distress" are the images of anxiety. Connecting alternations and transformations is the image of progression and regression. The hard and soft are the images of day and night. The six lines['] (3) movement is the way of the three extremes. This is why the [sequence[8]] of the *Changes* is that in which the gentleman dwells and finds contentment, and the beginnings[9] of the lines[10] are that in which he delights and plays. When the gentleman dwells he observes its images and plays with its statements; when he moves he observes its alternations and plays with its prognostications; therewith "From heaven blessing it; auspicious; there is nothing not beneficial."[11]

The hexagram statements are phrased like[12] images. The line statements are phrased like (4) alternations. "Auspicious" and "inauspicious" are phrased in its loss and gain. "Regret" and "distress" are phrased like little flaws. "There is no trouble" is phrased[13] in patching mistakes. This is why [the] arraying of the noble and mean resides in position, taking the great and little to the extreme[14] resides in the hexagrams, distinguishing the "auspicious" and "inauspicious" resides in the statements, worrying about "regret" and "distress" resides in the divisions,[15] and stirring "no trouble" resides in planning. This is why there are great and little hexagrams (5) and dangerous and easy statements. As for the statements, each points to where it is going.

The *Changes* is compliant[16] with heaven and earth. Therefore, it is able completely to assay the way of all under heaven. Looking up to observe the heavenly markings, and looking down to observe the patterns of the earth, this is why it knows the reasons for dark and light. Observing the beginning[17] and reverting to the end, therefore it knows the explanations of death and life. Seminal fluids and vapor make up beings and wandering souls make up alternations; therefore it knows the seminal[18] shape of ghosts and spirits. Compared[19] together with heaven and (6) [earth], therefore it is not deflected.[20] Knowing universally among the ten-thousand beings, the Way is equal[21] with all under heaven; therefore, it does not go too far. Walking squarely without leaving anything out,[22] delighting in heaven and knowing fate, therefore it is not worried. Being content with the earth and sincere in humaneness, therefore it is able to (love).[23] Revolving throughout the

天地之化而不過. 曲萬物而不遺, 達諸晝夜之道而知. 古 (故) 神無方, 《易》無體.

一陰一陽 (7) 之胃 (謂) 道. 係之者, 善也. 成之者, 生 (性) 也. 仁者見之胃 (謂) 之仁, 知 (智) 者見之胃 (謂) 知 (智), 百生 (姓) 日用而弗知也. 故君子之道鮮. 耵 (聖) 者仁勇, 鼓萬物而不與衆人同憂, 盛德大業至矣幾 (哉). 富有之胃 (謂) 大業, 日新之胃 (謂) (8) 誠德, 生之胃 (謂) 馬 (象), 成馬 (象) 之胃 (謂) 鍵 (乾), 敎 (爻) 法之胃 (謂) 川 (坤), 極數知來之胃 (謂) 占, 迥 (通) 變之胃 (謂) 事, 陰陽之胃 (謂) 神.

夫 《易》, 廣矣, 大矣. 以言乎遠則不過, 以言乎近則精而正, 以言乎天地之間則備. 夫鍵 (乾), 其靜也圈, 其 (9) 動也榴, 是以大生焉. 夫川 (坤), 其靜也歙, 其動也辟, 是以廣生焉. 廣大肥 (配) 天地, 變迥 (通) 配四 [時], 陰 [陽] 之合肥 (配) 日月, 易閒 (簡) 之善肥 (配) 至德.

子曰: 《易》, 其至乎, 夫 《易》, 耵 (聖) 人之所崇德而廣業也. 知崇膻 (禮) 卑, (10) 崇效天, 卑法地, 天地設立 (位), 《易》行乎其中. 誠生 [存存?], 道義之門.

耵 (聖) 人具以見天之業而□疑 (擬) 者 (諸) 其刑 (形) 容, 以馬 (象)

192

transformations of heaven and earth, it does not go too far; winding among the ten-thousand beings it does not leave any out; and penetrating it in the way of day and night it knows. Therefore, spirits have no direction and the *Changes* has no body.

One yin and one yang (7) is called the Way. What is tied[24] to it is goodness; what completes it is life.[25] When the humane see it, they call it humane. When the wise see it, they call it wise. The hundred families daily use it but do not know it. Therefore, the way of the gentleman is [rare]. The sage's humane use[26] drums up the ten-thousand beings and yet does not partake of the same worries as the masses of men.[27] His full virtue and great enterprise are perfect indeed![28] Bountifully having it is called the great enterprise; daily renewing it is called (8) sincere[29] virtue; giving life to it is called the image[30]; completing the image is called "The Key"; imitating[31] the model is called "The Flow"; going to the limits of numbers to know what is coming is called the prognostication; uniting the alternations is called serving; the yin and yang[32] is called spirit.

The *Changes* is broad indeed, is great indeed. In speaking in terms of the distant, then it does not go too far.[33] In speaking in terms of the near, then it is seminal[34] and upright. In speaking in terms of what is between heaven and earth, then it is complete. As for "The Key," its stillness is curled,[35] its (9) movement shakes,[36] and thereby greatness comes to life with it. As for "The Flow," its stillness is gathered,[37] its movement is opened, and thereby broadness comes to life in it. The broad and great match heaven and earth. Alternations unite and match the four [seasons]. The joining[38] of the yin and [yang] matches the sun and the moon. The goodness of the *Changes*' simplicity matches perfect virtue.

Confucius said: "How perfect the *Changes* is! The *Changes* is the virtue that the sage esteems and the enterprise he broadens. Knowing the esteemed and embodying[39] the base, (10) the esteemed emulates heaven and the base imitates earth. Heaven and earth construct positions, and the *Changes* moves in their midst. [Completing the inborn nature and maintaining it so], is the gate of the Way's propriety."

The sage is complete[40] in order to see heaven's enterprise[41] and [.. imitates][42] it in its form and appearance in order to give image to

其物義, [是] 故胃 (謂) 之馬 (象). 耴 (聖) 人具以見天下之動而觀
其會同, 以行其疾 (典) 膿 (禮). 係 (繫) 辭焉, 以 (11) 斷其吉凶, 是
故胃 (謂) 之教 (爻). 言天下之至業而不可惡也. 言天下之至業而
不亂, 知之而後言, 義之而後動矣. 義以成其變化. 嗚額 (鶴) 在
陰, 其子和之. 我有好爵, 吾與璽 (爾) 贏之. 曰君子居 (12) 其室,
言善則千里之外應之, 倪 (況) 乎其近者乎. 出言 而不善, 則十里
之外回之, 倪 (況) 乎其近者乎? 言出乎身, 加於民. 行發乎近, 見
乎遠. 言行, 君子之區 (樞) 幾 (機). 區 (樞) 幾 (機) 之發, 營辰之
關也. 言行, 君子之 (13) 所以動天地也. 同人先號逃 (咷) 而後哭.
子曰: 君子之道, 或出或居, 或謀或語. 二人同心, 其利斷金, 同人
之言, 其臭如蘭. 初六, 藉用白茅, 无咎. 子曰: 苟足 (措) 者 (諸)
地而可矣. 藉之用茅, 何咎之有, 慎之至 (14) 也. 夫且茅之爲迚
也, 薄用也, 而可重也. 慎此迚也以往, 其毋所失之. 勞謙, 君子有
冬 (終), 吉. 子曰: 勞而不代 (伐), 有功而不聽德, 厚之至也. 語以
其功下人者也. 德言成, 膿 (禮) 言共 (恭) 也. 濂 (謙) 也者, 至共
(恭) 以存其立 (位) 者 (15) 也. 抗 (亢) 龍有愍 (悔). 子曰: 貴而

194

the propriety of its beings. [This] is why it is called image. The sage is complete in order to see the movements of all under heaven and observes their coming together in order to move their canons and rituals.[43] He appends statements to it in order (11) to determine their auspiciousness and inauspiciousness. This is why it is called a line. Said in terms of the perfect enterprise[44] of all under heaven, it cannot be despised. Said in terms of the perfect enterprise of all under heaven, it is not disordered.[45] Only after knowing[46] it does one speak; only after making it proper[47] does one move. Propriety is used to complete its alternations and transformations.[48]

"A calling crane in the shade, its young harmonizes with it: We have a fine chalice, I will down it with you"[49] means[50] that when the gentleman dwells (12) in his chamber and speaks of the good[51] then even those from beyond a thousand *li* respond to him; how much more so those near to him! If he utters any words and they are not good, then even those beyond a thousand *li* will turn away from him; how much more so those near to him! Speech comes out of the person but acts on the people. Actions start in the near but are seen from afar. Speech and action are the pivot and fulcrum of the gentleman. The pivot and fulcrum's activation is the master of renown and disgrace.[52] Speech and action are the means by which the gentleman (13) moves heaven and earth.[53] As for "Gathering men at first weeping and wailing, but later crying (*sic*),"[54] Confucius said: "The way of the gentleman, whether going out or dwelling, whether silent[55] or conversing, is that when two men are of the same heart their benefit will cut metal. As for the speech of united men, its fragrance is like that of the orchid." Of the Initial Six, "For the mat use white cogongrass; there is no trouble,"[56] Confucius said: "Even if it were placed[57] on the ground it would be acceptable; to use cogongrass for the mat, what trouble could there be? This is the extreme of caution (14). Moreover, as for cogongrass being woven, it is thin in use and can be doubled over. Being cautious about this weaving, then in traveling there will be no place where you lose it." With respect to "Toiling modestly; the gentleman has an end; auspicious,"[58] Confucius said: "Toiling but not bragging,[59] and having achievement but not regarding oneself as virtuous is the extreme of sincerity. He who talks about his achievement is a lowly man. Virtue speaks of completion[60]; ritual speaks of collectivity.[61] As for modesty, it is being extremely collective-minded in order to maintain its position." (15) With respect to "Resisting dragon; there is regret,"[62] Confucius said: "It is noble but

無立 (位), [高而無民], 賢人在其下, □立 (位) 而无輔, 是以動而有悔 (悔) 也. 不出戶牖, 无咎. 子曰: 亂之所生, 言語以爲階, 君不閉則失臣, 臣不閉則失身, 幾 (機) 事不閉則害盈, 是以君子 (16) 慎閉而弗 [出也. 子曰: 作《易》者, 其知盜] 乎? 《易》曰: 負且乘, 致寇至, 負] 之事也者, 小人之事也. 乘者, 君子之器也. 小人而乘君子之器, 盜思奪之矣. 上曼 (慢) 下暴, 盜思伐之. 曼 (慢) 暴謀, 盜思奪之. 易曰: 負且乘, (17) 致寇至, 盜之招也.

　　[《易》有聖人之道四] 焉, 以言 [者, 上 (尙) 其辭]. 以動者, 上 (尙) 其變. 以 [制器者, 上 (尙) 其象. 以卜筮者], 上 (尙) 其占. 是故君子將有爲, 將有行者, 問焉 [而以] 言. 其受命也如錯, 無又 (有) 遠近幽險. 述 (18) 知來勿 (物), 非天之至精, 其孰能 [與于此]. 參五以變, [錯綜其數, 通] 其變, 述 [成天下之文, 極其數, 遂定天下之象, 非天下] 之至變, 誰能與於此. [《易》, 無思也], 無爲也. [寂] 然不動, 欽而述達天 (19) 下之故, 非天下之至神, 誰 [能與於此?] 夫《易》耵 (聖) 人 [之所以極深而] 達幾也. 唯深, 故達天下之誠. 唯幾,

196

without position, high [but without the people]. The worthy man is beneath him, standing but without support[63]; this is how he moves but has regrets." With respect to "Not going out of door or window; there is no trouble,"[64] Confucius said: "That which disorder brings to life is conversation being regarded as ranked. If the lord does not shut himself away, then he will lose his minister; if the minister does not shut himself away, then he will lose his person; if incipient affairs are not shut away, then they will harm fullness.[65] This is how the gentleman (16) is cautious about shutting himself away and not [going out." Confucius said: "Did the one who made the *Changes* know about bandits]? The *Changes* says 'Carrying on the back [and riding in a cart brings robbers to arrive.']"[66] The business of [carrying on the back] is the business of the little man. A cart is the vehicle of the gentleman. If the little man rides in the gentleman's vehicle, bandits will think to usurp him. For the high to be arrogant and the low to be violent, bandits will think to attack them. With arrogant and violent plans, bandits will think to usurp them.[67] When the *Changes* says 'Carrying on the back and riding in a cart (17) brings robbers to arrive,' it is the beckoning of bandits."

[The *Changes* has four (aspects) of the sage's way] in it: in terms of words [, it esteems its statements]; in terms of movements, it esteems its alternations; in terms of fashioning implements, it esteems its images; and [in terms of divination,] it esteems its prognostications. This is why when the gentleman is about to do anything or about to go anywhere, he asks of it [in] words. As for his receipt of the mandate, it is like a reversal[68]: there is no distant or near, dark or precipitous[69]; consequently (18) he knows beings that are to come. If it were not the perfect seminal essence of heaven, who would be capable [of participating in this]? The *Changes* proceeds by threes and fives, [weaving its numbers, and connecting] its changes; consequently, [he completes the (markings:) culture of all under heaven. It takes numbers to their limit; consequently, he settles] the images [of all under heaven; if it were not] the most perfect alternation [of all under heaven], who would be able to participate in this? [The *Changes* is without thought,] without action. [Quiet]-ly unmoving, following a feeling[70] it penetrates (19) the reasons of all under heaven; if it were not the most perfect spirituality of all under heaven, who [would be able to participate in this?] The *Changes* is [that by which] the sage [goes to the limits of the deep] and reaches the pivot. Only because it is deep is he therefore able to reach the sincerity of all under heaven; only because it is pivotal [is he therefore able to complete] the responsibility

[故能成天下] 之勢. 唯神, 故不疾而 [速, 不行而] 至. [子曰:《易》有] 耵 (聖) 人之道 [四焉者], 此言之 [冑 (謂)] 也.

天 (20) 一, 地二, 天三, 地四, 天五, 地六, 天七, 地八, 天九, 地十. [子曰: 夫《易》] 可 (何) 爲者也. 夫《易》, 古物定命, 樂天下之道, 如此而已者也. 是故耵 (聖) 人以達天下之志, 以達 [天下之業, 以] 斷 [天下之疑. 是故蓍] 之德, 員 (圓) 而神. 卦 (21) 之德, 方以知. 六肴 (爻) 之義, 易以工. 耵 (聖) 人以此佚心, 內藏於閉, [吉凶與] 民同顝 (願), 神以知來, 知以將往, 其誰能爲 [於] 茲? 古之忈 (聰) 明叡知神武而不羞者也虖? 是其 [明於天道] 察於民故, 是闉 (闔) 神物以前民 (22) 民用. 耵 (聖) 人以此齋戒, 以神明其德夫. 是故闉 (闔) 戶冑 (謂) 之川 (坤), 辟門冑 (謂) 之鍵 (乾). 一闉 (闔) 一辟冑 (謂) 之變, 往來不窮冑 (謂) 之迵 (通). 見之冑 (謂) 之馬 (象), 刑 (形) 冑 (謂) 之器, □而用之冑 (謂) 之法. 利用出入, 民一用之冑 (謂) 之神.

是故易有大恒, 是 (23) 生兩樣 (儀). 兩樣 (儀) 生四馬 (象), 四馬 (象) 生八卦, 八卦生吉凶, 吉凶生六 (大) 業. 是故法馬 (象) 莫大乎天地. 變迵 (通) 莫大乎四時, 垂馬 (象) 著明,

198

[of all under heaven]; only because it is spiritual is he therefore not abrupt but [rapid, does not go but] arrives. [When Confucius said "The Changes has four (aspects)] of the sage's way [in it]," this is what [is meant] by these words.

Heaven (20) is one, earth two; heaven three, earth four; heaven five, earth six; heaven seven, earth eight; heaven nine, earth ten.[71]

[Confucius said: "As for the Changes], (it can:) what is it that it does? The Changes strengthens beings and fixes fate,[72] taking pleasure in[73] the way of all under heaven. It is like this and nothing more. This is why the sage uses it to penetrate the will of all under heaven, and uses it to penetrate[74] [the enterprise of all under heaven, in order] to cut off [the doubts of all under heaven. This is why the milfoil]'s virtue is round and spiritual, and the hexagrams' virtue (21) is square and thereby knowing; the six lines' propriety is changeable and thereby accomplished.[75] The sage uses these in order to ease[76] his heart. Internally[77] storing them within his enclosure, [auspiciousness and inauspiciousness partake] of the same wishes[78] as the people. Being spiritual in order to know what is to come, and knowledgeable in order to lead what has gone, who would be able to act[79] [in] this? Is it that of antiquity which is perceptive and illumined, keen and knowledgeable, spiritual and martial and does not worry?[80] This is that in which it [illuminates the way of heaven] and examines into the reasons of the people; this is the closing[81] of the spiritual being in order to advance the uses of the people,[82] (22) and the people use it. The sage through this fasts and warns in order spiritually to illuminate his virtue. This is why shutting the window is called 'The Flow' and opening the gate is called 'The Key.' One shutting and one opening is called alternation. The going and coming not being exhausted is what is called connection. Seen, it is called an image; as form, it is called an implement; [fashioned] and used, it is called a model; and being beneficial to use it to go out and come in, the people as one using it, it is called spiritual. This is why the Changes has great constancy.[83] This (23) gives life to the two properties; the two properties give life to the four images; the four images give life to the eight trigrams; the eight trigrams give life[84] to auspiciousness and inauspiciousness, and auspiciousness and inauspiciousness give life to the great enterprise. This is why in modeling the images, there is none greater than heaven and earth; of the uniting of alternations, there is none greater than the four seasons; of revealing images and making

莫大乎日月, 榮莫大乎富貴. 備物至用, 位成器以爲天下利, 莫大乎耶 (聖) 人. 深備錯根, 柘險至遠, (24) 定天下吉凶, 定天下之勿勿者, 莫善乎蓍龜. 是故天生神物, 耶 (聖) 人則之. 天變化, 耶 (聖) 人效之. 天垂馬 (象), 見吉凶而耶 (聖) 人馬 (象) 之. 河出圖, 雒出書, 而耶 (聖) 人則之. 《易》有四馬 (象), 所以見也. 毄 (繫) 辭焉, 所以告也. 定之以吉 (25) 凶, 所以斷也. 《易》曰: 自天右 (祐) 之, 吉, 無不利. 右 (祐) 者, 助之也. 天之所助者, 順也. 人之所助也者, 信也. 膿 (禮) 信, 思乎順, □上 (尙) 賢, 是以自天右 (祐) 之, 吉, 无不利也.

　　子曰: "書不盡言, 言不盡意. 然則耶 (聖) 人之意, 其義可見已乎? (26) 子曰: 耶 (聖) 人之位 (立) 馬 (象) 以盡意, 設卦以盡請 (情) 僞. 毄 (繫) 辭焉, 以盡其〈言〉, 變而迵 (通) 之以盡利. 鼓之舞之以 [盡] 神. 鍵 (乾) 川 (坤), 其 [《易》] 之經與? 鍵 (乾) 川 (坤) [成] 列, 易位乎其中. 鍵 (乾) 川 (坤) 毀則無以見 《易》矣. 《易》不可則見則鍵 (乾) 川 (坤) 不可見, 鍵 (乾) 川 (坤) 不可見則 (27) 鍵 (乾) 川 (坤) 或幾乎息矣. 是故刑 (形) 而上者胃 (謂) 之道, 刑 (形) 而下者胃 (謂) 之器, 爲而施之胃 (謂) 之變, 誰 (推) 而舉

200

apparent the brightness, there is none greater than the sun and moon; of renown[85] there is none greater than wealth and nobility; of making beings whole and bringing about (their) uses and establishing and completing implements to be used for the benefit of all under heaven, there is none greater than the sage; and in plumbing completeness to revert to the root,[86] hooking the precipice to reach the distant, (24) settling the auspiciousness and inauspiciousness of all under heaven, and settling[87] the diligence[88] of all under heaven, there is none better[89] than the milfoil and the turtle. This is why heaven gives life to the spiritual beings, and the sage takes their measure. Heaven[90] alternates and transforms, and the sage emulates it. Heaven reveals images to show the auspicious and inauspicious, and the sage imagines them. The River gave forth the diagram, and the Luo gave forth the document, and the sage took their measure. The *Changes* has four images, and thereby it is apparent. Statements were appended to it, and thereby it announces. It was settled with auspiciousness (25) and inauspiciousness, and thereby it is divided."

When the *Changes* says "From heaven blessing it; auspicious; there is nothing not beneficial," "blessing it" is to help it.[91] That which is helped by heaven is compliant; that which is helped by man is sincere. Ritual and sincerity cause one to think of compliance, [and also] thereby to esteem the worthy. This is the meaning of "from heaven blessing it; auspicious; there is nothing not beneficial." Confucius said: "Writing does not fully express words, and words do not fully express ideas. Nevertheless, of the ideas of the sages, how their meaning can be seen!"[92] (26) Confucius said: "The sage established images[93] in order fully to express ideas, constructed the hexagrams in order fully to express the real and the artificial, appended statements to them in order fully to express their <words>,[94] alternated and connected them in order fully to express their benefit, and drummed them and caused them to dance in order [fully to express] their spirituality. 'The Key' and 'The Flow,' how they are the classics[95] of the [*Changes*]! 'The Key' and 'The Flow' [completed] their arrayal, and the *Changes* was established in their midst. If 'The Key' and 'The Flow' were destroyed, then there would be nothing with which to see the *Changes*. If the *Changes* could not then be seen, then 'The Key' and 'The Flow' could not be seen. If 'The Key' and 'The Flow' could not be seen,[96] then (27) 'The Key' and 'The Flow' would just about be at an end! This is why that which is above forms is called the Way, and that which is below forms is called implements. To do[97] and to put into action[98] is called to alternate, and to push and lift

諸天下之民胃 (謂)之 事業. 是 [故] 夫馬 (象), 耺 (聖) 人具以見天下之請 (情) 而不疑 (擬) 者 (諸) 其刑 (形) 容, 以馬 (象) 其物義, 是故胃 (謂) 之 (28) 馬 (象). 耺(聖) 人有以見天下之動而觀其會同, 以行其疾 (典) 膿 (禮). 毄 (繫) 辭焉, 以斷其吉凶. 是故胃 (謂) 之敎 (爻). 極天下之請 (情) 存乎卦, 鼓天下之動者存乎辭, 化而制之存乎變, 誰 (推) 而行之存乎迵 (通), 神而化之存乎其 (29) 人. 謀而成, 不言而信, 存乎德行.

八卦成列, 馬 (象) 在其中矣. 因而動之, 敎 (爻) 在其中矣. 剛柔相誰 (推), 變在其中矣. 毄 (繫) 辭而齊之, 動在其中矣. 吉凶悐 (悔) 閵 (吝) 也者, 生乎動者也. 剛柔也者, 立本者也. 變迵 (通) 也者, (30) 聚者也. 吉凶者, 上勝者也. 天地之道, 上觀者. 日月之行, 上明者. 天下之動, 上觀天者也. 夫鍵 (乾), 藞然視人易. 川 (坤), 魋然視人閒. 敎 (爻) 也者, 效此者也. 馬 (象) 也者, 馬 (象) 此者也. 效 (爻) 馬 (象) 動乎內, 吉凶見乎外, 功業 (31) 見乎變, 耺 (聖) 人之請 (請) 見乎辭. 天地之大思曰生, 耺 (聖) 人之大費曰立立 (位), 何以守立 (位) 曰人, 何以聚人曰材, 理材正辭, 愛民安行曰義.

among the people under heaven is called service and enterprise.[99] This [is why] the sage completes the images in order to make apparent the real characteristics[100] of all under heaven, but does not doubt[101] them in their form and appearance in order to give image to the propriety of their beings. This is why they are called (28) images. The sage has them in order to make apparent the movements of all under heaven, observes their union in order to give motion to their canons and rituals, and appends statements to them in order to decide their auspiciousness and inauspiciousness. This is why they are called lines. (He) takes the real characteristics of all under heaven to their extreme and causes them to reside in the hexagrams; drums the movements of all under heaven and causes them to reside in the statements; transforms and regulates[102] them and causes them to reside in the alternations; pushes and puts them into motion and causes them to reside in the unity; makes them spiritual and transforms them and causes them to reside in his (29) person; and plans[103] and completes them, not speaking but being trustworthy, and causes them to reside in virtuous action."

The eight trigrams complete their arrayal, and the images are in their midst. According with and moving[104] them, the lines are in their midst. The hard and the soft pushing against each other, alternation is in their midst. Appending statements and equalizing[105] them, move-ment is in their midst. As for "auspicious," "inauspicious," "regret," and "distress," they are what come to life in movement. As for the hard and soft, they are what establish the basis. As for alternation and connection (30), they are what gathers.[106] Auspiciousness and inauspiciousness are what raise up victory.[107] The way of heaven and earth is what is observed on high. The motion[108] of the sun and the moon is what is illumined on high. The movement of all under heaven is what on high observes heaven.[109] "The Key" loftily[110] shows men the change. "The Flow" loweringly shows men the crack. As for the lines, they emulate these. As for the images, they give image to these. Emulation and images move within, and auspiciousness and inauspiciousness are apparent with-out, achievement and enterprise (31) are apparent in the alternations, and the real characteristics of the sage are apparent in the statements. The great thought[111] of heaven and earth is called life. The great expen-diture[112] of the sage is called establishing position.[113] What is used to maintain position is called man.[114] What is used to gather men together is called resources. To bring order to resources and to make upright the statements, to love the people and to pacify actions[115] is called propriety.

古者戲是 (氏) 之王天下也, 印 (仰) 則觀馬 (象) 於天, 府 (俯) 則觀法於地, 觀鳥獸之文與 (32) 地之義 (宜), 近取諸身, 遠取者 (諸) 物, 於是始作八卦, 以達神明之德, 以類萬物之請 (情). 作結繩而爲古 (罟), 以田以漁, 蓋取者 (諸) 羅也. 肆戲是 (氏) 沒, 神戎 (農) 是 (氏) 作, 斲木爲枛 (耜), 斲木爲耒槈 (耨). 槈 (耨) 耒之利, 以敎天下, 蓋 [取] (33) 者 (諸) 益也. 日中爲疾, 至天下之民, 聚天下之貨, 交易而退, 各得其所欲, 蓋取者 (諸) 筮 (噬) 盍 (嗑) 也. 神戎 (農) 是 (氏) 沒, 黃 [帝] 堯舜是 (氏) 作, 迵 (通) 其變, 使民不亂, 神而化之, 使民宜之. 《易》, 多 (終) 則變, 迵 (通) 則久, 是以自天右 (祐) 之, (34) 吉, 无不利也. 黃帝堯舜陲 (垂) 衣常 (裳) 而天下治, 蓋取者 (諸) 鍵 (乾) 川 (坤) 也. 杅木爲周 (舟), 剡木而爲楫, 齎 (濟) 不達, 至 (致) 遠以利天下, 蓋取者 (諸) 奐也. 備牛乘馬, [引] 重行遠, 以利天下, 蓋取者 (諸) 隋也. 重門擊柝, 以挨 (俟) 抮客, 蓋取 (35) 余 (餘) 也. 斷木爲杵, 枏 (掘) 地爲臼, 臼杵之利, 萬民以次, 蓋取者 (諸) 少過也. 弦木爲柧 (弧), 棪木爲矢, 柧 (弧) 矢之利, 以威天 [下], 蓋取者 (諸) 誄 (乖) 也. 上古穴居而野處, 後世耵 (聖) 人易之以宮室,

204

In antiquity, as for Mr. Xi's (i.e., Fu Xi) ruling all under heaven, looking up he observed the images in the heavens and looking down he observed the models in the earth. He observed the markings of the birds and animals and (32) the properties of the earth. Near at hand he took them from his body, and at a distance he took them from beings. With this he first made the eight trigrams in order to penetrate the virtue of spiritual brightness and to categorize the real characteristics of the ten-thousand beings. He made the knotting of ropes and made nets in order to hunt and to fish; he probably took it from *Luo*, "The Net."[116] When Mr. Xi died, Mr. Shen (Rong:) Nong acted, chopping wood to make a plowshare and bending wood to make a plowhandle and hoe, using the benefit of the plow and hoe to teach all under heaven; he probably took (33) it from *Yi*, "Increase."[117] When the sun was centered he made (fast:) markets, (reaching:) causing the people under heaven to come and gathering together the goods under heaven, exchanging and retreating, each getting that which he wished[118]; he probably took it from *Shi Ke*, "Biting and Chewing."[119] When Mr. Shen Nong died, the Yellow [Emperor], Yao and Shun acted, connecting the alternations and causing the people not to be disordered.[120] Making them spiritual and transforming them, they caused the people to regard them as appropriate. When the change comes to an end then it alternates,[121] and connected then it is long-lived, thereby "from heaven blessing it; (34) auspicious; there is nothing not beneficial." The Yellow Emperor, Yao and Shun allowed their jackets and skirts to hang down and all under heaven was governed; they probably took it from "The Key" and "The Flow." They hollowed wood to make boats, scorched wood and made oars,[122] assisting what does not reach to arrive at the distant in order to benefit all under heaven; they probably took it from *Huan*, "Dispersal."[123] They made ready oxen and hitched horses to [pull] the heavy to travel to the distance in order to benefit all under heaven; they probably took it from *Sui*, "Following."[124] They doubled doors and struck clappers in order to attend to traveling[125] guests; they probably took (35) (it from) *Yu*, "Excess."[126] They split wood to make pestles and excavated the earth to make pits, the benefit of the pits and pestles being used by the ten-thousand people to spend the night; they probably took it from *Shaoguo*, "Small Surpassing."[127] They strung wood to make bows and pared wood to make arrows, the benefit of bows and arrows being used to awe all [under] heaven; they probably took it from *Guai*, "Perversion."[128] In high antiquity they dwelled in caves and located themselves in the wilds. The sages of later generations changed it with palaces and chambers,

上練下楣, 以寺風雨, 蓋取者 (諸) 大莊 (壯) 也. (36) 古之葬者, 厚
裹之以薪, 葬諸中野, 不封不樹, 葬期無數. 後世耵 (聖) 人易之以
棺椁 (槨), 蓋取者 (諸) 大過也. [上古結] 繩以治, [後] 世耵 (聖)
人易之以書契, 百官以治, 萬民以察, 蓋取者 (諸) 大有也.

是故《易》也者, 馬 (象). 馬 (象) 也者, (37) 馬 (象) 也. 緣
(彖) 也者, 制也. 肴 (爻) 也者, 效天下之動者也. 是 [故] 吉凶生而
悬 (悔) 闇 (吝) 著也.

陽卦多陰, 陰卦多 [陽, 其何故也? 陽卦] 奇, 陰 [卦耦. 其德]
行何也? 陽, 一君二民, 君子之馬 (象) 也.

《易》曰: 童童往 [來], 崩 (朋) 從璽 (爾) 思. 子曰: 天下 (38)
[何思何慮, 天下同歸而殊途, 一致而百慮. 天下何思何慮? 日往
則月來, 月往則日來. 日月相推而明生焉. 寒往則暑來, 暑往則寒
來, 寒暑相] 推 [而歲成焉. 往者屈也, 來者信 (伸) 也. 屈信 (伸)
相感而利生焉. 尺 (39) 蠖之屈, 以求信 (伸) 也. 龍蛇之蟄, 以存
身也. 精義入] 神, 以至 (致) 用. 利用安身, 以崇 [德也. 過此以往,
未之或知也. 窮神知化,

with a ridgepole at the top and eaves below in order to attend to the wind and rain; they probably took it from *Dazhuang,* "Great Maturity."[129] (36) With the burials of antiquity, they thickly interred[130] them with brushwood and buried them in the middle of the wilds, neither making a mound nor planting trees, and the burial period having no number. The sages of later generations changed it with inner and outer coffins; they probably took it from *Daguo,* "Great Surpassing."[131] [In high antiquity they knotted] ropes in order to govern. The sages of [later] generations changed it with writings and inscriptions, which the hundred officials used to govern and the ten-thousand people used to examine; they probably took it from *Dayou,* "The Great Possession."[132]

This is why the *Changes* is images. Images (37) are imaged.[133] The hexagram statements regulate.[134] The line statements emulate the movements of all under heaven. This is [why] "auspicious" and "inauspicious" come to life and "regret" and "distress" are manifest.

Yang hexagrams have a majority of yin lines, and yin hexagrams have a majority of [yang lines. What is its reason? Yang hexagrams] are odd numbered, and yin [hexagrams are even numbered.] What is the motion [of its virtue]? Yang is one ruler and two people, the image of the gentleman.

The *Changes* says: "So undecided going and [coming], a friend follows you in thought."[135] Confucius said: "As for all under heaven, (38) [what thoughts, what considerations does it have. All under heaven returns to the same place but by different routes, arriving at one place but with one hundred considerations. What thoughts, what considerations does all under heaven have! The sun goes and then the moon comes; the moon goes and then the sun comes. The sun and moon push against each other and then brightness is born from it. The cold goes and then the heat comes; the heat goes and then the cold comes. The cold and heat] push [against each other and the year is completed from it. That which goes contracts; that which comes extends. Contraction and extension feel for each other and benefit comes to life from it. The contraction of the inchworm (39) is to seek extension. The hibernation of the dragon is to maintain its body. Seminal essence and propriety enter into] spirituality in order to bring about use. Benefit and use content the body in order to exalt [virtue. Surpassing this in order to go, perhaps one still does not know it. Exhausting spirituality to know

德之盛也. 《易》曰: 困于石, 據] 于疾 (蒺) 利 (藜), 入于其宮, 不見其妻, 凶. 子曰: 非其 [所困而困焉,] 名 (40) 必辱, 非其所勮而據焉, 身必危. 既辱且危, 死其 (期) 將至, 妻可得見 [耶? 《易》曰: 公用射隼于高墉之上獲之, 無不利. 子曰]: 隼者, 禽也. 弓矢者, 器也. 射之者, 人也. 君子臧器於身, 待者而童 (動), 何 (41) 不利之又 (有)? 動而不繒, 是以出而又 (有) 獲也. 言舉成器而動者也. 子曰: 小人 [不恥不仁, 不畏不義, 不見利不勸, 不] 畏不誅 (懲), [小] 誅 (懲) 而大戒, 小人之福也. 《易》曰: 構校滅止 (趾), 無咎也者, 此之胃 (謂) 也. 善不責 (積) 不足以 (42) 成名, 惡不責 (積) 不足以滅身. 小人以小善爲無益也而弗爲也, 以小惡 [爲無傷而弗去也, 故惡責 (積) 而不可] 蓋也, 罪大而不可解也. 《易》曰: 何校滅耳, 凶. 君子見幾而作, 不位多 (終) 日. 《易》曰: 介于石, (43) 不多 (終) [日, 貞] 吉. 介于石, 毋用多 (終) 日, 斷可識矣. 君子知物知章, 知柔 [知剛, 萬夫之望.

若夫雜物撰德, 辨] 是與非, 則下中敎 (爻) 不備, 初大要. 存亡吉凶, 則將可知矣.

208

transformation is the fullness of virtue. The *Changes* says: "Entangled in stone, and grounded] in thistles: Entering into his palace, and not seeing his wife; inauspicious."[136] Confucius said: "It is not that in which he is entangled that entangles him, but that his reputation (40) will necessarily be shamed; it is not that in which he is grounded that grounds him, but that his person will necessarily be in danger. Being shamed and in danger, when the time of death is about to arrive can he get to see the wife[?" The *Changes* says: "The duke herewith shoots a hawk on top of a high wall, bagging it; there is nothing not beneficial."[137] Confucius said:] "A hawk is game. A bow and arrow are implements. The one who shoots it is a man. If the gentleman keeps implements to his person and waits upon it[138] to move, what (41) could there be not beneficial! Moving and not attaching a line to the arrow,[139] and thereby going out and having something bagged, speaks of one who raises up completed implements and moves."[140] Confucius said: "The little man [is not embarrassed by not being humane, is not awed by not being proper; he does not see benefit without being encouraged, is not] awed unless reproved. [A little] reproof and a great warning are the good fortune of the little man. As for the *Changes* saying 'Meeting with stocks on the feet and with a foot cut off; there is no trouble,'[141] it is this meaning. If goodness is not accumulated it will not suffice (42) to complete a reputation; if badness is not accumulated it will not suffice to destroy a person. The little man considers little goodnesses to be of no increase, and so does not do them; considers little badnesses [to be of no harm and so does not dispense with them; therefore, the badness accumulates and cannot] be capped, the guilt becomes great and cannot be undone. The *Changes* says: 'Carrying a cangue on the shoulders and with an ear cut off; inauspicious.'[142] The gentleman sees the pivot and acts, not waiting[143] until the end of the day. The *Changes* says: 'Strengthened with stone; (43) not to the end [of the day; determination] is auspicious.'[144] To be 'strengthened with stone,' but not[145] to use it 'to the end of the day' can definitely be recognized. The gentleman knows beings[146] and knows patterns, knows the soft [and knows the hard; he is the expectation of the ten-thousand fellows."[147]

As with the various beings and manifest virtues, in distinguishing] right and wrong then the bottom and middle lines are not complete; the initial line is greatly important. Existence and loss, auspiciousness and inauspiciousness can then be known.[148]

鍵 (乾), 德行恒易, 以知險. 夫川 (坤), (44) 虇然天下 [之至] 順也. 德行恒閒 (簡), 以知 [阻]. 能說之心, 能數諸侯之 [慮, 定天下之吉凶, 成天下之勿勿者, 是故] 變化具爲, 吉事又 (有) 羊 (祥). 馬 (象) 事知器, 筭 (算) 事知來. 天地設馬 (象), 耵 (聖) 人成能. 人謀鬼謀, 百姓與能. 八 (45) 卦以馬 (象) 告也. 教 (爻) 順以論語. 剛柔雜處, 吉 [凶] 可識. 動作以利言, 吉凶以請 (情) 遷. [是故] 愛惡相攻, [而吉凶生], 遠近相取, [而惡 (悔) 閵 (吝) 生], 請 (情) 偽相欽, 而利害生. 凡《易》之請 (情), 近而不相得則凶, 或害之, 則惡 (悔) (46) 且哭 (吝). 將反則 [其] 辭亂, 吉人之辭寡, 趮人之辭多, 無善之人其辭斿, 失其所守其辭屈. (47)

The virtuous action of "The Key" is constantly changing in order to know the dangerous.[149] As for "The Flow," (44) loweringly it is the [perfect] compliance of all under heaven. Its virtuous action is constantly cracked in order to know [obstructions]. It can be made happy in the heart, can count[150] it in the lord's [considerations, to settle the auspicious and inauspicious of all under heaven and to complete the diligence of all under heaven. This is why] alternations and transformations thoroughly[151] act and auspicious affairs have auspices. By imagining affairs one knows implements, and by calculating affairs one knows what is to come. Heaven and earth construct images, and the sage completes ability. Men plan and ghosts plan, and the hundred families partake of the ability. The eight (45) trigrams announce through images. The lines comply[152] through assayed[153] phrases. The hard and soft are variously situated, and auspiciousness [and inauspiciousness] can be recognized. Movements and actions[154] are stated in terms of benefit, and the auspicious and inauspicious shift in terms of real characteristics. [This is why] when loving and despising are in conflict with each other, auspiciousness and inauspiciousness come to life; when the distant and near take from each other, ["regret" and "distress" come to life]; when the real and the artificial cheat each other, benefit and harm come to life. In all of the real characteristics of the *Changes,* when those near do not mutually gain then it is inauspicious; or harming it, then it is both regretful (46) and distressed. When one is about to turn about[155] then [its] statements are disordered,[156] and the statements of the auspicious man are few while the statements of the unruly man are numerous. As for the man without goodness, his statements will wander; when he loses that to which he should hold, his statements will be crooked. (47)

THE
PROPERTIES
OF THE
CHANGES

易之義

子曰: 易之義誰 (唯) 陰與陽, 六畫而成章. 曲句焉柔, 正直焉剛. 六剛無柔, 是謂大陽, 此天 [之義也.] □□□□□□□□□□□□方. 六柔無剛, 此地之義也. 天地相衛 (率), 氣味相取, 陰陽流刑 (形), 剛 (1) 柔成□. 萬物莫不欲長生而亞 (惡) 死, 會心者而台 (以) 作易, 和之至也. 是故鍵 (乾) □□□□□□□□□□□□□□□□□□義沾下就, 地之道也. 用六贛 (坎) 也, 用九盈也. 盈而剛, 故易曰 “直 (2) 方大, 不習, [吉]” 也. 因不習而備, 故易曰 “見群龍無首, 吉” 也. 是故鍵 (乾) 者得□□□□□□□□□□□□□□□□□□□□畏也. 容 (訟) 者, 得之疑也. 師者, 得之栽也. 比者, 得鮮也. 小蓄 (畜) 者, [得] 之 (3) 未□也. 履者, 誣之□行也. 益者, 上下交矣. 婦 (否) 者, [陰] 陽姦矣.

214

Confucius said: "The properties of the *Changes* are only the yin and yang, six lines creating a pattern. Being broken off in the middle of it, it is soft; straight across, it is hard. Six hards without a soft is called the Great Yang; this is the property of heaven. .. .. square. Six softs without a hard; this is the property of earth. Heaven and earth embrace each other, vapor and flavor infuse each other, the yin and yang flow into form, and the hard (1) and soft complete .. . Of the ten-thousand beings there is none that does not desire long life and despise death. The joining of hearts and through it the making of the *Changes* is the epitome of harmony. This is why *Jian*, 'The Key,' .. .. appropriate to moisten that below is the Way of the earth.

"The use of six is to be hollow; the use of nine is to be filled. To be filled is then to be hard. Therefore the *Changes* says: 'Straight, (2) square, and great; not repeated; [auspicious].'[1] Because it is not repeated and yet is complete, therefore the *Changes* says: 'See the flock of dragons without heads; auspicious.'[2] This is why *Jian*, 'The Key,'[3] is obtained .. .. awe. (*Rong*:) *Song*, 'Lawsuit,'[4] is obtained from doubts. *Shi*, 'The Troops,'[5] is obtained from cutting. *Bi*, 'Alliance,'[6] is obtained from scarcity. *Xiaoxu*, 'Little Storage,'[7] [is obtained] from (3) not yet ... *Lü*, 'Treading,'[8] is the .. motion of indecision. *Yi*, 'Increase,'[9] is the merging of the top and bottom. *Fu*, 'The Wife,'[10] is the transgression of [yin] and yang.

下多陰而紓(?) □□□□□□□□□□□□□□□□□□而
周, 所以人背(?) 也. 無孟 (妄) 之卦, 有罪而死, 无功而賞, 所以
畜(?), 故 (4) □. □之卦, 歸而強士諍(?) 也. 孺 (需) □□□□□□
□□□知未騰勝也. 容失諸□□□□□□□□□□□□□□□
□□□遠也. 大有之卦, 孫 (遜) 位也. 大牂 (壯), 小腫 (動) 而大
從, □□□也. 大蓄 (畜), 兌而誨 (5) [也]. 隋 (隨) 之卦, 相而能戒
也. □□□□□□□□□□无爭而後(?) ☒者, 得☒說, 和說
而知畏. 謹 (艮) 者, 得之代邢也. 家 [人] 者, 得處也. 井者, 得之
徹 (6) 也. 均 (姤) 者, □□□□□□□□□□□□□□□□□□
也. 豐者, 得☒之卦, 草木(?) ☒而從于不壹(?). 均 (姤) 之卦, 足而
知余(?). 林 (臨) 之卦, 自誰 (推) 不先瞿 (懼). 觀之卦, 盈而能乎
(虛). (7) 齎 (晉?) 之卦, 善近而□□□□□□□□□□□□□□
□□其☒絕(?) 誘也. ☒乎□□□□□□□忠身失量, 故曰慎而
侍 (待) 也. 筮 (噬) 聞 (嗑) 紫紀, 恒言不 (8) 已, 容 (訟) 獄凶得也.
勞之☒易☒者☒行也. 損以☒也. 大牂 (壯), 以卑陰也. 歸妹, 以
正女 [也]. (9) 既齎 (濟) 者, 亨余比貧☒而知路, 凡☒埭也. 子曰:
☒ (10) □禁□也. 子曰: ☒既窮□而☒ "[晉] 如秋 (愁) 如", 所以
辟 (避) 怒☒ (11) □□□□ "[不] 事王 [侯]", □□之謂也. 不求(?)
則不足以難☒. 易曰☒ (12) □□□□則危, 親傷□□. [易] 曰 "何
校"

216

"When the bottom (trigram) has more yin and is pure .. ..
.. .. and everywhere, men thereby turn their
backs(?) on it. With the hexagram *Wumeng*, 'Pestilence,'[11] there is guilt
and death, no accomplishment but reward through greed(?), and therefore (4) … With the hexagram .., there is return and the strong sires are
tranquil. With *Ru*, 'Moistened,'[12] .. .. know that there is
not yet soaring victory. (*Rong:*) *Song*, 'Lawsuit,' loses it in .. ..
.. .. distant. With the hexagram *Dayou*, 'The Great
Possession,'[13] there is retreat from position. With (*Dachuang:*) *Taizhuang*,
'Great Maturity,'[14] the little move and the great follow, ... With
Daxu, 'Great Storage,'[15] there is enjoyment but regret (5). With the
hexagram *Sui*, 'Following,'[16] there is assistance and the ability to warn.
.. .. no contention and thereafter . . . , gaining . . .
joy, and through harmonious joy one knows awe. (*Jin*, 'Caution':) *Gen*,
'Stilling,'[17] is taken from substituting models(?). *Jia[ren]*, 'Family Members,'[18] is taken from being situated. *Jing*, 'The Well,'[19] is taken from
getting to the bottom (of things). (6) *Gou*, ('Dirt':) 'Meeting,'[20] .. .. ..
.. .. *Feng*, 'Abundance,'[21] is obtained from . . .
hexagram, grasses and trees . . . and follows from not being one (?).
With the hexagram *Gou*, 'Meeting,' there is sufficiency and one knows
of excess(?). With the hexagram *Lin*, 'The Forest,'[22] one pushes oneself
without fretting beforehand. With the hexagram *Guan*, 'Looking Up,'[23]
one is replete and yet able to be empty. (7) With the hexagram (*Ji:*) *Jin*,
'Aquas,'[24] one is good at drawing near and yet .. ..
.. .. its . . . cutting off seduction. . . . in .. .. loyal to
oneself but loses the measure, therefore it says 'be cautious and wait.'[25]
Shi Ke, 'Biting and Chewing,'[26] is tense and taut; constantly speaking but
not (8) stopping, one obtains the inauspiciousness of lawsuits and trials.
Causing it to toil . . . *Changes* . . . one . . . motion. *Sun*, 'Decrease,'[27] is
to . . . . (*Dachuang:*) *Taizhuang*, 'Great Maturity,' is to humble the yin.
Guimei, 'Returning Maiden,'[28] is to make the female upright. (9) *Jiji*,
'Already Completed,'[29] receives excess and allies with poverty . . . and
yet knows (the road:) defeat, in all cases . . . to expel."

Confucius said: ". . . (10) .. prohibit .. ." Confucius said: ". . . already
exhausted .. and . . .'aquatically, gloomily,'[30] one thereby avoids anger . . .
(11) .. .. '[does not] serve the king [or lord]'[31] .. .. is what is meant.
If one does not seek then it will not suffice to make difficult . . . .
When the *Changes* says: . . . (12) .. .. .. then danger, relatives will be
wounded and .. .. . When [the *Changes*] says: 'Carrying a cangue on the

217

則凶, "屢 (屨) 校" 則吉, 此之謂也. 子曰: 五行□□□□□□□□□□□用, 不可學者也, 唯其人而已矣. 然其利(?) □□□□□□□□□□□□□□□□□ (13) 贊於神明而生占也, 參 天 雨 地而義 數也, 觀變於陰陽而立卦也, 發揮於 [剛] 柔而 [生爻也, 和順於道德] 而理於義也. 窮理盡生 (性) 而至於命□□□□□□□□□□理也. 是故位 (立) (14) 天之道曰陰與陽, 位 (立) 地之 道曰柔與剛, 位 (立) 人之道曰仁與義. 兼三財 (才) 兩之, 六畫而 成卦. 分陰分陽, [迭用柔剛, 故] 易六畫而爲章也. 天地定立 (位), [山澤通氣], 火水相射, 雷風相槫 (薄), 八卦相厝 (錯). 數 (15) 往 者順, 知來者逆, 故易達數也. 子曰: 萬物之義, 不剛則不能僮 (動), 不僮 (動) 則無功, 恒僮 (動) 而弗中則□, [此剛] 之失也. 不 柔則不靜, 不靜則不安, 久靜不僮 (動) 則沈, 此柔之失也. 是故鍵 (乾) 之 "炕 (亢) 龍", 壯之 "觸蕃 (藩)", (16) 句 (姤) 之離角, 鼎之 "折足", 酆 (豐) 之虛盈, 五繇者, 剛之失也, 僮 (動) 而不能靜者 也. 川 (坤) 之 "牝馬", 小蓄 (畜) 之 "密雲", 句 (姤) 之 [適 (蹢)] 屬 (躅), [漸] 之繩 (孕) 婦, 肫 (屯) 之

218

shoulders'[32] then it is inauspicious, while 'Wearing stocks on the feet'[33] then it is auspicious, this is what is meant."

Confucius said: "The five phases .. .. use, that which cannot be studied is only the person and that is all. Nevertheless, its benefit .. .. (13) drawing on the spiritual brightness and so giving life to the prognostication, joining with the three of heaven and the two of earth and so making proper the numbers, observing the alternations in the yin and yang and so establishing the hexagrams, elaborating the [hard] and soft and so [giving life to the lines, harmoniously complying with the Way and its virtue] and so bringing order to propriety, thoroughly plumbing order and (life:) inner-nature (xing) and so arriving at the mandate .. .. order. This is why (positioning:) establishing (14) heaven's way is called yin and yang, establishing earth's way is called the soft and the hard, and establishing man's way is called humaneness and propriety. Bringing together these three qualities and doubling them, six lines complete a hexagram. By dividing yin and yang, [and successively using the soft and hard, therefore] the Changes' six lines make patterns. Heaven and earth settle their positions, the mountains and marshes interchange their vapors, fire and water assault each other, and thunder and wind incite each other, and the eight trigrams move above and below each other. Enumerating (15) the past is compliant, while knowing the future is retrograde; therefore the Changes penetrates numbers."[34]

Confucius said: "The property of the ten-thousand beings is that if they are not hard they are not able to move, and if they do not move they are without achievement; but if they are constantly moving and not centered then ..; [this is hardness's] loss. If they are not soft they are not tranquil, and if they are not tranquil they are not peaceful; but if they are long tranquil and not moving then they sink; this is softness's loss. This is why the following five line statements, Jian, 'The Key,' 's 'blazing dragon,'[35] Zhuang (i.e., Taizhuang), 'Great Maturity,' 's 'butted fence'[36] (16), Gou, 'Meeting,' 's fastened (sic) horn,[37] Ding, 'The Cauldron,' 's 'bro-ken leg,'[38] and Feng, 'Abundance,' 's voiding and filling,'[39] are (examples of) hardness's loss, of moving and not being able to be tranquil. The following five line statements, Chuan, 'The Flow,' 's 'mare,'[40] Shaoshu, 'Small Harvest,' 's 'dense clouds,'[41] Gou, 'Meeting,' 's 'balkiness,'[42] [Jian, 'Advancing']'s pregnant woman,[43] and Zhun, 'Hoarding,' 's 'weeping

"泣血", 五翳者, 陰之失也, 靜而不能僮 (動) 者也. 是故天之義剛建 (健) 僮 (動) 發 (17) 而不息, 其吉保功也. 無柔救 (救) 之, 不死必亡. 僮 (動) 陽者亡, 故火不吉也. 地之義柔弱沈靜不僮 (動), 其吉 [保安也, 無] 剛□之, 則窮賤遺亡. 重陰者沈, 故水不吉也. 故武之義保功而恒死, 文之義 (18) 保安而恒窮. 是故柔而不狂(?枉), 然後文而能勝也; 剛而不折, 然而後武而能安也. 易曰 "直方大, 不 [習, 吉"] □□□之屯於文武也, 此易贊也. 子曰: 鍵 (乾) 六剛能方, 湯武之德也. "潛龍勿用" 者, 匿也. (19) "見蠶 (龍) 在田" 也者, 德也. "君子冬 (終) 日鍵 (乾) 鍵 (乾)", 用也. "夕沂 (惕) 若厲, 無咎". 息也. "或鱬 (躍) 在淵", 隱 [而] 能靜也. "翟 (飛) 蠶 (龍) [在天"], □而上也. "炕 (亢) 龍有悔", 高而爭也. "群龍無首", 文而耴 (聖) 也. 川 (坤) 六柔相從順, 文之至也. 君 (20) 子 "先迷後得主", 學人之謂也. "東北喪崩 (朋), 西南得崩 (朋)", 求賢也. "履霜堅冰至", 豫□□也. "直方大, [不習, 吉,] □□□ [也]. "含章可貞", 言美請 (情) 也. "聒 (括) 囊, 無咎",

blood,'[44] are (examples of) yin's loss, of being tranquil and not being able to move.

"This is why the property of heaven is to be hard and vigorous and to move (17) without rest, its auspiciousness being to protect achievement. (But) if there were no softness to rescue it, (even) if it did not die it would certainly be lost. Doubled yang is lost; therefore fire is not auspicious. The property of earth is to be soft and weak and to be tranquil without moving, its auspiciousness being to [protect peace. (But) if there were no] hardness to .. it, then it would be thoroughly demeaned and left behind. Doubled yin sinks; therefore water is not auspicious. Therefore, the property of the martial is to protect achievement and constantly to die, while the property of the cultured (18) is to protect peace and constantly to be exhausted. This is why it is only after being soft but not warped that the cultured is able to be victorious; only after being hard but not broken that the martial is able to be peaceful. The *Changes* says: 'Straight, square, and great; not [repeated; auspicious'[45]; ... . being pure in both the cultured and the martial, this is the invocation of the *Changes*."

Confucius said: "That the six hard lines of *Jian*, 'The Key,' are able to be square is the virtue of (kings) Tang and Wu. 'Submerged dragon; do not use'[46] is (an example of) concealment (19); 'Appearing dragon in the fields'[47] is (an example of) virtue; 'The gentleman to the end of the day is so initiating'[48] is (an example of) use; 'In the evening he is wary as if there is danger; there is no trouble'[49] is (an example of) rest; 'And now jumping in the depths'[50] is (an example of) being shaded [and yet] being able to be tranquil; 'Flying dragon [in the heavens]'[51] is (an example of) .. and yet high; 'Blazing dragon; there is regret'[52] is (an example of) being high and yet contending; 'The flock of dragons without heads'[53] is (an example of) being cultured and sagely.

"*Chuan*, 'The Flow,''s six soft lines are mutually compliant, the epitome of culture (or King Wen). The gentleman's (20) 'first being lost and afterwards finding his ruler'[54] is said of a scholar; 'to the northeast to lose a friend and to the southwest to gain a friend'[55] is (an example of) seeking worthies; 'Treading on frost: the firm ice will arrive'[56] is (an example of) caution .. .. ; 'Straight, square, and great; [not repeated; .. ']'[57] .. .. ; 'Containing a pattern; it is permissible to determine'[58] is said of beautiful characteristics; 'Tying the sack; there is no trouble'[59] is (an

語無聲也. "黃常 (裳) 元吉", 有而弗發也. (21) "龍單 (戰) 于野", 文而能達也. "或從王事, 无成有冬 (終)", 學而能發也. 易曰 "何校", 剛而折也. "鳴嗛 (謙)" 也者, 柔而□ [也]. [胅之] "黃牛", 文而知勝矣. 渙之緣 (彖) 辭, 武而知安矣. 川 (坤) 之至德, 柔而反於方; 鍵 (乾) 之至德, (22) 剛而能讓. 此鍵 (乾) 川 (坤) 之厽 (參) 說也. 子曰: 易之用也, 段 (殷) 之无道, 周之盛德也. 恐以守功, 敬以承事, 知 (智) 以辟 (避) 患, □□□□□□□□文王之危知, 史說(?) 之數書, 孰能辯焉? 易曰 (按此字衍) 又 (有) 名焉曰鍵 (乾). 鍵 (乾) 也者, 八卦 (23) 之長也. 九也者, 六肴 (爻) 之大也. 爲九之狀, 浮首兆 (頯) 下, 蛇身傴曲, 其爲龍類也. 夫蠠 (龍), 下居而上達者□□□□□□□□□而成章. 在下爲楮 (潛), 在上爲炕 (亢). 人之陰德不行者, 其陽必失類. 易 (24) 曰 "潛龍勿用", 其義潛清勿使之謂也. 子曰: 廢則不可入于謀, 勝則不可與戒, 忌者不可與親, 繳□□□□□□. [易] 曰 "潛龍 [勿用]", "炕 (亢) 龍有悔", 言其過也. 物之上撼 (盛) 而下絕者, 不久大立 (位), 必多其 (25) 咎.

222

example of) conversing without sound; 'Yellow skirts; prime auspiciousness'[60] is (an example of) having and yet not developing it (21); 'The dragon fights in the wilds'[61] is (an example of) being cultured and yet able to penetrate; 'Someone follows the king's service; there is no completion, but there is an end'[62] is (an example of) studying and being able to develop."

When the *Changes* says "Carrying a cangue on the shoulders,"[63] it is to be hard and yet to be broken; "Calling modesty"[64] is to be soft and yet ..... [*Yuan*, "Wielding"'s] "yellow ox"[65] is to be cultured and yet to know victory; *Huan*, "Dispersal,"'s hexagram statement[66] is to be martial and yet to know peace; *Chuan*, "The Flow,"'s perfect virtue is to be soft and yet to return to the square; *Jian*, "The Key,"'s perfect virtue (22) is to be hard and yet able to yield. These are the three explanations of *Jian*, "The Key," and *Chuan*, "The Flow."

Confucius said: "As for the use of the *Changes*, Yin's being without the way (brought about) Zhou's full virtue. Being fearful in order to maintain achievement, being respectful in order to uphold affairs, being knowledgeable in order to avoid calamity, ... King Wen's knowledge of danger and Scribe Shui's (?) number books; who could debate with them? The *Changes* (says)[67] has a name in it that is called *Jian*, 'The Key.' As for *Jian*, it is the senior of the eight trigrams (23). As for the number nine, it is the greatest of the six lines. The appearance of the number nine is a floating head facing downward, a snakelike body coiled around; this is in the category of dragons. As for dragons, they dwell below yet reach on high, ... and complete patterns. When below they are submerged; when on high they are blazing. If man's yin virtue is not put in motion, his yang will necessarily lose its category. When the *Changes* (24) says 'Submerged dragon; do not use,' it means that one should submerge into the clear and not serve."

Confucius said: "The discarded one cannot enter into plans; the victorious one cannot partake of warnings. The jealous cannot be drawn close to, while the arrogant .. .. When [the *Changes*] says 'Submerged dragon; [do not use]' and 'Blazing dragon; there is regret,' it speaks of its excesses. When beings reach the pinnacle of fullness and cut themselves off from that below, they will not long perpetuate the great position but will necessarily increase their (25) trouble. When the

易曰 "炕 (亢) 龘 (龍) 有悔", 大人之義不實于心, 則不見于德; 不單于口, 則不澤于面. 能威能澤, 謂之龘 (龍). 易 [曰 "見龍在田, 利] 見大人", 子曰: 君子之德也. 君子齊明好道, 日自見以待用也. 見男 (用) 則 (26) 僮 (動), 不見用則靜. 易曰 "君子冬 (終) 日鍵 (乾) 鍵 (乾), 夕沂(惕) 若厲, 無咎". ·子曰: 知息也, 何咎之有? 人不淵不䍐 (躍) 則不見□□□□□反居其□□. 易曰 "或䍐 (躍) 在淵, 無咎". ·子曰: 恒䍐 (躍) 則凶, 君子䍐 (躍) 以自見, 道以自 (27) 成. 君子窮不忘達, 安不忘亡, 靜居而成章, 首福又 (有) 皇. 易曰 "翟 (飛) 龘 (龍) 在天, 利見大人", 子曰: 天□□□□□□□□□□□□□□文而溥(?). 齊明而達矣. 此以劃 (專) 名, 孰能及□? 易曰 "見群 (28) 龘 (龍) 无首", 子曰: 讓善之謂也. 君子群居莫乩 (亂) 首, 善而治, 何談其和也? 龍不侍 (待) 光而僮 (動), 無階而登, □□□□□□□□□□□□, 此鍵 (乾) 之羊 (詳) 說也. 子曰: "易又 (有) 名曰川 (坤), 雌道也. 故曰

224

Changes says 'Blazing dragon; there is regret,' if the propriety of the great man is not sincere of heart then he will not display it in virtue; if he is not simple of mouth, then he will not be (moist:) kind in complexion. Being able to be awe-inspiring and kind is what is called a dragon."

As for the *Changes* [saying "Appearing dragon in the fields; beneficial] to see the great man," Confucius said: "This is the virtue of the gentleman. The gentleman equalizes his brightness and enjoys the Way, daily displaying himself in order to await being used. When he is used then (26) he moves; when he is not used then he is tranquil."

As for the *Changes* saying "The gentleman to the end of the day is so initiating, in the evening is wary as if there is danger; there is no trouble," Confucius said: "If one knows to stop, what trouble could there be? If man is neither in the depths nor jumping, then he will not see .. .. but will return to dwell in his .. .. ."

As for the *Changes* saying "And now jumping in the depths; there is no trouble," Confucius said: "If one is constantly jumping then it is inauspicious. The gentleman jumps in order to display himself, speaks in order to complete (27) himself. When the gentleman is impoverished he does not forget success, and when at peace does not forget losses; he dwells tranquilly and completes patterns, his head fortunate and august."

As for the *Changes* saying "Flying dragon in the heavens; beneficial to see the great man," Confucius said: "The heavens .. .. culture and spread out, equalizing brightness and penetrating. To transmit fame in this way, who could reach ..?"

As for the *Changes* saying "See the flock (28) of dragons without heads," Confucius said: "This means yielding to the good. The gentleman dwells in groups and does not disorder the (head:) leadership, the good ruling; how could he be jealous of the harmony? The dragon does not await radiance to move; even without stairs he still climbs, ... This is the detailed explanation of *Jian*, 'The Key.'"

Confucius said: "The *Changes* has a name called *Chuan*, 'The Flow'; it is the way of the feminine. Therefore, it says 'The determination of a

"牝馬之貞", (29) 童獸也; 川 (坤) 之類也. 是故良馬之類, 廣前而景後, 遂臧, 尙受而順, 下安而靜, 外又 (有) 美刑 (形), 則中又 (有) □□□□□□□乎戻以來群, 文德也. 是故文人之義, 不侍 (待) 人以不善, 見亞 (惡) 墨 (默) 然弗 (30) 反, 是謂以前戒後, 武夫昌慮, 文人緣序. 易曰 "先迷後得主", 學人謂也, 何先主之又 (有)? 天氣作□□□□□□□, 其寒不凍 (凍), 其暑不曷 (渴). 易曰 "履霜堅冰至", 子曰: 孫 (遜) 從之謂也. 歲之義, (31) 始于東北, 成于西南. 君子見始弗逆, 順而保斩. 易曰: "東北喪崩 (朋), 西南得崩 (朋), 吉." 子曰: 非吉石也. 其□□□□與賢之謂也. [武夫] 又 (有) 栿 (拂), 文人有輔, 栿 (拂) 不橈 (撓), 輔不絶, 何不吉之又 (有)? 易曰: "直方大, 不習, (32) 吉", 子曰: 生 (性) 文武也, 雖强學, 是弗能及之矣. 易曰 "含章可貞, 吉", 言美請 (情) 之謂也. 文人僮 (動), 小事時說, 大 [事] 順成, 知毋過數而務柔和.

226

mare,'[68] (29) which is a young animal, the category of *Chuan*. This is why the category of a fine horse is to be broad in the front and tall in the rear and consequently it can be stabled. Ahead it is led and complies; below it is sturdy and tranquil. If on the outside it has a beautiful form, then on the inside it will have ... ... being askew in order to bring along the group is the virtue of being cultured. This is why the propriety of the man of culture is not to attend on others treating them as not good, and silently not to turn away even after being despised (30).[69] This is called using the prior to warn the latter. The military man prizes deliberation, while the man of culture stresses succession.

When the *Changes* says "First lost but later gains his ruler,"[70] it is said of students; how could there be any notion of them first being ruler? The heavenly vapor acts ... ..., its cold does not freeze and its heat does not wither."

As for the *Changes* saying "Treading on frost: the firm ice will arrive,"[71] Confucius said: "This means to follow compliantly. The property of the year (31) is to begin in the northeast and to be completed in the southwest. The gentleman sees the beginning and does not transgress against it, but complies with and protects against abrupt occurrences."[72]

As for the *Changes* saying "To the northeast to lose a friend, to the southwest to gain a friend; auspicious,"[73] Confucius said: "This is not about an auspicious stone; it is said of its ... ... together with worthies. The [military man] has a flail; the man of culture has a support. If the flail is not bent and the support is not broken, what inauspiciousness could there be?"

As for the *Changes* saying "Straight, square, and great; not repeated; (32) auspicious,"[74] Confucius said: "Culture and military bearing are inborn; even if one were to insistently study them, these would not be able to reach it."

As for the *Changes* saying "Containing a pattern: it is permissible to determine; auspicious,"[75] it speaks of the beautiful characteristics. When the man of culture moves, he speaks in a timely fashion about small affairs and the great [affairs] are fluently completed; he knows not to exceed the number but to strive to be soft and harmonious.

227

易曰 "或從事, 無成又 (有) 冬 (終)". 子曰: 言詩書之謂也. 君子笱 (苟) 得其 (33) 冬 (終), 可必可盡也. 君子言于无罪之外, 不言于又 (有) 罪之內, 是謂重福. 易曰 "利 [永] 貞", 此川 (坤) 之羊 (詳) 說也. 子 [曰]: 易之要, 可得而知矣. 鍵 (乾) 川 (坤) 也者, 易之門戶也. 鍵 (乾), 陽物也; 川 (坤), 陰物也. 陰陽合德而剛柔有膿 (體), (34) 以膿 (體) 天地之化. 又 (有) 口能斂之, 无舌罪, 言不當其時則閉慎而觀. 易曰 "聒 (括) 囊, 無咎", 子曰: 不言之謂也. □ □□□ [何] 咎之又 (有)? 墨 (默) 亦毋譽, 君子美其慎而不自箸 (著) 也. 淵深而內其華. 易曰 "黃常 (裳) 元吉", 子 (35) 曰: 尉 (蔚) 文而不發之謂也. 文人內其光, 外其龍, 不以其白陽人之黑, 故其文茲 (滋) 章 (彰). 易⊘□□旣沒, 又 (有) 爵□□□□□居其德不忘. "蠠 (龍) 單 (戰) 于野, 其血玄黃", 子曰: 耺 (聖) 人信戈 (哉)! 隱文且靜, 必見之謂也. (36) 龍七十變而不能去其文, 則文其信于 (按此字衍) 而達神明之德也. 其辯名也, 雜而不戉 (越), 于指 (稽) 易□, 衰世之僮 〈意〉與? 易□□□□□而 [察] 來者也. 微顯贊絕, 巽而恒當, 當名辯物, 正言巽辭而備.

As for the *Changes* saying "Someone follows the service (*sic*[76]); there is no completion, but there is an end," Confucius said: "This speaks of the *Poetry* and the *Documents*. If the gentleman gains his (33) end, it can be necessary and can be finished. The gentleman speaks outside of innocence and does not speak inside of guilt; this is called doubled good fortune, what the *Changes* calls '[beneficial] for the permanent determination.' This is the detailed explanantion of *Chuan*, 'The Flow.'"

Confucius [said]: "The essentials of the *Changes* can be known. Jian, 'The Key,' and Chuan, 'The Flow,' are the gate and window of the Changes. Jian *is the penis,* Chuan *the vagina. The yin and yang join their virtues and the hard and soft are embodied (34), embodying the transformations of heaven and earth.*[77] Having a mouth, if one is able to (collect:) control it, there will be no slips of the tongue; if words do not match the moment, then one closes up with caution and observes." As for the *Changes* saying "Tying the sack; there is no trouble,"[78] Confucius said: "This means not to speak. ... . [what] trouble could there be? Being silent there is also no renown; the gentleman regards caution as beautiful and does not show himself off. The depths are deep and contain his flower."

As for the *Changes* saying "Yellow skirts; prime auspiciousness,"[79] Confucius (35) said: "This means making culture flourish and yet not speaking out. The man of culture holds his radiance on the inside, and puts his dragon on the outside. He does not use his white to (yang:) harm the black of others. Therefore, his culture is nurtured and patterned. The *Changes* ... . being lost, there would be merit .. .. dwelling, his virtue would not be forgotten."

As for "The dragon fights in the wilds, its blood is black and yellow,"[80] Confucius said: "The sage is trustworthy indeed. This is said of shading one's culture and keeping tranquil, and yet necessarily being seen. (36) If the dragon changes seventy times and yet it does not lose its markings then the markings are trustworthy and *reach the virtue of spiritual brightness. As for discriminating*[81] *its names, they are varied but do not overstep their limits. In pointing at the* Changes .. ,[82] *is it the movement*[83] of a declining age? The Changes [*makes manifest what has gone*] and [*investigates*] *what is to come. The minute becomes lustrous and praises what is cut off,*[84] *becomes manifest and is constantly on the mark. It is complete by discriminating things with matching names and by choosing phrases with correct words.*

本生 (性) 仁義, 所 (37) 行以義 (儀) 剛柔之制也. 其稱名也少, 其取類也多, 其指閒 (簡), 其辭文, 其言曲而中, 其事隱而單. 因齎 (濟) 人行, 明 [失得之報, 易之] 興也; 於中故 (古) 乎? 作易者, 其又 (有) 患憂與? 上卦九者, 贊以德而占以義者 (38) 也. 履也者, 德之基也. 嗛 (謙) 也者, 德之枋也. 復也者, 德之本也. 恒也者, 德之固也. 損也者, 德之脩也. 益 [也者], 德之譽也. 困也者, 德之欲也. 井者, 德之地也. 渙者, 德制也. 是故占曰履, 和而至; (39) 嗛 (謙), 奠 (尊) 而光; 復, 少而辨于物; 恒, 久而弗厭; 損, 先難而後易; 益, 長裕而與; 宋 (困), 窮而達; 井, 居其所而遷; [渙], □□□ 而救. 是故履, 以果 (和) 行也; 嗛 (謙), 以制禮也; 復, 以自知也; 恒, 以一德也; 損, 以遠害也; 益, 以興 (40) 禮也; 困, 以辟 (避) 咎也; 井, 以辯義也; 渙, 以行權也. 子曰: 渙而不救, 則比矣. 易之爲書也難前, 爲道就罷 (遷), □□□僮 (動) 而不居, 周流六虛, 上下無常, 剛柔相易也, 不可爲典要, 唯變所次, 出入又 (有) 度, 外內 (41) 內 (按此字衍) 皆瞿 (懼), 又知患故, 无又 (有) 師保而親若父母. 印率其辭, 楺 (揆) 度其方, 无又 (有) 典常. 後 (苟) 非其人, 則道不 [虛行].

230

The basis gives life to humaneness and propriety. What is put into motion (37) through propriety is the regulation of the hard and soft. *The names it mentions are few but the categories it adopts are many; what it points to is simple and yet its phrases are cultured; its words are oblique but centered, its affairs shaded yet straightforward. According with it helps men to act, illustrating [the rewards of loss and gain.*

As for the Changes'] *rise, was it in middle antiquity? As for the one who created the* Changes, *did he have anxieties and worries?* The nine of the upper trigram is what is praised as virtuous and prognosticated as proper (38). Lü, *"Treading,"* is the foundation of virtue. Qian, *"Modesty,"* is the (grain:) handle of virtue. Fu, *"Returning,"* is the basis of virtue. Heng, *"Constancy,"* is the sturdiness of virtue. Sun, *"Decrease,"* is the refining of virtue. Yi, *"Increase,"* is the renown of virtue. Kun, *"Entangled,"* is the wish of virtue. Jing, *"The Well,"* is the ground of virtue. Huan, *"Dispersal,"* is virtue's regulation. This is why in prognosticating one says of Lü, *"Treading,"* that it is harmonious and arrives; (39) *of* Qian, *"Modesty," that it is venerated and radiant; of* Fu, *"Returning," that it is few but discriminates among beings; of* Heng, *"Constancy," that it endures and yet does not oppress; of* Sun, *"Decrease," that it is at first difficult but later easy; of* Yi, *"Increase," that it grows to fullness and gives; of* (Song:) Kun, *"Entangled,"*[85] *that it is exhausted and yet penetrates; of* Jing, *"The Well," that it dwells in its place and yet shifts; of* Huan, *"Dispersal," ... . and yet rescues. This is why* Lü, *"Treading," is used to fructify*[86] *movements;* Qian, *"Modesty," is used to regulate ritual;* Fu, *"Returning," is used to know oneself;* Heng, *"Constancy," is used to unite virtue;* Sun, *"Decrease," is used to distance harm;* Yi, *"Increase," is used to stimulate (40) ritual;* Kun, *"Entangled," is used to avoid trouble;* Jing, *"The Well," is used to discriminate propriety;* and Huan, *"Dispersal," is used* to exercise authority. Confucius said: "If one disperses but does not rescue, then it is alliance."

As a book the Changes *puts the difficult first, but as a Way accords with shifts.*[87] *... ...*[88] *moves and does not dwell, circulating throughout the six empty spaces. The upper and lower are not fixed, and the hard and the soft change into each other; it cannot be canonized or essentialized. It only alternates the sequence,*[89] *the coming and going having measure, the inside and outside (41) all being fearful and yet still knowing the reasons for anxiety. It does not have a master to protect it and yet it is close like a father and mother. One leads from its statements and takes the measure of its prescriptions, yet there is no canon or fixity.* (Later:) *if you are not its man, then the Way will not [emptily move].*

□□无德而占, 則易亦不當. 易之義, 贊始 [反] 夂 (終) 以爲質, 六肴 (爻) 相雜, 唯侍 (時) 物也. 是故 [其初] (42) 難知而上易知也, 本難知也而末易知也. □則初如疑 (擬) 之, 敬以成之, 夂 (終) 而无咎. □□□□□□□□脩道, 鄉物巽德, 大明在上, 正其是非, 則□□□□□□□□□□占, 危戔 (哉). □□不 (43) 當, 疑德占之, 則易可用矣. 子曰: 知者觀其緣 (彖) 辭而說過半矣. 易曰 "二與四同 [功而異位, 其善不同, 二] 多譽, 四多瞿 (懼), 近也. 近也者, 嗛 (謙) 之謂也. 易曰: 柔之 [爲道, 不利遠者, 其] 要无 [咎, 其用] 柔若 [中也. 易] (44) 曰: 三與五同功異立 (位), 其過□□, [三] 多凶, 五多功, [貴賤] 之等☐ (45)

.. .. to prognosticate without virtue, then even the *Changes* will not be appropriate. The property of the *Changes* is *to praise the beginning and [return] to the end in order to give it substance. The six lines are mutually varied; they are only time and beings. This is why [its first line] (42) is difficult to know but its top line is easy to know, its basis is difficult to know but its end is easy to know.. . then with the first line if you (doubt:) imitate it, then being respectful in order to complete it,* in the end there will be no trouble.. .. .. refining the Way. With inclined beings and manifest virtue, the great illumination is at the top line, correcting what is right and wrong, then .. .. to prognosticate is dangerous indeed. .. .. not (43) to match, to prognosticate about it while imitating virtue, then the *Changes* can be used indeed.

Confucius said: "The wise observe its hexagram statements and explain more than half." The *Changes* says: *"The second and fourth lines have the same [merit and yet have different positions, their goodness being not the same: that the second line] has much renown while the fourth has much fear is because of their proximity."* Proximity means modesty. The *Changes* says: *"When the soft [serves as the Way, it does not benefit the distant, but its] essence is without [trouble, and its use] is soft like [the center."* The Changes] (44) says: *"The third and fifth lines have the same merit but different positions, their excesses .. .. . [That the third line] has much inauspiciousness while the fifth line has much merit, is due to the ranking of [noble and mean] . . .* (45).

233

THE
ESSENTIALS

☒反疏 (4) ☒矣 (5) ☒至命者也. 易☒ (6) 明而甚☒行其義, 長其
慮, 脩其☒易矣. 若夫祝巫 (7) 卜筮龜☐☐☐☐☐☐☐☐☐☐☐☐☐
☐☐☐☐☐☐☐☐☐☐☐☐ ☐☐☐巫之師☐☐☐☐☐☐無德,
則不能知易, 故君子龥 (尊) 之. ☐☐☐ ☐☐☐☐☐☐子曰: 吾好
學而龨 (纔) (8) 聞要, 安得益吾年乎? 吾☐焉而產道, ☐焉益之,
☐而貴之, 難☒危者安其立 (位) 者也; 亡者保 [其存者也; 亂者有
其治者也. 是故] 君子安不忘危, 存不忘亡, 治不 [忘亂. 是以身安
而國] 家可保也. 易曰 "其亡其亡, 毄 (繫) 于 (9) 枹 (苞) 桑." 夫子
曰: 德薄而立 (位) 龥 (尊), ☐☐鮮不及. 易曰 "鼎折足, 復 (覆) 公
莝 (餗)", 言不勝任也. 夫子曰: 顏氏之子其庶幾乎? 見幾又 (有)
不善, 未嘗弗知; 知之, 未嘗復行之. 易 (10) 曰 "不遠復, 無菫
(祗) 誨 (悔), 元吉." 天地昷, 萬勿 (物) 潤, 男女購 (構) 請 (精) 而
萬物成.

. . . returns sparsely (4) . . . the highest mandate. The *Changes* . . . (6) bright and very . . . puts its propriety into motion, lengthening its deliberations, and refining its . . . *Changes* indeed. It is like when priests and magicians divine by turtle shell and stalk .. .. the magician's master .. .. without virtue, then he is not able to know the *Changes*; therefore, the gentleman venerates it. .. .. Confucius said: "I am fond of studying but only now have heard its essentials; how can I get to increase my years? Wherein will I .. and give birth to the Way, wherein .. increase it .. and ennoble it. Difficulty . . . *those in danger secure their positions; those lost protect [their existence; those disordered have their governors. This is why] when the gentleman is at peace he does not forget danger, maintaining what he has he does not forget loss, and when governed he does not [forget disorder. It is by this that when the person is at peace, the state] and family can be protected."* The Changes *says: "It is lost, it is lost, tied to a bushy mulberry."*[1] *The Master said: "When virtue is thin but one's position is venerated, ... rarely does it not reach it. When the* Changes *says: 'The cauldron's broken leg, overturns the duke's stew,'*[2] *it speaks of not being capable of bearing responsibility."*[3]

The Master said: "Was not Mr. Yan's son almost there? When he saw at the incipience that there was anything not good, he never failed to know it; knowing it, he never failed not to redo it." The Changes (10) *says: "Returning from not a great distance: without reverence or regret; prime auspiciousness."*[4] *Heaven and earth are warmed and the ten-thousand things moistened. Males and females unite their seminal fluids and the ten-thousand beings are completed.*

易 [曰] "三人行則損一人, 一人行則 [得] 其友", 言至一也. 君子
安其身而後動, 易其心而後評, 定位而後求. 君子脩於此三 (11)
者, 故存也. 危以動, 則人弗與也; 無立 (位) 而求, 則人弗予也. 莫
之予, 則傷之者必至矣. 易曰 "莫益之, 或繫之, 立心勿恒, 凶",
此之謂也. ・夫子老而好易, 居則在席, 行則在囊. 子贛曰: 夫
(12) 子它日教此弟子曰: "悳 (德) 行亡者, 神需 (靈) 之趨; 知 (智)
謀遠者, 卜筮之蔡", 賜以此爲然矣. 以此言取之, 賜緟 (?) 行之爲
也. 夫子何以老而好之乎? 夫子曰: 君子言以榘 (榘) 方也. 前羊
(祥) 而至者, 弗羊 (祥) 而好 (?) 也. (13) 察其要者, 不趨 (詭) 其德.
尙書多於 (闕) 矣, 周易未失也, 且又 (有) 古之遺言焉. 予非安其
用也. [子贛曰: 賜] 聞於夫 [子曰] 必 (?) 於□□□□如是, 則君子
已重過矣. 賜聞諸夫子曰孫 (遜) 正而行義, 則人不惑矣. 夫 (14)
子今不安其用而樂其辭, 則是用倚於人也, 而可乎? 子曰: 校 (謬)
戈 (哉), 賜! 吾告女 (汝), 易之道□□□□而不□□□百生 (姓)
之□□□易也. 故易剛者使知瞿 (懼), 柔者使知剛, 愚人爲而不
忘 (妄), 僸 (漸) 人爲而去詐. 文 (15) 王仁, 不得其志以成其慮, 紂
乃無道, 文王作, 諱而辟 (避) 咎,

When the Changes *[says] "If three men walk then they will lose one man; if one man walks then he will gain his friend,"[5] it speaks of arriving at unity. The gentleman secures his person and only then moves, puts his heart at ease and only then hollers out, settles his position and only then seeks. The gentleman refines himself in these three (11) things, and therefore is maintained. If one moves because of being endangered, then others will not join with him; if one seeks without position, then others will not give to him. If no one gives to him, then those who harm him will necessarily arrive. When the* Changes *says "No one increases him; someone hits him; establishing the heart without constancy; inauspicious,"[6] it means this.[7]*

When the Master aged he delighted in the *Changes*; when at home it was at his mat, and when traveling it was in his pack. Zi Gong said: "Master, (12) at another time you taught this disciple saying, 'The loss of virtuous action leads to a tendency to spiritualism, and the (desire) to know the future leads to the consulting of divination.' I took this to be the case. Having accepted this maxim, I have striven to put it into practice. How is it that now that the Master has aged he could delight in it?" The Master said: "A gentleman's words are squared with a carpenter's rule. It is what comes before the auspices and not the auspices themselves in which I delight. (13) Examining the essentials does not pervert its virtue. To the *Book of Documents* there are many hindrances, but the *Zhouyi* has not yet been lost. Moreover, there are sayings in it bequeathed from antiquity. It is not that I am content with its use."

[Zi Gong said: "I] heard the Master say that one must in .. .. like this, then the gentleman will already take mistakes seriously. I have heard from the Master that if one follows the upright and puts propriety into practice then people will not be confused. If the Master (14) now is not content with its use but enjoys its statements, then this is a case of use that is dependent on others; is that acceptable?" Confucius said: "(Corrected:) How wrong you are! Ci (i.e., Zi Gong), I will tell you, the Way of the *Changes* .. .. and not .. .. .. the hundred families' .. .. .. *Changes*. Therefore, the hardness of the *Changes* causes one to know fear, and its softness causes one to know the hard.[8] Stupid people use it and do not forget; shameful people use it and eschew deceit. King Wen (15) was humane, but he did not succeed in his ambitions to complete his plans. Zhou (i.e., Shang king Di Xin) was then without the Way. King Wen acted, and by observing prohibitions avoided trouble, and

239

然後易始興也. 予樂其知之□□□之□□□予何日 (?) 事紂乎?
子贛曰: 夫子亦信其筮乎? 子曰: 吾百占而七十當, 唯周梁山之占
也, 亦必 (16) 從其多者而已矣. 子曰: 易, 我復其祝卜矣, 我觀其
德義耳也. 幽贊而達乎數, 明數而達乎德, 又 (?) 仁□者而義行之
耳. 贊而不達於數, 則其爲之巫; 數而不達於德, 則其爲之史. 史
巫之筮, 鄉 (17) 之而未也, 好之而非也. 後世之士疑丘者, 或以易
乎? 吾求其德而已, 吾與史巫同涂而殊歸者也. 君子德行焉求福,
故祭祀而寡也; 仁義焉求吉, 故卜筮而希也. 祝巫卜筮其後乎? 孔
子 (18) 繇 (籀) 易, 至于損益一〈二〉卦, 未尚 (嘗) 不廢書而嘆,
戒門弟子曰: 二厽 (參) 子! 夫損益之道, 不可不審察也, 吉凶之□
也. 益之爲卦也, 春以授夏之時也, 萬勿 (物) 之所出也, 長日之至
也, 產之 (?) 室也, 故曰 (19) 益. 損者, 秋以授冬之時, 萬勿 (物) 之
所老衰也, 長 [夕之] 所至也, 故曰產. 道窮□□□□□□□. [益
之] 始也吉, 其多 (終) 也凶. 損之始凶, 其多 (終) 也吉. 損益之道,
足以觀天地之變, 而君者之事已. (20) 是以察於損益之總 (?) 者,
不可動以憂 (憙). 故明君

240

only thereafter did the *Changes* first arise. I delight in its wisdom's ... ..
.. it .. .. .. how could I say to serve (King) Zhou?"

Zi Gong said: "Does the Master also believe in milfoil divination?"
The Master said: "I am right in (only) seventy out of one hundred
prognostications. Even with the prognostications of Liangshan of Zhou
one necessarily (16) follows it most of the time and no more." The
Master said: "As for the *Changes,* I do indeed put its prayers and divinations last,[9] only observing its virtue and propriety. Intuiting the commendations to reach the number, and understanding the number to
reach virtue, is to have humaneness (?) and to put it into motion properly.
If the commendations do not lead to the number, then one merely acts
as a magician; if the number does not lead to virtue, then one merely
acts as a scribe. The divinations of scribes and magicians tend (17) toward
it but are not yet there, delight in it but are not correct. Perhaps it will
be because of the *Changes* that sires of later generations will doubt me.
I seek its virtue and nothing more. I am on the same road as the scribes
and magicians but end up differently. The conduct of the gentleman's
virtue is to seek blessings; that is why he sacrifices, but little; the
righteousness of his humaneness is to seek auspiciousness; that is why
he divines, but rarely. Do not the divinations of priests and magicians
come last!"

When Confucius (18) chanted the *Changes,* when he reached the
(one:) two hexagrams *Sun,* "Decrease," and *Yi,* "Increase," he invariably
put down the book and sighed, admonishing his disciples saying: "My
sons; you cannot not examine the way of *Sun,* 'Decrease,' and *Yi,*
'Increase'; it is the .. of auspiciousness and inauspiciousness. As a hexagram, *Yi,* 'Increase,' is the time of spring giving way to summer, when
the ten-thousand beings come out, the height of the long days, the chamber of birth. Therefore it is called (19) Increase. As for *Sun,* 'Decrease,'
it is the time of autumn giving way to winter, when the ten-thousand
beings age and decline, the height of the long night; therefore, it is
called the way of birth being exhausted .. .. The beginning
[of Increase] is auspicious, but its end is inauspicious. The beginning of
Decrease is inauspicious, but its end is auspicious. The way of Decrease
and Increase is sufficient to observe the alternations of heaven and earth,
and the lord's service is finished (in it). (20) Thereby examining into
the completeness of Decrease and Increase, one cannot be moved by
sadness or happiness. Therefore, the enlightened lord does not for a

不時不宿, 不日不月, 不卜不□□□□□□□□□地之也, 此謂易道. 故易又 (有) 天道焉, 而不可以日月生 (星) 辰盡稱也, 故爲之以陰陽. 又 (有) 地道 (21) 焉, 不可以水火金土木盡稱也, 故律之以柔剛. 又 (有) 人道焉, 不可以父子君臣夫婦先後盡稱也, 故要之以上下. 又 (有) 四時之變焉, 不可以萬勿 (物) 盡稱也, 故爲之以八卦. 故易之爲書也, 一類不足以亟 (極) (22) 之, 變以備其請 (情) 者也, 故謂之易. 又 (有) 君道焉, 五官六府不足盡稱之, 五正之事不足以至之, 而詩書禮樂不□百篇, 難以致之. 不問於古法, 不可順以辭令, 不可求以志善. 能者繇 (由) 一求之, 所謂 (23) 得一而君 (群) 畢者, 此之謂也. 損益之道, 足以觀得失矣.

《要》千六百冊八 (24)

moment or a night, not for a day or a month, not divine by turtle shell or milfoil, and yet knows auspiciousness and inauspiciousness and complies with heaven and earth[10]; this is called the Way of the *Changes.* Therefore, the *Changes* has the way of heaven in it, and yet you cannot use the sun, moon, stars, and planets to exhaust its names; therefore it is done with the yin and the yang. It has the way of earth (21) in it, and yet you cannot use water, fire, metal, earth, and wood to exhaust its names; therefore it is regulated with the soft and the hard. It has the way of man in it, and yet you cannot use father, son, ruler, minister, husband, wife, first, and last to exhaust its names; therefore they are summarized with high and low. It has the alternations of the four seasons in it, and yet you cannot use the ten-thousand beings to exhaust its names; therefore it is done with the eight trigrams. Therefore, since as a book the *Changes* cannot be encompassed by a single category (22), there are alternations in order to complete its characteristics; therefore it is called the *Changes.* There is the way of the ruler in it, and yet the five officials and the six bureaus are not sufficient to exhaust its names, the services of the five governors are not sufficient to reach it, and even with the *Poetry, Documents, Rituals,* and *Music* do not .. one hundred chapters, it would be difficult to bring it about. If you do not ask about the ancient models, you cannot follow it through stated commands and cannot seek it through recorded goodness. Those who are able seek it from the one; what is called (23) gaining the one and everything being complete means just this. The way of Decrease and Increase is sufficient to observe gain and loss." *The Essentials,* 1648 (graphs). (24)

MU HE
AND
ZHAO LI

繆和

繆和問於先生曰: 請問《易》渙之九二曰: 渙, 賁其階, 每 (悔) 亡. 此辭吾甚疑焉. 請問此之所冑 (謂). [先生] 曰: 夫《易》, 明君之守也. 吾□□不達, 問學不上與 (歟)? 恐言而貿易, 失人之道, 不然, 吾志亦願之. 繆和 (1) 曰: 請毋若此, 願聞其說. 子曰: 渙者, 散也. 賁階, 幾也, 時也. 古之君子, 時福至則進取, 時亡則以讓, 夫福至而能既焉, □走其時, 唯恐失之, 故當其時而弗能用也. 至於其失之也, 唯欲爲人用, (2) 剴 (豈) 可得也才 (哉)? 將何無每 (悔) 之又 (有)? 受者昌, 賁福而弗能葴者窮, 逆福者死. 故其在《詩》也曰: 女弄不敝衣常 (裳), 士弄不敝車輪. 无千歲之國, 无百歲之家, 无十歲之能. 夫福之於人也, 既焉, 不 (3) 可得而賁也. 故曰賁福又 (有) 央 (殃). 耴 (聖) 人知福之難得而賁也,

MU HE

Mu He asked of his teacher, saying: "I beg to ask about the Nine in the Second line of *Huan,* 'Dispersal,' 'Dispersal rushes its stairs; regret is gone'; I have grave doubts about this statement. I beg to ask what this means." [The teacher] said: "The *Changes* is the guard of the enlightened lord. I .. .. have not penetrated it, and my scholarship is not up to it. I am afraid to speak and to detract from the *Changes,* losing the way of man; otherwise, I would surely be pleased to do it." Mu He (1) said: "Please don't be like this; I want to hear its explanation." The master said: "*Huan* means to scatter. 'To rush the stairs' is the pivot, the instant. With the lords of antiquity, at the instant that good fortune arrived they advanced and took it; at the instant it was gone they therewith yielded. When good fortune has arrived and you are able to have it, but .. running for time you only fear losing it, then even at that time you will not be able to use it. And coming to when you do lose it, if you only wish to be used by others, (2) how could you ever succeed! How would you ever be 'without regret'? He who receives it flourishes, but he who rushes to good fortune and is not able to cover it will be impoverished, and he who goes against good fortune will die. Therefore, in the *Poetry* it says: 'The female acts and does not wear out the jacket or skirt; The male acts and does not wear out the cart or wheel.'[1] There are no thousand-year-old states, no hundred-year-old families, and no ten-year-old capabilities. Good fortune's relationship with man is that if you aready have it, then you cannot (3) succeed in rushing to it. Therefore it says 'to rush to good fortune there is disaster' (*sic*). The sage knows how difficult good fortune is to get and rushes to it; this is

247

是以又 (有) 矣. 故《易》曰: 渙, 賁其階, 每 (悔) 亡. 則□言於能賁其時, 悔之亡也. ·繆和問於先生曰: 凡生於天下者, 无愚知 (智) 賢不宵 (肖), 莫不 (4) 願利達顯榮. 今《周易》曰: 困, 亨, 貞, 大人吉, 无咎, 又 (有) 言 [不] 信. 敢問大人何吉於此乎? 子曰: 此耵 (聖) 人之所重言也. 曰又 (有) 言不信, 凡天之道, 壹陰壹陽, 壹短壹長, 壹晦壹明, 夫人道凸 (雝) 之. 是故 (5) 湯□□王, 文王絢 (拘) 於 (牖) 里, [秦繆公困] 於 [殽, 齊桓 (桓) 公] 辱於長頜 (勺), 戉 (越) 王勾賤 (踐) 困於 [會稽], 晉文君困 [於] 驪氏, 古古 (衍一字) 至今, 柏 (伯) 王之君, 未嘗憂困而能□□曰美亞 (惡) 不□□□也. 夫困之為達也, 亦猶 (6) □□□□□其□□□□□□□□□□□□□□, 故《易》曰: 困, 亨, 貞, 大人吉, 无 [咎, 又 (有) 言] 不信, [此] 之胃 (謂) 也. 繆和問於先生曰: 吾年歲猶少, □□□□□□□□□□敢失忘吾者. 子曰: 何 (7) ☑□□□《書》,《春秋》,《詩》語蓋☑ (8) 者莫不願安☑者☑ (9) 以高下, 故□□禹之取天 [下者], 當此卦也. 禹□其四枝 (肢), 苦其思□, 至於手足駢 (胝) 胝, 煩 (顏) 色□□□□, ☑能□細, 故上能而果□□ (10) 下□號耵 (聖) 君, 亦可胃 (謂) 多 (終) 矣, 吉孰大焉? 故曰: 勞 [嗛], 君子又 (有) 多 (終), 吉, 不亦宜乎? 今又 (有) 土之君, 及至布衣□□□□□□□其妻奴 (孥) 粉白黑涅□□□□□□□□□□矣, 日中必傾 (?), □非能□而 (11) 又 (有) 功名於天下者, 殆无又 (有) 矣.

248

why he has it. Therefore, when the *Changes* says 'Dispersal rushes its stairs; regret is gone,' then .. it speaks about being able to rush to the moment and regret will be gone."

Mu He asked his teacher, saying: "Of everything that is born under heaven, whether stupid or wise, good or bad, nothing does not (4) wish for profit and fame. Now the *Zhou Changes* says 'Entangled: Receipt; determination for the great man is auspicious; there is no trouble; there are words that are [not] trustworthy.'[2] Might I dare to ask what auspiciousness there is for the great man in this?" The master said: "These are words that the sage regards as weighty. When it says 'there are words that are not trustworthy,' in all cases the Way of heaven is one yin and one yang, one short and one long, one dark and one bright, and man's Way matches it. This is why (5) Tang .. ... king, King Wen was imprisoned at Youli, [Duke Mu of Qin was entangled] at [Yao, Duke Huan of Qi] was shamed at Changshao, King Goujian of Yue was entangled at [Kuaiji], and Lord Wen of Jin was entangled [by] Madame Li; from antiquity to the present, such rulers as elders and kings have never been saddened by being entangled and been able .. ... saying 'beauty and ugliness do not .. .. ..' . That being entangled can be a breakthrough is just like (6) .. .. its .. .., therefore when the *Changes* says: 'Entangled: Receipt; determination for the great man is auspicious; there is no [trouble; there are words] that are not trustworthy,' this is what it means."

Mu He asked of his teacher, saying: "I am still young, ... dare to lose and forget myself." The master said: "How (7) .. .. the sayings of the *Documents, Spring and Autumn,* and *Poetry* are just . . . (8) none do not wish to be content . . . (9) to elevate the lowly, therefore .. .. Yu's taking of all under heaven matches this hexagram. Yu .. his four limbs and worked his mind .. , to the extent that his arms and legs were callused and his brow and face .. .. able .. minute, therefore when those above are capable and really .. .. (10) those below .. call them 'sage kings,' this can also be said to have an 'end'; what could be more auspicious than it? Therefore, when it says: 'Toiling [modesty]; the gentleman has an end; auspicious,'[3] is it not also appropriate? Today, lords of the land, and even extending to cloth and clothes .. .. their consorts and slaves powder white and black and dye .. .. , in the middle of the day necessarily collapse, .. not able .. and yet (11) are renowned for merit probably do not exist."

故曰: 勞嗛, 君 [子又 (有)] 冬 (終), 吉, 此之胃 (謂) 也. ·蓼 (繆)

和問先生曰: 吾聞先君其□義錯 (措) 法, 發 [號] 施令於天下也,

皎焉若□□□□□□世, 循者不惑眩焉. 今《易》 [豐] 之 (12) 九

四曰: 豐其剖, 日中見斗, 遇其夷主, 吉, 何胃 (謂) 也? 子曰: 豐者,

大也; 剖者, 小也, 此言小大之不惑也.□君之爲爵, 立賞慶也, 若

膿 (禮) 埶然, 大□□□□□□使下, 君能令臣, 是以動則又

(有) (13) 功, 靜則又 (有) 名, 死埶尤矣, 賞祿甚厚, 能弄傅君而國

不損敵者, 蓋无又 (有) 矣. 日中見斗, 夫日者, 君也; 久〈斗〉者,

臣也. 日中而久〈斗〉見, 君將失其光□□□□□幾失君之德

矣. 遇者, 見也. 見夷 (14) 主者, 其始夢 (萌) 兆而亟見之者也. 其

次秦蓼 (繆) 公, 荊莊, 晉文, 齊桓 (桓) 是也. 故《易》曰: 豐其剖,

日中見斗, 遇其夷主, 此之胃 (謂) 也. ·呂昌問先生曰:《易》屯

之九五曰: 屯其膏, 小貞吉, 大貞凶, 將何 (15) 胃 (謂) 也? 夫

《易》, 上耴 (聖) 之治也. 古君子處尊思卑, 處貴思賤, 處富思

貧, 處樂思勞. 君子能思此四者, 是以長又 (有) 其 [利] 而名與天

地俱. 今《易》曰: 屯其膏, 此言自閏 (潤) 者也. 夫處上立 (位)

厚自利而不自 (16) 血 (恤) 下, 小之猶可, 大之必凶.

250

Mu He asked his teacher, saying: "I have heard that with past lords their .. propriety was articulated with their laws, and that when they issued [commands] and promulgated statutes under heaven they were clear about it as if .. .. world, and those who followed them were not confused or dazzled by them. Now when the Nine in the Fourth line (12) of the *Changes*' [*Feng*, 'Abundance'] states: 'Making abundant his curtain; in the middle of the day one sees the Dipper; meeting his placid ruler; auspicious,' what does it mean?" The master said: "'Abundant' is great, while a 'curtain' is little; this speaks of the little and great not being confused... the lords' being ennobled establishes awards and celebrations; if the rites are well grounded, then the great .. .. serve the lowly, and the lord is able to command his ministers; this is why when he acts he has (13) merit and when at rest has fame. There are probably no cases in which the foundation is misaligned, awards and emoluments are very rich, and one is able to manipulate the lord that the state is not diminished. As for 'In the middle of the day one sees the Dipper,' the 'day' (i.e., the sun) is the lord and the 'Dipper' is the minister. If in the middle of the day the lord is about to lose his brightness .. .. almost loses the lord's virtue. To 'meet' is to see. To see the 'placid (14) ruler' means abruptly to see it as soon as it first sprouts. Next after it are Duke Mu of Qin, (King) Zhuang of Jing (i.e., Chu), (Lord) Wen of Jin, and (Duke) Huan of Qi. Therefore, when the *Changes* says: 'Making abundant his curtain; in the middle of the day one sees the Dipper; meeting his placid ruler,' this is what it means."

Lü Chang asked the teacher, saying: "The Nine in the Fifth line of the *Changes*' *Zhun*, 'Hoarding,' hexagram says: 'Hoarding its fat; little determination is auspicious, great determination is inauspicious'; what is this supposed (15) to mean?" "The *Changes* is the rule of the highest sage. In antiquity the gentleman occupied the venerable position but thought of the mean, occupied the honored position but thought of the humble, occupied the rich position but thought of the poor, occupied the happy position but thought of the belabored. It is because the gentleman was able to think of these four things that he was able long to have [benefit] and his fame was congruent with that of heaven and earth. Now when the *Changes* says 'Hoarding its fat,' this saying is self-revealing. If one is situated in a high position and richly benefits oneself but does not of himself (16) commiserate with the lowly, this is still acceptable in little cases but is necessarily inauspicious for the great.

且夫君國又 (有) 人而厚斂 (斂) 致正以自封也, 而不顧其人, 此除也. 夫能見其將□□□□□, 未失君人之道也, 其小之吉, 不亦宜乎? 物未夢 (萌) 兆而先知之者, 耴 (聖) 人之志 (17) 也, 三代所以治其國也. 故 《易》 曰: 屯其膏, 小貞吉, 大貞凶, 此之胃 (謂) 也. ·呂昌問先生曰: [天] 下之士, 皆欲會□□□□□□□□樓與以相高也, 以爲至是也. 今 《易》 渙之六四曰: 渙其群, 元吉, 此 (18) 何胃 (謂) 也? 子曰: 異才 (哉), 天下之士所貴. 夫渙者, 散; 元者, 善之始也; 吉者, 百福之長也. 夫群黨僴 (朋) □□□□□□□比□相譽, 以奪君明, 此古亡國敗家之法也, 明君之所行罰也, 將何 (19) 元吉之又 (有) 矣? 呂昌曰: 吾聞類大又 (有) 爲耳, 而未能以辨也, 願先生少進之, 以明少者也. 子曰: 明君□□□□□□□然立爲刑辟, 以散其群黨, 埶爲賞慶爵死, 以勸其下群臣, 黔首男 (20) 女, 夫人, 渴 (竭) 力盡知, 歸心於上, 莫敢僴 (朋) 黨侍 (待) 君, 而主將何求於人矣? 其曰渙其群, 元吉, 不亦宜乎? 故□□□□小星, 參 (三) 五在東, 蕭 (肅) 蕭 (肅) 宵正 (征), 蚤 (早) 夜在公, 是命不同, 彼此之胃 (謂) 也. ·

252

Moreover, in the case of rulers of states there are those who richly gather power in order to establish themselves but do not think of their people; this is rejected. Those who are able to see what they lead to .. .. have not lost the way of the lord of men, is it not also appropriate that in little cases it should be auspicious? When beings have not yet sprouted and yet one has prior knowledge of them, this is the will of the sage (17), the means by which the Three Dynasties (i.e., Xia, Shang, and Zhou) ruled their states. Therefore, when the *Changes* says: 'Hoarding its fat; little determination is auspicious, great determination is inauspicious,' this is what it means."

Lü Chang asked the teacher, saying: "All of the sires under [heaven] wish to join .. .. compare in height with a multistoried building, regarding this as having made it. Now when the Six in the Fourth line of the *Changes' Huan,* 'Dispersal,' says: 'Dispersing his flock; prime auspiciousness,' what does this (18) mean?" The master said: "Different indeed is what the sires under heaven regard as honorable. *Huan,* 'Dispersal,' is to scatter; 'prime' is the beginning of goodness; 'auspiciousness' is the height of the hundred good fortunes. Flocks and cliques and friends and .. .. ally .. praise each other in order to snatch away the lord's brightness; from of old this has been the model of losing the state and defeating the family, and the reason for which the enlightened lord has put punishments into effect; what (19) 'prime auspiciousness' could there be?"

Lü Chang said: "I have heard that there are great categories in it, and yet one cannot use them to make discriminations. I wish that the teacher would enter into this a little to enlighten me." The master said: "If the enlightened lord .. .. so establishes rule by punishment in order to scatter flocks and cliques, and grounds awards and ennoblements in order to encourage his lower ministers and the males (20) and females of the common people, and if the people exert all of their strength and knowledge and are loyal to their superior, none daring to treat their lord through cliques, then what would the ruler need to seek from the people? When it says 'Dispersing his flock; prime auspiciousness,' isn't it really appropriate? Therefore, ... the little stars, Shen and Wu in the east, so quietly journeying at night, both morning and night on the job, this is the difference of fate, the meaning of this and that."

呂昌問先生曰: (21) 夫古之君子, 其思慮舉錯 (措) 也, 內得於心, 外度於義, 外內和同, 上順天道, 下中地理, 中適人心, 神□□□ □□□□筈之聞. 今《周易》曰: 蒙, 亨, 非我求董 (童) 蒙, 董 (童) 蒙求我, 初筮吉, 再參讀 (瀆), 讀 (瀆) 則 (22) 不吉, 利貞. 以 昌之和〈私〉, 以爲夫設身無方, 思索不察, 進退無節, 讀 (瀆) 焉 則不吉矣, 而能亨其利者, 古又 (有) 之乎? 子曰: □ [又 (有)] 也, 而又 (有) 不然者. 夫內之不咎, 外之不逆, 筈筈然能立志於天下, (23) 若此者, 成人也. 成人也者, 世無一夫, 剴 (豈) 可强及輿才 (哉)? 故言曰: 古之馬及古之鹿, 今之馬 [及] 今之鹿. 夫任人□ 過, 亦君子□. [呂] 昌曰: 若子之言, 則《易》蒙上矣. 子曰: 何必 若此, 而不可察也. 夫蒙者, (24) 然少未又 (有) 知也. 凡物之少, 人之所好也, 故曰: 蒙, 亨. 非我求童蒙, 童蒙求我者, 又 (有) 知 (智) 能者不求无能者, 无能者 [求又 (有)] 能者, 非我求童蒙, 童 蒙求我. 初筮吉者, 聞其始而知其冬 (終), 見其本而知其 [末, 故] (25) 曰初筮吉. 再參讀 (瀆), 讀 (瀆) 則不吉者, 反覆問之而讀 (瀆), 讀 (瀆) 弗敬, 故曰不吉. 弗知而好學, 身之賴也, 故曰利 [貞]. 君子於仁義之道也, 雖弗身能, 剴 (豈) 能已才 (哉). 日夜不 休, 冬 (終) 身不卷 (倦),

Lü Chang asked the teacher, saying: (21) "With the gentlemen of antiquity, their thoughts and considerations were raised up and articulated, within getting it in their hearts and without measuring it by propriety; with both outside and inside being harmonious, above they complied with the way of heaven, below they were centered on the pattern of the earth, and in the middle they arrived at the heart of man. The spirit .. .. the renown of purity. Now the *Zhou Changes* says: 'Folly: Receipt; it is not we who seek youthful folly, youthful folly seeks us. The initial milfoil divination is auspicious, but if two or three times drawn out, being drawn out then (22) it is not auspicious; beneficial to determine.'[4] Taking my own situation, for the fellow to construct his person without boundaries, for his thoughts not to be examined, for his advancing and retreating to be without measure, then drawing this out would indeed not be auspiciousness, and yet in antiquity could there have been receipt of its benefit?" The master said: ".. is, and yet is not so. To be untroubled within and nontransgressive without, purely able to establish your will under heaven is the way (23) to be a complete person. As for the complete person, there is not a single fellow in the world who could force and carry him! Therefore, the saying goes: 'The horses and deer of antiquity are the horses and deer of the present.' One who shoulders men .. excesses, is also a gentleman .. " Lü Chang said: "If it is as you say, then the *Changes*' *Meng*, 'Folly,' is the highest." The master said: "Why must it be like this, and yet not be able to be examined? *Meng* (24) is to be small, to be sure, and not yet to have knowledge. All beings when small are what others are fond of; therefore when it says: 'Folly: Receipt; it is not we who seek youthful folly, youthful folly seeks us,' it means that those who have knowledge and ability do not seek those without ability but those without ability seek those with ability, it is not we who seek youthful folly but youthful folly that seeks us. 'The initial milfoil divination is auspicious' means that when one hears of the beginning he knows of its end, sees the root and knows its [branches; therefore], (25) it says 'The initial milfoil divination is auspicious.' 'If two or three times drawn out, being drawn out then it is not auspicious' means that in asking about it over and over again and drawing it out, drawing it out is not to respect it; therefore it says 'not auspicious.' To be fond of studying when one does not know something is the support of the person; therefore it says 'beneficial [to determine].' The gentleman's relationship with the Way of humaneness and propriety is that even if he is personally unable, still how would he be able to quit: not resting either day or night, throughout his life

255

日日載載, 必成而 (26) 後止, 故《易》曰: 蒙, 亨, 非我求童蒙, 童蒙求我. 初筮吉, 再參瀆 (瀆), 瀆(瀆)則 不吉, 利貞, 此之胃 (謂) 也. ·吳孟問先 [生曰]:《易》中復之九二, 其辭曰: 鳴鶴在陰, 其子和之, 我又 (有) 好爵, 吾與壐 (爾) 羸之, 何胃 (謂) [也? 子] (27) 曰: 夫《易》, 耴 (聖) 君之所尊也, 吾庸與焉乎? 吳子〈孟〉曰: 惡又 (有) 然, 願先生式 (試) 略之, 以爲毋忘, 以匡弟子. □□□□□□□者所獨擅也, 道之所見也, 故曰在陰. 君者, 人之父母也: 人者, 君之子 (28) 也. 君發號出令, 以死力應之, 故曰其子和之. 我又 (有) 好爵, 吾與壐 (爾) 羸之者, 夫爵祿在君在人□君不徒□□□□臣□□其人也, 訢焉而欲利之; 忠臣之事其君也, 驩然而欲明之, 驩訢交迵 (通), (29) 此耴 (聖) 王之所以君天下也, 故《易》曰: 鳴鶴 [在] (原缺) 陰, 其子和之, 我又 (有) 好爵, 吾與壐 (爾) 羸之, 其此之胃 (謂) 乎? ·莊但 [問] 於先生曰: 敢問於古今之世, 聞學談說之士君子, 所以皆牧焉勞其四枳 (肢) 之力, 渴 (竭) 其腹心 (30) 而索者, 類非安樂而爲之也. 以但之私心論之, 此大者求尊嚴顯貴之名, 細者欲富厚安樂 [之] 實, 是以皆□□必勉輕奮 (?) 其所敎幸於天下者, 殆此之爲也. 今《易》溓之初六, 其辭 (31) 曰: 嗛嗛 [君子], 用涉大川,

256

untiring, day after day carrying on, he stops only after the work (26) is completed. Therefore, when the *Changes* says 'Folly: Receipt; it is not we who seek youthful folly, youthful folly seeks us. The initial milfoil divination is auspicious, but if two or three times drawn out, being drawn out then it is not auspicious; beneficial to determine,' this is what it means."

Wu Meng asked the teach[-er, saying]: "The Nine in the Second line statement of the *Changes' Zhongfu, 'Central Return,'* hexagram reads: 'A calling crane in the shade, its young harmonizes with it; We have a good chalice, I will down it with you'; what does this mean?" [The master] (27) said: "The *Changes* is what is revered by the sagely lord; what do I have to do with it?" Wuzi (i.e., Wu Meng) said: "How could it be so! I wish that my teacher would try to outline it, considering that his disciple won't forget it and thus will be corrected." [The master said]: .. .. alone being monopolized, the way's being seen, therefore it says 'in the shade.' The lord is the father and mother of the people, and the people are the children of the lord (28). The lord issues commands and puts out statutes and they exert all of their strength to respond to them; therefore it says 'its young harmonizes with it.' 'We have a good chalice, I will down it with you' means that title and emolument are with the lord and with the people .. lord not only .. .. minister .. .. his people, informs them and wishes to benefit them. A loyal minister's service to his lord is joyous and he wishes to enlighten him. With joy informing and interrelating with him (29) is what the sage king uses to lord over all under heaven; therefore, when the *Changes* says 'A calling crane in the shade, its young harmonizes with it; We have a good chalice, I will down it with you,' doesn't it mean just this!"

Zhuang Qu [asked] of the teacher, saying: "I dare to ask whether in the worlds of antiquity and today the reason that sires and gentlemen of scholarship and explanations have all labored their limbs and exhausted their minds in their searches (30) is not because they find satisfaction in them? From my own personal perspective, the great ones among these seek a venerable and illustrious name, while the trivial wish for the substance of wealth and satisfaction. This is probably why all those who .. .. insist on rising above their lot in life act in this way. Now when the Initial Six line statement of the *Changes' Qian, 'Modesty,'*[5] (31) hexagram says: 'So modest is the gentleman; herewith fording the great river;

吉, 將何以此論也? 子曰: 夫務尊顯者, 其心又 (有) 不足者也. 君子不然, 畛焉不 [自] 明也, 不自尊□□高世□嗛之初六, 嗛之明夷也. 取 (聖) 人不敢又 (有) 立 (位) 也, 以又 (有) 知爲无知 (32) 也, 以又 (有) 能爲无能也, 以又 (有) 見爲无見也. 憧焉无敢設也. 以使其下, 所以治人請 (情), 牧群臣之僞也. □□君子者, 夫(?) □□□□然以不□□於天下, 故奢多 (侈) 廣大旅 (游) 樂之鄉不敢渝其身焉, (33) 是以而 〈天〉 下驩然歸之而弗猒 (厭) 也. 用涉大川, 吉者, 夫明夷離下而川 (坤) 上. 川(坤) 者, 順也. 君子之所以折其身者, 明察所以□□□□□, 是以能既致天下之人而又 (有) 之. 且夫川 (坤) 者, 下之爲也. 故曰用 (34) 涉大川, 吉. 子曰: 能下人若此, 其吉也, 不亦宜乎? 舜取天下也, 當此卦也. 子曰: 蔥 (聰) 明叡知守以愚, 博聞强試 (識) 守 [以] □, □□□貴而守以卑, 若此故能君人, 非舜其孰能當之? ·張射問 (35) 先生曰: 自古至今, 天下皆貴盛盈. 今 《周易》 曰: 嗛, 亨, 君子又 (有) 冬 (終), 敢問君子何亨於此乎? 子曰: 所問是也. □□□□□□埶死爵立 (位) 之尊, 明厚賞慶之名, 此先君之所以勸其力也 (36) 宜矣. 彼其貴之也, 此非取 (聖) 君之所貴也. 夫取 (聖) 君卑膿 (體) 屈貌以舒孫 (遜), 以下其人, 能至天下之人而又 (有) 之, □□□□□□孰能以此冬 (終)? 子曰: 天之道,

auspicious,' how can we use this theory?" The master said: "He who strives to be venerated and illustrious will necessarily be unsatisfied in his heart. The gentleman is not like this. Circumspect, he does not show off and is not conceited .. ... high world .. *Qian*'s Initial Six, which is the *Mingyi*, 'Calling Pheasant,' line of *Qian*.[6] The sage does not dare to have position, and takes having knowledge as being without knowledge (32), takes having ability as being without ability, takes having vision as being without vision; he understands it but does not dare to set himself up. It is by serving those under him that he governs men's emotions and shepherds the artifices of the flock of ministers. .... gentleman, ... so through his not .. .. under heaven, therefore even in the midst of luxury and vast pleasure he does not dare to change his person. (33) This is why all under heaven joyously return to him and do not feel oppressed. 'Herewith fording the great river; auspicious' derives from *Mingyi* ䷣ hexagram having *Li* ☲ (trigram)[7] at the bottom and *Chuan* ☷ (trigram) at the top.[8] *Chuan*, 'The Flow,' means compliant. The reason that the gentleman bends his body to investigate why .. .. , this is why after bringing together the people under heaven he is able to have them. Moreover, *Chuan* is the action of the low; therefore, it says 'herewith (34) fording the great river; auspicious.'" The master said: "To be able to place oneself under others like this, is its auspiciousness not also appropriate? Shun's accepting all under heaven matched this hexagram." The master said: "Perspicacity and knowledge are maintained through stupidity; erudition and awareness are maintained [through] .. ; .. .. .. honor are maintained through baseness. In this way therefore he was able to lord over men; if not Shun, who would have been able to match this?"

Zhang She asked (35) the teacher, saying: "From antiquity to the present, all under heaven have always honored fullness. Now the *Zhou Changes* says: 'Modesty: Receipt; the gentleman has an end.' Might I dare to ask what 'receipt' the gentleman has in this?" The master said: "What you have asked is correct. It is appropriate that the reason the prior lords exerted their strength is because of .. .. the veneration of respect and titles and the fame of riches and awards (36). But whereas others honor these things, they are not what the sage lords honored. The sage lords debase their bodies and draw back their teeth in order to extend compliance, and through lowering their persons are able to reach and to have the people under heaven. .. .., who would be able to have this 'end'?" The master said: "The way of heaven is high

禀 (崇) 高神明而好下, 故萬勿 (物) 歸命焉; 地之 (37) 道, 精博以

尙而安卑, 故萬勿 (物) 得生焉; 耴 (聖) 君之道, 尊嚴夐知而弗以

驕人, 嗛然比 (?) 德而好後, 故□□《易》曰: 嗛, 亨, 君子又 (有)

冬 (終). 子曰: 嗛者, 嗛然不足也; 亨者, 嘉好之會也. 夫君人 (38)

者, 以德下其人, 人以死力報之, 其亨也, 不亦宜乎? 子曰: 天道毀

盈而益嗛, 地道銷 [盈而] 流嗛, [鬼神害盈而福嗛], [人道] 惡盈而

好嗛. 嗛者, 一物而四益者也; 盈者, 一物而四損者也, 故耴 (聖)

君以 (39) 爲豐荏, 是以盛盈. 使祭服忽, 屋成加茸, 宮成杊隅, 嗛

之爲道也, 君子貴之, 故曰嗛, 亨, 君 [子又 (有) 冬 (終).] 盛盈□

□下, 非君子其孰當之? ·李羊問先生曰:《易》歸妹之上六曰:

女承匡, 无實, 士 (40) 刲羊, 无血, 无攸利, 將以辭, 是何明也? 子

曰: 此言君臣上下之求者也. 女者, 下也. 士者, 上也. 承者, □□,

[匡] 者□之名也. 刲者, 上求於下也. 羊者, 衆也. 血者, 邺也. 攸

者, 所也. 夫賢君之爲死埶爵立 (位) (41) 也, 與實俱, 群臣榮其

死, 樂其實, 夫人盡忠於上. 其於小人也, 必談博知其又 (有) 无而

□□□□□□行, 莫不勸樂以承上求, 故可長君也. 貪亂之君不

然, 群臣虛立 (位), 皆又 (有) 外志, 君无賞祿

and spiritual and yet is fond of the lowly; therefore the ten-thousand beings owe their fate to it. The way of earth (37) is seminally broad in order to elevate and yet is content with the base; therefore the ten-thousand beings get life from it. The way of the sage lord is venerated and knowledgeable and yet is not thereby arrogant to the people, modestly allying with virtue and being fond of coming last, therefore .. .. the *Changes* says: 'Modesty: Receipt; the gentleman has an end.'" The master said: " 'Modesty' means being modestly unsatisfied. 'Receipt' is the conjunction of goodnesses. If one who is lord over men (38) uses virtue to put himself below them, they will then exert themselves to repay him; is his 'receipt' not appropriate?" The master said: "The heavenly way destroys fullness and adds to modesty; the earthly way dispels fullness and gives flow to modesty; [ghosts and spirits harm fullness and give fortune to modesty, and the human way] hates fullness and is fond of modesty. Modesty is but one thing and yet has these four advantages, while fullness is but one thing and yet has these four disadvantages. Therefore, the sage lord considers (39) it to be florescence, and this is why he is full. The sacrificial clothes being haphazard, or the room being completed and adding a mat, or the palace being completed and carving out a corner, this is the way of modesty and the gentleman honors it. Therefore it says: 'Modesty: Receipt; the gentle[man has an end].' Fullness .. .. low, if not the gentleman, who would be able to match it?"

Li Yang asked the teacher, saying: "The Top Six[9] line of the *Changes'* *Guimei*, 'Returning Maiden,' has as its statement: 'The woman holds up the basket without fruit, the man (40) stabs the sheep without blood; there is no place beneficial'; how do you explain this?" The master said: "This speaks of the seeking between lord and minister, high and low. The 'woman' is the low, and the 'man' the high. To 'hold up' is .. .. and [basket] is the word for ..; to 'stab' is the high seeking from the low, and the 'sheep' is the multitude, while 'blood' is to commiserate and 'place' locates an event. The wise lord's acting for respect and title (41) is in tandem with substance: the flock of ministers glories in his effort and enjoys his substance, and the people are all loyal to the one above. But the petty man must talk about his erudition, what he has and does not have and yet .. .. motion, nothing does not encourage them to uphold what the one above seeks; therefore he can long be lord. The greedy and disordered lord is not like this: the many ministers have empty positions, all having external aims, and the lord has no awards

261

(42) 以勸之. 其於小人也, 賦斂無根 (限), 耆 (嗜) 欲无猒 (厭), 徵求无時, 財盡而人力屈, 不朕 (勝) 上求, 衆又 (有) 離□□□□□□所以亡其國以及其身也. 夫明君之畜其臣也不虛, 忠臣之事其君也又 (有) 實, 上下迵 (通) 實, 此 (43) 所以長又 (有) 令名於天下也. 夫忠言請 (情) 愛而實弗隋 (隨), 此鬼神之所疑也, 而兄 (況) 人乎? 將何所利? [故《易》] 曰女承 [匡, 无] 實, 士刲羊, 无血, 无攸利, 此之胃 (謂) 也. 孔子曰: 夫无實而承之, 无血而卦 (刲) 之, 不亦不知 (智) 乎? (44) 且夫求於无又 (有) 者, 此凶之所產也. 善乎胃 (謂) □无所利也. ·子曰: 君人者又 (有) 大德於臣而不求其報, □則不□□要, 晉齊宋之君是也. 臣人者, 又 (有) 大德 [於] □□□□□□□□□□□□□ (45) □□王子比干, 五 (伍) 子 (?) □□子隼是也, 君人者, 又 (有) 大德於臣而不求其報, □道也, 臣者 [有德於人] 而不求其報, 死道也. 是故耴 (聖) 君求報□□□□□□□□□□□□□□□ (46) □□□□□□□也, □其在《易》也復之六二曰: 休復, 吉, 則此言以□□□□□也, 又 (有) □□□□□□□☑將何吉之求矣. ·子曰: 昔者先君□□□□□□□□□□□□□□□□ (47) □□□□□□不相□□□前不相☑正之成也, 故人□□□□□□□□□□□□□□□□猶恐人之不順也, 故其在《易》☑□□□□□□□□□□□□□□□无成, 子 (48) [曰] □□□□□□□□□□□□□幹事, 食舊德以自厲□□□□□□□

(42) with which to encourage them. But the petty man taxes without restraint, desires oppressively, and makes levies out of season; even when resources are exhausted and the people's strength is contracted, they cannot satisfy what the one above seeks, and the multitude are caught .. .. and that is why he loses his state and himself as well. The enlightened lord's nurturing of his ministers is not empty, and the loyal minister's serving of his lord has substance; the high and low unifying their substances is why (43) they long have a commanding name under heaven. If loyalty speaks of love and yet there is no substance behind it, this would be doubted even by the ghosts and spirits, and how much more so by men; where would there be any benefit in it? [Therefore, when the *Changes*] says: 'The woman holds up the [basket without] fruit, the man stabs the sheep without blood; there is no place beneficial,' this is what it means." Confucius said: "That it is without substance and yet one upholds it, that it is without blood and yet one stabs it, is this not ignorant? (44) Moreover, seeking from what does not have it is the product of inauspiciousness. It is well put that 'there is no place beneficial.'"

The master said: "If the lord has great virtue with respect to his ministers and yet does not seek to be repaid, .. then not .. .. want, such were the lords of Jin, Qi, and Song. If a minister has great virtue [with respect to] .. .. (45) .. .. such were the prince Bi Gan, Wu Zi-[xu], and .. Zizhun. If the lord has great virtue with respect to his ministers and yet does not seek to be repaid, this is the way of ..; if a minister [has virtue with respect to] .. and yet does not seek to be repaid, this is the way of respect. This is why the sage lord seeks repayment .. .. (46) .. .., .. . When in the Six in the Second line of the *Changes' Fu*, 'Returning,' hexagram, it says 'Beneficent return; auspicious,' then this speaks of .. .. There is .. .. , what seeking of auspiciousness would there be?"

The master said: "In former times, the prior lords .. .. (47) .. .. not mutually .. .. .. the front not mutually . . . the completion of correctness; therefore, men .. .. still fear others' not complying with them; therefore, in the *Changes* . . . . without completion. The master (48) .. .. manage affairs, 'eating old virtue' in order to endanger himself .. ..

□□□□□□□□□□□也, 夫產於今之世而□□□□□□□□□□□□□□□□不亦宜乎? (49) [故曰: 食] 舊德, 貞, 厲. 或從王事, 无成. ·子曰: 恆之初六曰: 夐恆, 貞凶, 无 [攸利. 子] 曰, 夐, 治□□□□□□□□□□□□□用人之所非也, 凶必☒, [故曰: 夐恆, 貞凶, 无攸] 利. ·子曰: 恆人之九三曰: (50) [不恆其德], 或承之羞, 貞 [藺]. 子曰: 不恆其 [德] (原缺) 者, 言其德行之無恆也, 德行無道, 則親疏無辨, 親疏無辨 [則] 必將□□□□□□□不藺, 故曰: 不恆其德, 或 [承之羞, 貞藺. 子曰: 烜之] 九五曰: 恆其德貞, 婦人 (51) 吉, 夫子凶. 婦德一人之爲, [不] 可以又 (有) 它; 又 (有) 它矣, 凶□產焉, 故曰, 恆其德, 貞, 婦人吉, 其男德不☒□□□□□又 (有) □德必立而好比於人, 賢不宵 (肖), 人得其宜□□則吉, 自恆也則凶. 故曰: 恆其德, 貞, 婦人 (52) 吉, 夫子凶. ·子曰: 川 (坤) 之六二曰: 直方大, 不習, 无不利. 子曰: 直方者, 知之胃 (謂) 也; 不習者, □□□□□□□□也; 无不利者, 无過之胃 (謂) 也; 夫贏德以與人過, 則失人和矣. 非人之所習也,

264

.. .. , is born of today's world and yet .. ..
.. .. , is it not appropriate? (49) [Therefore, it says: 'Eating] old
virtue; determination is dangerous. Someone follows the king's service,
without completion.' "[10]

The master said: "The Initial Six line of *Heng*, 'Constancy,' says:
'Distant constancy; determination is inauspicious; there is no [place
beneficial.'" The master] said: "'Distant' means to govern .. ..
.. .. using that which men negate, inauspiciousness necessarily . . .
[therefore, it says: 'Distant constancy; determination is inauspicious;
there is no place] beneficial.'"

The master said: "The Nine in the Third line of *Heng*, 'Constancy,'
says: (50) '[Not making constant his virtue], he perhaps receives its
disgrace; determination is [distressful].'" The master said: "'Not making
constant his virtue' says that his virtuous conduct is without constancy;
if virtuous conduct is without the Way then there will be no discrimination between near and far relations, and if there is no discrimination
between near and far relations [then] this will necessarily lead to .. .. ..
.. .. not distress; therefore it says: 'Not making constant his virtue,
he perhaps [receives its disgrace; determination is distressful.'"

The master said]: "The Nine in the Fifth line of *Heng*, 'Constancy,'
says: 'Making constant his virtue; determination is auspicious for the
wife (51), inauspicious for the husband.' A wife's virtue acts for a single
person; she may [not] have any other; if she has another, inauspiciousness .. is born of it. Therefore it says: 'Making constant his virtue; determination is auspicious for the wife.' The male's virtue is not .. ..
.. have .. virtue necessarily established and yet be fond of allying with
others; whether worthy or not good, if a man gets what is appropriate
to him .. then it is auspicious, but if he is constant to himself then it is
inauspicious. Therefore it says: 'Making constant his virtue; determination is auspicious for the wife (52), inauspicious for the husband.'"

The master said: "The Six in the Second line of *Chuan*, 'The Flow,'
says: 'Straight, square, and great; not repeated; nothing not beneficial.'"
The master said: "'Straight' and 'square' is said of knowledge; 'not repeated' .. .. ; 'nothing not beneficial' is said of there being
no excesses. If emaciated virtue is combined with human excesses,
then you will lose human harmony. If it is not that which men repeat,

265

則近害矣, 故 (53) 曰: 直方大, 不習, 无不利. ·湯出軷 (巡) 守, 東北又 (有) 火, 曰: 彼何火也? 又 (有) 司對曰: 漁者也. 湯遂□□□□子之祝 [曰: 古者蛛] 蝥作罔 (網), 今之人緣序. 左者, 右者, 尙 (上) 者, 下者, 率突乎土者皆來 (離) 乎吾罔 (網). 湯 (54) 曰: 不可, 我教子祝之曰: 古者蛛蝥作罔 (網), 今之 [人] (原缺)緣序. 左者使左, 右者使右, 尙 (上) 者使尙 (上), 下者使下, □□□□□□□□. 諸侯聞之曰: 湯之德及禽獸魚鱉矣, 故共 (供) 皮敝 (幣) 以進者卅又 (有) (55) 餘國. 《易》卦其義曰: 顯比, 王用參毆, 失前禽, 邑 [人] (原缺) 不戒, 吉, 此之胃 (謂) 也. ·西人擧兵侵魏野而□□□□□□□□□□而逐出見諸大夫, 過段干木之閭而式, 其僕李義曰: 義聞之, 諸侯 (56) 先財而後財; 今吾君先身而後財, 何也? 文侯曰: 段干木富乎德, 我富於財; 段干木富 [於義], [我富於地. 財不如德, 地不如義. 德而不吾] 爲者也, 義而不吾取者也, 彼擇取而不我與者也, 我求而弗 (57) 得者也, 若何我過而弗式也? 西人聞之曰: 我將伐无道也. 今也文侯尊賢□□□□□兵□□□□□□□□□何何而要之, 局而窘 (?) 之, 獄獄吾君敬女, 而西人告不足. 《易》卦其義 (58) 曰: 又 (有) 覆惠心, 勿問, 元吉, 又 (有) 復惠我德也. ·

then it will be near to harm. Therefore, (53) it says: 'Straight, square, and great; not repeated; nothing not beneficial.'"

When Tang went out on procession, to the northeast there was a fire; he said: "What fire is that?" A supervisor responded, saying: "A fisherman's." Tang consequently .. .. Zi Zhu, [saying: "In antiquity, the spider] made a net, and the men of today follow in line. Whether to the left or to the right, above or below, all those who run along or through the ground are caught in my web." Tang (54) said: "That is not acceptable. I taught Zi Zhu, saying: 'In antiquity, the spider made a net, and the [men] of today follow in line. For those to the left he caused it to be to the left; for those to the right he caused it to be to the right; for those above he caused it to be above, and for those below he caused it to be below, ...'" The many lords heard this and said: "Tang's virtue reached even the animals and fishes," and therefore there were more than forty states that sent in pelts and cloth to submit to him (55). When the *Changes* diagrams its meaning, saying, 'Lustrously ally; the king herewith thrice drives the hunt, losing the front catch; the city men are not warned; auspicious,'[11] this is what it means.

The western men (i.e., Qin) raised troops to invade the wilds of Wei and .. .. and consequently (Lord Wen of Wei) went out and presented himself to the great officers, passing Duangan Mu's village he saluted. His servant Li Yi said: "I have heard that the many lords (56) put resources first and their person[12] last; now how is it that my lord puts his person first and resources last?" Lord Wen said: "Duangan Mu is rich in virtue, while I am rich in resources. Duangan Mu is rich [in propriety, while I am rich in land. Resources are not as good as virtue, and land is not as good as propriety. If there is virtue and I do not] act for it, or if there is propriety and I do not take it, while they snatch it and do not give it to me or I seek it and do not (57) get it, then how could I go past (his village) and not salute him?" The western men heard it and said: "We are about to attack but without the Way. Now Lord Wen honors the worthy .. .. weapons .. .."
"What could he want with it, bowing and enfeoffing him, imprisoning my lord and respecting you, and yet the western men report dissatisfaction. The *Changes* diagrams its meaning (58), saying: 'There is a return with a kind heart; do not question it; prime auspiciousness; there is a return that treats kindly my virtue.'"[13]

吳王夫跋 (差) 攻當夏, 大子辰歸冰八管, 君問左右. 冰□□□□
□□□□□□□□, 注冰江中上流, 與士飲, 其下流江水未加凊
而士人大說 (悅), (59) 斯壘爲三逐而出毁 (擊) 荆人, 大敗之, 襲其
郢, 居其君室, 徙其祭器. 察之, 則從八管之冰始也. [易卦其義曰:
鳴溓, 利用] 行師征 (征) 國. ·越王句賤 (踐) 即已克吳, 環周而
欲均荆方城 (60) 之外. 荆王聞之, 恐而欲予之. 左史倚相曰: 天下
吳爲強, 以戉 (越) 戔 (踐) 吳, 其銳者必盡, 其餘不足□也. 是知
晉之不能以踐尊□, 齊之不能隃 (踰) 驕 (鄒) 魯而與我爭於吳也,
是恐而來觀 (61) 我也. 君曰: 若何則可? 左史倚相曰: 請爲長轂五
百乘, 以往分於吳地. 君曰: 若 (諾). 逐爲長轂五 [百] 乘, 以往分
[於吳地], 其先君作□而不服者, 請爲君服之. 曰且, 越王曰: 天下
吳爲強, 吾 (62) 旣戔 (踐) 吳, 其餘不足以辱大國. 士人請辭, 又
曰: 人力所不至, 周 (舟) 車所不達, 請爲君服之. 王胃 (謂) 大夫
重□□□不退兵□□□□□不可. 天下吳爲強, 以我戔 (踐) 吳,
吾銳者旣盡, 其餘不足用 (63) 也, 而吳衆又未可起也, 請與之分
於吳地. 逐爲之封於南巢至於北蘄, 南北七百里, 命之曰倚 [相
之] 封. 《易》卦 [其義曰: 暌] 孤, 見豕負途, 載鬼一車, 先張之
柧, 後說之壺, 此之胃 (謂) 也. (64) ·

268

When King Fuchai of Wu (r. 495–477 B.C.) attacked in the summer, his eldest son Chen returned with ice from Baguan. The lord asked those around him, ice .. .., putting ice into the headwaters of the river and giving it to the troops to drink, the waters downstream will not be any clearer and yet the troops are very happy. (59) Si Lei formed three divisions and went out and hit the men of Jing (i.e., Chu), greatly defeating them; assaulting their capital Ying, he resided in their lord's chambers and made off with their sacrificial vessels. If you investigate it, it all began with the ice of Baguan. [The *Changes* diagrams its meaning, saying: "Calling modesty; beneficial herewith] to move troops to campaign against the state."[14]

King Gou Jian of Yue (r. 496–465 B.C.), having already conquered Wu, surrounded Zhou and wanted everything outside of the Jing (i.e., Chu) cities (60). The king of Chu heard it, and fearful, wanted to give it to him. The Scribe of the Left Yi Xiang said: "Under heaven Wu was strong, but Yue stepped on Wu, the sharp among them necessarily being extinguished and what is left of them is not sufficient ... From this one knew that Jin would not be able to step up to the honorable .., and Qi would not be able to get over Zou and Lu to contend with us with respect to Wu; these would fear and come to observe (61) us." The lord said: "What then can be done?" Scribe of the Left Yi Xiang said: "I would request five hundred heavy chariots to go and divide [the land of Wu]; that their past lord made .. and did not submit, I would ask that you cause them to submit." The next morning the king of Yue said: "Under heaven Wu was strong, and I (62) have already stepped on Wu; what is left of them is not sufficient to disgrace our great state." The sire requested to decline, saying: "Their men and power will not reach us, and their boats and chariots will not penetrate us; I request that you cause their lord to submit." The king said to the great officer Zhong ".. .. .. not to withdraw troops .. .. is not acceptable. Under heaven Wu was strong; for us to step on Wu, our sharp troops are already extinguished, and what is left of them is not sufficient to be used (63). And yet Wu's multitudes cannot yet be raised; I request that we divide the land of Wu with them." Consequently he caused him to be enfeoffed from South Chao as far as North Zhan, seven hundred li from north to south, calling it Yi Xiang's fief. When the *Changes* diagrams [its meaning saying: "Perverse] solitude: seeing a pig with mud on its back and one cart carrying ghosts; the first drawn bow is later released into the jar," it is this meaning.[15] (64)

荆莊王欲伐陳, 使沈尹樹往觀之. 沈尹樹反 (返), 至令曰: 其城郭脩, 其倉實, 其士好學, 其婦人組疾, 君 [曰]: 如是則陳不可伐也. 城郭脩, 則其守固也; 倉廩實, 則人食足也; 其士好學, 必死上也; (65) 其婦組 [疾], 其財足也, 如是陳不可伐也. 沈尹樹曰: 彼若若君之言則可也, 彼與君之言之異. 城郭脩, [則] 人力渴 (竭) 矣; 倉廩實, [則□] 之人也; 其士好學, 則又 (有) 外志也; 其婦組疾, 則士祿不足食也, (66) 故曰陳可伐也. 遂舉兵伐陳, 克之. 《易》卦其義曰: 入於左腹, 稚 (穫) 明夷之心, 于出門廷. ·趙閒 (簡) 子欲伐衛, 使史黑 [往睹之, 期以] 卅日, 六十日焉反 (返). 閒 (簡) 子大怒, 以爲又有) 外志也. 史黑曰: 吾君殆乎大過矣. 衛使 (67) 據 (蘧) 柏 (伯) 王〈玉〉相, 子路爲浦 (輔), 孔子客焉, 史子突焉, 子贛出入於朝而莫之留也. 此五人也, 一, 治天下者也, 而皆在衛□□□□□□□又 (有) 是心者, 倪 (況) □□而伐之乎? 《易》卦其義曰: 觀國之光, 利用 (68) 賓於王. 《易》曰: 童童往來, 仁不達也; 不克征 (征), 義不達也; 其行塞, 道不達也; 不明晦, 明不達 [也]. □□□□□□□□□□□□□善 (?), 義達矣; 自邑告命, 道達矣; 觀國之光, 明達矣. 《繆和》(69)

King Zhuang of Jing (i.e., Chu) wanted to attack Chen, and sent Shen Yinshu to go and observe it. Shen Yinshu returned and went to report, saying: "Their city walls are well maintained, their granaries are full, their sires are fond of studying, and their wives weave with alacrity." The lord [said]: "If it is like this, then Chen cannot be attacked. If the city walls are well maintained, then their defense will be stout; if the granaries are full, then the people will have enough to eat; if the sires are fond of studying, they will certainly respect their superiors; (65) and if the wives weave with [alacrity], their resources will be sufficient. Like this, Chen cannot be attacked." Shen Yinshu said: "Though it is acceptable to put it the way the lord has, there is also a different analysis from yours. [If] the city walls are well maintained, the people's strength will be sapped; [if] the granaries are full, .. men; if the sires are fond of studying, they will have external ambitions; and if the wives weave with alacrity, the sires will be clothed but without enough to eat. (66) Therefore I say that Chen can be attacked." Thereupon they raised arms and attacked Chen, conquering them. The *Changes* diagrams its meaning, saying: "Entering into the left belly, bagging the calling pheasant's heart; going out of the gate and courtyard."[16]

Zhao Jianzi wanted to attack Wei, and sent Scribe Hei [to go and scout it, giving him] thirty days. He returned in sixty days. Jianzi was greatly angered, assuming that he had some external ambitions. Scribe Hei said: "My lord is about to make a great mistake. Wei had (67) Jubo Yu serving as minister and Zi Lu serving as tutor, while Confucius was a retainer there, Scribe Zi Tu was there, and Zi Gong came and went at court, and yet none of them was kept on. Of these five men, any one of them could govern the world, and all of them are at Wei .. .. had this heart, how would .. ... and attack them?" The *Changes* diagrams its meaning, saying: "Looking up at the state's radiance; beneficial herewith (68) to be entertained in audience by the king."[17] When the *Changes* says: "So undecided going and coming,"[18] it means that humaneness is not reached; "cannot campaign"[19] means that propriety is not reached; "his motion is blocked"[20] means that the way is not reached; "not bright or dark"[21] means that brightness is not reached. .. .. well, propriety is reached indeed; "from the city announce the mandate"[22] means that the way is reached indeed; "looking up at the state's radiance"[23] means brightness is reached indeed. *Mu He* (69)

昭力問曰:《易》又 (有) 卿大夫之義乎? 子曰: 師之左次, 與闌 輿之衞, 與獷豕之牙, 參者, 大夫之所以治其國而安其□□. 昭力 曰: 可得聞乎? 子曰: 昔之善爲大夫者, 必敬其百姓之順德, 忠信 以先之, 脩其兵甲 (1) 而衞之, 長賢而勸之, 不乘脎 (勝) 名以敎 其人, 不羞卑隃以安社禝 (稷), 其將督諎 (?) 也, 吐 (?) 言, 以爲人 次; 其將報□, □□□一, 以爲人次; 其將取利, 必先其義, 以爲人 次. 《易》曰: 師左次, 无咎. 師也者, 人之聚也; 次 (2) 也者, 君之 立 (位) 也. 見事而能左 (佐) 其主, 何咎之又 (有)? 問闌輿之義. 子 曰: 上正 (政) 衞國以德, 次正 (政)衞國以力, 下正 (政) 衞 [國] 以 兵. 衞國以德者, 必和其君臣之節, 不 [以] (原缺) 耳之所聞, 敗目 之所見, 故權臣不作. 同父子之 (3) 欲, 以固其親, 賞百姓之勸,

Zhao Li asked, saying: "Does the *Changes* have meaning for ministers and great officers?" The master said: "The three lines: 'The troops camp on the left,'[24] 'a barrier-cart's defense,'[25] and 'the crying pig's teeth,'[26] are what the great officer uses to govern his state and pacify his …. ." Zhao Li asked: "May I hear of it?" The master said: "In former times those who were good at being great officers necessarily respected the compliant virtue of their hundred families, loyally putting them first, training their armies (1) and defending them, raising worthy ones and encouraging them, and neither taking advantage of fame for victory to teach the people nor being shamed by rusticity to pacify the ancestral altars. In making their overseer's reports, they put them in coarse words, considering themselves after others; in making repayments .., ... one, considering themselves after others; and in accepting benefits, they necessarily put propriety first, considering themselves after others. The *Changes* says: 'The troops camp on the left; there is no trouble.' The 'troops' are the multitude of men; 'to camp' (2) is the position of the lord. Seeing affairs and being able to (stand to the left of:) assist his ruler, what trouble could there be?" (Zhao Li) asked the meaning of "barrier cart." The master said: "The highest government defends the state with virtue; the next government defends the state with strength, and the lowest government defends the state with arms. Defending the state with virtue necessarily harmonizes the measures of the lord and ministers, not letting what the ears hear overcome what the eyes see; therefore, strong ministers do not act. It unites the desires of fathers and sons (3) in order to firm their relations, awards encouragement to the hundred families in

以禁諱 (違) 教, 察人所疾, 不作苛心, 是故大國屬力焉, 而小國歸德焉. 城郭弗脩, 五兵弗□, 而天下皆服焉. 《易》曰: 闌輿之衛, 利又 (有) 攸往. 若輿且可以闌然衛之, 倪 (況) 以 (4) 德乎? 可 (何) 不吉之又 (有)? 又問獑豕之牙何胃 (謂) 也? 子曰: 古之伎强者也, 伎强以侍 (待) 難也. 上正 (政) 衛兵而弗用, 次正 (政) 用兵而弗先也, 下正 (政) 銳兵而後威. 幾兵而弗用者, 調愛其百生 (姓) 而敬其士臣, 强爭其時而讓其 (5) 成利. 文人爲令, 武夫用國. 脩兵不解 (懈), 卒伍必固; 權謀不讓, 怨弗先昌. 是故其士驕而不頃 (?), 其人調而不野, 大國禮之, 小國事之, 危國獻焉, 力國助焉, 遠國依焉, 近國固焉. 上正 (政) 陲 (垂) 衣常 (裳) 以來 (6) 遠人, 次正 (政) 橐弓矢以伏天下. 《易》曰: 獑豕之牙, 吉. 其豕之牙, 成而不用者也. 又 (有) 槩 (笑) 而後見, 言國脩兵不單 (戰) 而威之胃 (謂) 也. 此大夫之用也, 卿大夫之事也. ·昭力問曰: 《易》又 (有) 國君之義乎? 子曰: 師之王參賜命, (7) 與比之王參毆, 與奈 (泰) 之自邑告命者, 三者國君之義也. 昭力曰: 可得聞乎? 子 [曰]: 昔之君國者, 君親賜其大夫, 親賜其百官, 此之胃 (謂) 參祒.

274

order to prohibit deviant teachings, and inspects men's illnesses and does not belabor their hearts. This is why the great state encompasses power within it and the little state brings virtue back to it. Even if a city's walls are not well maintained and the five arms are not .. , still all under heaven will submit to it. The *Changes* says: 'A barrier-cart's defense; beneficial to have someplace to go.' If even a cart can be used as a barrier to defend it, how much more so using (4) virtue! How could there be anything not auspicious about it?" (Zhao Li) also asked about the meaning of "the crying pig's teeth." The master said: "In antiquity those who were strong of arm were strong of arm in preparation for difficulties. The highest government has defensive arms but does not use them, the next government uses arms but never first, while the lowest government sharpens its arms and only thereafter is imposing. Being armed and yet not using them harmonizes the hundred families and shows respect to the sires and ministers while contending for time and yielding its (5) completion of benefit. The man of culture makes the commands and the military man uses the state. Training arms assiduously, the units will certainly be sturdy; conspiring and not yielding, resentment will not first well up. This is why their sires will be proud but not askew, their people harmonious and not rustic. The great state treats them with ritual, while the little state causes them to serve. Endangered states will present them with tribute and strong states will help them; distant states will rely on them and near states will be sturdy with them. The highest government lets its robes hang down in order to cause (6) the distant people to come, while the next government sheathes its bows and arrows in order to cause all under heaven to bow down. The *Changes* says: 'The crying pig's teeth; auspicious.' The pig's teeth are complete and yet it doesn't use them. To be seen only when smiling is said of the state's being imposing by maintaining its arms but not fighting. This is the use of the great officer, the service of the minister and great officer."

Zhao Li asked, saying: "Does the *Changes* have meaning for the lord of a state?" The master said: "The three lines: 'The king thrice awards the command' of *Shi*, 'The Troops,'[27] (7) and 'the king thrice drives' of *Bi*, 'Alliance,'[28] and 'from the city announce the mandate' of *Tai*, 'Greatness,'[29] have meaning for the lord of a state." Zhao Li said: "May I hear of it?" The master [said]: "In former times the lord of a state personally made awards to his great officers and personally made awards to the hundred officials; this is called the three signals. In cases

君之自大而亡國者, 其臣屬以最 (聚) 謀, 君臣不相知, (8) 則遠人無勸矣, 亂之所生於忘者也. 是故君以愛人爲德, 則大夫共 (恭) 悳 (德), 將軍禁單 (戰); 君以武爲德, 則大夫薄人矣, □□□柢 (?); 君以資財爲德, 則大夫賤人, 而將軍走利, 是故失國之罪必在君之 (9) 不知大夫也. 《易》曰: 王參賜命, 无咎. 爲人君而能亟賜其命, 无〈夫〉國何失之又 (有)? 又問比之三毆何胃 (謂) 也? 子曰: □□□□□□人以裹 (?), 教之以義, 付之以刑, 殺當罪而人服. 君乃服小節以先人曰義, (10) 爲上且猶又 (有) 不能, 人爲下, 何无過之又 (有)? 夫失之前, 將戒諸後, 此之胃 (謂) 教而戒之. 《易》 [曰比] 之王參毆, 失前禽, 邑人不戒, 吉. 若爲人君毆省其人, 孫 (遜) 戒在前, 何不吉之又 (有)? 又問曰: 柰 (泰) 以 (衍一字, 已塗去) 之自邑告命 (11) 何胃 (謂) 也? 子曰: 昔之賢君也, 明以察乎人之欲亞 (惡), 詩書以成其慮, 外內親賢以爲紀岡 (綱), 夫人弗告, 則弗識, 弗將不達, 弗遂不成. 《易》曰柰 (泰) 之自邑告命, 吉, 自君告人之胃 (謂) 也. ・昭力問先 (12) 生曰: 君卿大夫之事旣已聞之矣, 參 (?) 或又 (有) 乎? 子曰: 士數 (疑衍一字) 言數百, 猶又 (有) 所廣用之,

276

where the lord is self-important and (loses:) forgets the state and his ministers dangerously join together to plot, if the lord and ministers do not know each other (8) then distant people will not be encouraged; this is how disorder is generated from forgetfulness. This is why if the lord takes loving the people to be virtue then the great officers will uphold virtue and the generals will prohibit warfare. If the lord takes martial valor to be virtue, then the great officers will oppress the people ... ... If the lord takes resources to be virtue, then the great officers will devalue the people and the generals will rush to benefit. This is why the guilt of losing a state must reside with the lord's (9) not knowing the great officers. The *Changes* says: 'The king thrice awards the command; there is no trouble.' If one serves as the lord of men and is able urgently to award his commands, what loss will the state have?" (Zhao Li) also asked about the meaning of *Bi*'s "thrice drives." The master said: ".. .. .. people with ordinances, teaches them with propriety, treats them with punishments, and when killing matches the guilt then the people will obey. The lord's bringing the small measures under control in order to put the people first is called propriety (10), but being above and yet still not being able to consider the people below, how could there be any absence of trouble? Losses up front should warn those behind; this is called teaching and warning them. The *Changes*' .. .. 'the king thrice drives, losing the front catch; the city men are not warned; auspicious.' If the lord of men drives and inspects his people, humbly warning them up front, how could there be anything not auspicious?" (Zhao Li) also asked, saying: "What does *Tai*'s 'from the city announce the mandate' (11) mean?" The master said: "The worthy lords of former times were enlightened in order to investigate into the wishes and dislikes of the people and (had) the *Poetry* and *Documents* in order to complete their considerations. Without and within they drew near to the worthy in order to serve as their network. As for the people, if you do not report to them, then they will not know it; if you do not lead them, they will not penetrate, and if you do not follow them, they will not complete it. When the *Changes*' *Tai* says 'from the city announce the mandate; auspicious,' it is said of the lord reporting to the people."

Zhao Li asked his teacher (12), saying: "Having already heard of the affairs of the lord and ministers and great officers, is there perhaps a third?" The master said: "If even a sire speaks several hundred times, there will be much that is broadly useful; how much more so with the

兄 (況) 於《易》乎? 比卦六十又□, 冬 (終) 六合之內, 四勿之卦, 何不又 (有) 焉? □之潛斧, 啇夫之義也; 無孟之卦, 邑途之義也; (13) 不耕而穫 (穫), 戎夫之義也; 良月幾望, 處女之義也.《昭力》六千 (14)

Changes! Bi, 'Alliance,' hexagram's sixty and .. , bringing to an end all within the six enclosures, and the hexagram of the four prohibitions; what do they not have in them? ..'s submerged ax has meaning for a merchant[30]; *Wumeng,* 'Pestilence,' hexagram has meaning for city urchins; (13) not planting and yet harvesting has meaning for belligerent fellows[31]; and the fine moon almost being full has meaning for virgin girls."[32]
Zhao Li 6,000 (14)

NOTES

THE ORIGINS AND EARLY DEVELOPMENT
OF THE *YIJING*

1. For the best introduction to Shang oracle-bone inscriptions, see David N. Keightley, *Sources of Shang History: The Oracle-Bone Inscriptions of Bronze Age China* (Berkeley: University of California Press, 1978); for the topics divined, see pp. 33–35.

2. *Jiaguwen heji* 甲骨文合集, ed. Hu Houxuan 胡厚宣, 13 vols. (Beijing: Zhonghua shuju, 1982), #6834a.

3. Ibid., #6948a.

4. Ibid., #14001a.

5. Ibid., #35400.

6. H11:1; Xu Xitai 徐錫台, *Zhouyuan jiaguwen zongshu* 周原甲骨文綜述 (Xi'an: San Qin chubanshe, 1987), 11. For what is still the only extensive discussion of these Zhou oracle-bone inscriptions in a Western language, see Edward L. Shaughnessy, "Zhouyuan Oracle-Bone Inscriptions: Entering the Research Stage?" *Early China* 11–12 (1985–87), 146–163, and the following Forum pieces, pp. 164–94.

7. H31:1; Xu Xitai, *Zhouyuan jiaguwen zongshu*, 119. The two-stage nature of the inscriptions on this turtle shell was pointed out in Li Xueqin 李學勤, *Zhouyi jing zhuan suyuan* 周易經傳溯源 (Changchun: Changchun chubanshe, 1992), 129.

8. In my 1983 doctoral dissertation, "The Composition of the *Zhouyi*," I surmised, primarily on the basis of linguistic evidence contained within the hexagram and line statements of the *Yijing* itself, that divination with the *Yijing* originally entailed two stages, the first resulting in a particular hexagram, and the second in one of that hexagram's six lines (pp. 124–33); while this remains hypothetical with respect to *Yijing*

281

divination itself, that it has now been corroborated for Zhou dynasty divination in general perhaps offers further reason to suspect that it was indeed the case with *Yijing* divination as well.

9. Milfoil is a plant with numerous long stalks, which were used as counting rods, producing a result that could be expressed as a numeral. For a discussion of sets of numerals suggesting this sort of divination, see Zhang Zhenglang 張政烺, "Shishi Zhouchu qingtongqi mingwen zhong de Yi gua" 試釋周初青銅器銘文中的易卦, *Kaogu xuebao* 考古學報 1980.4, 404–15; for an English translation, see "An Interpretation of the Divinatory Inscriptions on Early Zhou Bronzes," trans. H. Huber, R. Yates, *et al.*, *Early China* 6 (1980–81), 80–96.

10. *Baoshan Chu jian* 包山楚簡, ed. Hubei sheng Jingsha tielu kaogudui (Beijing: Wenwu chubanshe, 1991), 34, Strips 216–17. For an introduction in English to these divination records, see Li Ling, "Formulaic Structure of Chu Divinatory Bamboo Slips," *Early China* 15 (1990), 71–86.

11. *Baoshan Chu jian*, 35–36, Strips 232–33.

12. *Chunqiu Zuozhuan zhengyi* 春秋左傳正義 (Shisanjing zhushu ed.), vol. 2, 2051 (44.349); for another English translation and the full context, see James Legge, *The Chinese Classics*, Vol. 5: *The Ch'un Ts'ew with the Tso Chuen* (1872; Rpt. Hong Kong: Hong Kong University Press, 1960), 619.

13. For an extensive discussion of this passage, and its implications for understanding how divination using the *Yijing* was performed, see Shaughnessy, "The Composition of the *Zhouyi*," 74–97.

14. The following discussion is adapted, with little change, from my article "The Origins of an *Yijing* Line Statement," *Early China* 20 (1995), 223–40.

15. *Chunqiu Zuo zhuan zhengyi*, vol. 2, 1648 (31.246); see also, Legge, *The Ch'un Ts'ew with the Tso Chuen*, 443, 447.

16. In the Mawangdui manuscript, *Jian*, "Advancing," is hexagram 60, while in the received text it is hexagram 53. Here I quote it in the form in which it is found in the received text, which varies from the manuscript text only in the final injunction, which there reads "beneficial to have that which robs" (*li suo kou* 利所寇).

17. Edward L. Shaughnessy, "Marriage, Divorce, and Revolution: Reading between the Lines of the *Book of Changes*," *The Journal of Asian Studies* 51.3 (August 1992), 594.

18. The translation given here is the text of the Mawangdui manuscript, in which *Jian*, "Advancing," is hexagram 60 (in the received

text it is hexagram 53). For the emendation of *e* 阿, "hill," for *lu* 陸, "land" in the final or Elevated Six line, see Shaughnessy, "The Composition of the *Zhouyi*," 192–193.

19. For the clearest examples of bottom-to-top low-to-high organization of images, see *Qin* 欽, "Feelings," hexagram 44 (in the received text, it is called *Xian* 咸 and is hexagram 31) and *Gen,* "Stilling," hexagram 9 (in the received text hexagram 52). For discussion of this feature, see Richard A. Kunst, "The Original 'Yijing': A Text, Phonetic Transcription, Translation, and Indexes, with Sample Glosses" (Ph.D. diss.: University of California, Berkeley, 1985), 38–43.

20. In the Mawangdui manuscript, *Ding,* "The Cauldron," is hexagram 56 (it is hexagram 50 in the received text).

THE MAWANGDUI *YIJING* MANUSCRIPT

1. For the *Laozi,* see Robert G. Henricks, *Lao-tzu Te-Tao Ching: A New Translation Based on the Recently Discovered Ma-wang-tui Texts* (New York: Ballantine Books, 1989). For comprehensive bibliographies of Mawangdui studies, see Zuo Songchao 左松超, "Mawangdui Han mu yanjiu ziliao mulu suoyin" 馬王堆漢墓研究資料目錄索引, *Zhongguo shumu jikan* 中國書目季刊 23 (1989), 95–115; Li Meili 李梅鹿, *Mawangdui Han mu yanjiu mulu* 馬王堆漢墓研究目錄 (Changsha: Hunan sheng bowuguan, 1992).

2. A transcription of the *Zhouyi* 周易 portion of the manuscript, i.e., the hexagram and line statements of the basic text, was published in 1984 (Mawangdui Han mu boshu zhengli xiaozu, "Mawangdui boshu 'Liushisi gua' shiwen" 馬王堆帛書六十四卦釋文, *Wenwu* 文物, 1984.3, 1–8), though complete photographs of this portion of the text have only recently been published, without transcription, in *Mawangdui Han mu wenwu* 馬王堆漢墓文物 (Added English title: The Cultural Relics Unearthed from the Han Tombs at Mawangdui), ed. Fu Juyou 傅舉有 and Chen Songchang 陳松長 (Changsha: Hunan chubanshe, 1992), 106–117. Other transcriptions of the *Zhouyi* are Zhang Liwen 張立文, *Zhouyi boshu jin zhu jin yi* 周易帛書今注今譯, 2 vols. (Taipei: Xuesheng shuju, 1991); Han Zhongmin 韓仲民, *Bo Yi shuolüe* 帛易說略 (Beijing: Beijing Shifan daxue chubanshe, 1992), 115–82; and Deng Qiubo 鄧球柏, *Baihua boshu Zhouyi* 白話帛書周易 (Changsha: Yuelu shushe, 1995), 1–172. Translations into modern Chinese are given in both Zhang Liwen and Deng Qiubo's books.

Mawangdui Han mu wenwu, which is more in the nature of a "coffee-table book" than a scholarly publication, also includes complete photographs of the portion of the manuscript bearing the *Xici* 繫辭 or *Appended Statements* commentary (pp. 118–26), in this case adding a preliminary transcription. Two superior transcriptions of the *Appended Statements* were published in *Daojia wenhua yanjiu* 道家文化研究 3 (1993): Zhang Zhenglang 張政烺, "Mawangdui boshu Zhouyi Xici jiaodu" 馬王堆帛書周易繫辭校讀, 27–35, and Chen Songchang 陳松長, "Boshu Xici shiwen" 帛書繫辭釋文, 416–23. A third, more convenient and more "literal" transcription is that of Huang Peirong 黃沛榮: "Mawangdui boshu Xici jiaodu" 馬王堆帛書繫辭校讀, *Zhouyi yanjiu* 周易研究 1992.4, 1–9. A transcription conveniently juxtaposed with the text of the received *Appended Statements* is also given in Han Zhongmin, *Bo Yi shuolüe*, 183–225; and a transcription and translation into modern Chinese is given in Deng Qiubo, *Baihua boshu Zhouyi*, 173–232.

Daojia wenhua yanjiu 3 also contains preliminary transcriptions, by Chen Songchang and Liao Mingchun 繆名春, of the commentaries *Ersanzi wen* 二三子問 or *The Several Disciples Asked*, *Yi zhi yi* 易之義 or *The Properties of the Changes*, and *Yao* 要 or *Essentials*; "Boshu Ersanzi wen Yi zhi yi Yao shiwen" 帛書二三子問易之義要釋文, pp. 424–35. Liao Mingchun has also provided excellent synopses of these commentaries; "Boshu Ersanzi wen jianshuo" 帛書二三子問簡說, pp. 190–95; "Boshu Yi zhi yi jianshuo" 帛書易之義簡說, pp. 196–201; and "Boshu Yao jianshuo" 帛書要簡說, pp. 202–6. A transcription of *Yao* that occasionally differs significantly from that of Chen Songchang and Liao Mingchun is Ikeda Tomohisa 池田知久, "Maōtei Kan bo hakusho Shūeki Yō hen no kenkyū" 馬王堆漢墓帛書周易要篇の研究, *Tōyō bunka kenkyūjo kiyō* 東洋文化研究所紀要 123 (1994), 111–207. Translations of these commentaries into modern Chinese are given in Deng Qiubo, *Baihua boshu Zhouyi*, 233–346.

The first transcription of the dual commentaries *Mu He* 繆和 and *Zhao Li* 昭力 to appear is that of Chen Songchang, "Mawangdui Boshu Mu He Zhao Li shiwen" 馬王堆帛書繆和昭力釋文, *Daojia wenhua yanjiu* 6 (1995), 367–80. Prior to this there had been only a synopsis by Liao Mingchun ("Boshu Mu He Zhao Li jianshuo" 帛書繆和昭力簡說, *Daojia wenhua yanjiu* 3 (1993), 207–15). Photographs of these other commentaries have not yet been published.

3. References to many of these will be found in the bibliography.

4. This chapter is a condensed version of my article "A First Read-

ing of the Mawangdui *Yijing* Manuscript," *Early China* 19 (1994), 47–73. That article provides more details and argumentation than it has been possible to include here.

5. *Hanshu* 漢書 (Zhonghua shuju ed.), 30.1704.

6. Edward L. Shaughnessy, "The Key and the Flow: Drying Out the Wet Woman of the *Yijing's Xici Zhuan*," paper presented to the annual meeting of the Association for Asian Studies, 11 April 1996, Honolulu, Hawaii.

7. *Jinshu* 晉書 (Zhonghua shuju ed.), 51.1432.

8. For a study arguing that the hexagram sequence of the Mawangdui manuscript is related to the Eight Palace (*ba gong* 八宮) sequence of Jing Fang 京房 (d. 37 B.C.), and thus that it is part of a long tradition, see Liu Dajun 劉大鈞, "Bo Yi chutan" 帛易初談, *Wenshizhe* 文史哲 1985.4, 53–60, translated as "A Preliminary Investigation of the Silk Manuscript *Yijing*," *Zhouyi Network* 1 (Jan. 1986), 13–26.

9. See, for instance, Han Zhongmin, *Bo Yi shuolüe*, 25.

10. This division of the text into two sections was first suggested in Yu Haoliang 于豪亮, "Boshu Zhouyi" 帛書周易, *Wenwu* 文物 1984.3, 22; Li Xueqin 李學勤, "Boshu Zhouyi de jidian yanjiu" 帛書周易的幾點研究, *Wenwu* 文物 1984.1, 46, maintains it.

11. See Yu Haoliang, "Boshu Zhouyi," 23; see, too, the remarks made by Zhang Zhenglang 張政烺 in "Zuotan Changsha Mawangdui Han mu boshu" 座談長沙馬王堆漢墓帛書, *Wenwu* 1974.9, 45–57.

12. In a postscript to his synopsis of the *Properties of the* Changes commentary, Liao Mingchun claims to have discovered a fragment bearing three barely legible characters that probably belongs in the final column of the text. He says that the second and third of these characters appear to be numerals, presumably indicating the number of characters in the text. However, he does not say what numerals they appear to be; Liao Mingchun, "Boshu Yi zhi yi jianshuo," 201.

13. Huang Peirong, "Mawangdui boshu Xici zhuan jiaodu," 3.

14. The first statement seems to have been Chen Guying 陳鼓應, "Yi zhuan Xici suoshou Laozi sixiang yingxiang—jianlun Yi zhuan nai Daojia xitong zhi zuo" 易傳繫辭所受老子思想影響————兼論易傳乃道家系統之作, *Zhexue yanjiu* 哲學研究 1989.1, 34–42, 52. This and other studies of Chen's were then included in his monograph *Lao Zhuang xinlun* 老莊新論 (Hong Kong: Zhonghua shuju, 1991). *Researches on Daoist Culture* (*Daojia wenhua yanjiu* 道家文化研究) began publication in June of 1992; seven volumes have appeared to date.

15. Wang Baoxuan 王葆玹, "Boshu Xici yu Zhanguo Qin Han Daojia Yi xue" 帛書繫辭與戰國秦漢道家易學, *Daojia wenhua yanjiu* 3, 73–88.

16. Liao Mingchun, "Lun boshu Xici yu jinben Xici de guanxi" 論帛書繫辭與今本繫辭的關係, *Daojia wenhua yanjiu* 3, 133–43.

17. For a point-by-point review of this debate, see Shaughnessy, "A First Reading of the Mawangdui *Yijing* Manuscript," 58–66. The nature of Daoism has also been reconsidered in a pair of Western-language studies published in the most recent issue of the journal *Early China:* Harold D. Roth, "Redaction Criticism and the Early History of Taoism," *Early China* 19 (1994), 1–46; Robin D. S. Yates, "The Yin-Yang Texts from Yinqueshan: An Introduction and Partial Reconstruction, with Notes on their Significance in Relation to Huang-Lao Daoism," *Early China* 19, 75–144.

18. For this suggestion, see Liao Mingchun, "Boshu Yi zhi yi jian-shuo," 198.

19. In addition to his transcription noted above (n. 2), Ikeda Tomohisa has also published a lengthy study of the thought of *Essentials;* "Maōtei Kan bo hakusho Shūeki Yō hen no shisō" 馬王堆漢墓帛書周易要篇の 思想, *Tōyō bunka kenkyūjo kiyō* 126 (1995), 1–105. Other studies of this commentary include Wang Bo 王博, "Yao pian lüelun" 要篇略論, *Daojia wenhua yanjiu* 6 (1995), 328–28; Liu Zhaozhuan 劉昭瑞, "Lun *Yi* zhi ming Yi—Jiantan boshu Yao pian" 論易之名易——兼談帛書要篇, *Daojia wenhua yanjiu* 6, 329–35; Xing Wen 邢文, "*Heguanzi* yu boshu Yao" 鶡冠子與帛書要, *Daojia wenhua yanjiu* 6, 336–49.

PRINCIPLES OF TRANSLATION

1. For the best introduction to dealing with Chinese manuscripts, see William G. Boltz, "Manuscripts with Transmitted Counterparts," in *New Sources of Early Chinese History: An Introduction to Reading Inscriptions and Manuscripts*, ed. Edward L. Shaughnessy (Berkeley: Society for the Study of Early China, 1996), in press.

2. After the Mawangdui manuscript, the next earliest text of the *Yijing* is that of the "Xiping Stone Classics," engraved between the years A.D. 175 and 183 during the reign of Emperor Ling of Han (r. 168–89). About twenty percent of this text has been recovered; see Ma Heng 馬亨, *Han shi jing jicun* 漢石經集存 (Beijing: Kexue chubanshe,

1957); Qu Wanli 屈萬里, *Han shi jing Zhouyi canzi jicheng* 漢石經周易殘字集成 (Nangang: Academia Sinica, 1961).

3. Richard Wilhelm, *The I Ching or Book of Changes*, translated by Cary F. Baynes (Princeton: Princeton University Press, 1967), 187.

4. This point is made by Zhang Liwen 張立文, *Zhouyi boshu jin zhu jin yi* 周易帛書今注今譯 (Taipei: Xuesheng shuju, 1991), 317.

5. Wilhelm, *The I Ching*, 211.

6. Richard John Lynn, *The Classic of Changes: A New Translation of the I Ching as Interpreted by Wang Bi* (New York: Columbia University Press, 1994), 482.

7. In this case, I assume that the *di* 弟 "younger brother" of the manuscript is the protograph of *di* 娣 "younger sister," as given in the received text.

8. See Xu Qinting 徐芹庭, *Zhouyi yiwen kao* 周易異文考 (Taipei: Wuzhou chubanshe, n.d.), 101–2.

9. *Ibid.*

THE *ZHOUYI*

1. *JIAN,* "THE KEY"

1. For *jian* 鍵, "key; linchpin," the received text, in which this is also hexagram 1, reads *qian* 乾, understood generally as "The Heavenly Principle" or "Vigor." In the Nine in the Third line, its only other occurrence in this hexagram, the word is used verbally, perhaps as *jian* 建, "to establish; to initiate."

2. For *xiang* 享, "reception; offering," the received text reads *heng* 亨, "receipt." The two words are closely cognate. For discussion of their nuances, see Kunst, "The Original *Yijing*," 181–89.

3. For *qin* 浸, "submersed," the received text reads *qian* 潛, "submerged."

4. For *ni* 泥, "muddy; ashen," the received text reads *ti* 惕, "wary."

5. For the unknown graph 鯩, which is composed of the "fish" signific and the phonetic *yue* 侖, the received text reads *yue* 躍, "to jump."

6. For *fei* 翡, "red-feathered sparrow," the received text reads *fei* 飛, "flying."

7. For *shang* 尙, "elevated; esteemed," the received text reads *shang* 上, "high, top."

8. For *kang* 抗, "to resist," the received text reads *gang* (or *kang*) 亢, "neck; haughty."

9. For *tong* 迵, "to penetrate; unified," the received text reads *yong* 用, "to use" (i.e., Use of the Nine).

2. *FU*, "THE WIFE"

1. For *fu* 婦, "wife," the received text, in which this is hexagram 12, reads (*fou*:) *pi* 否, "negation, nugatory; obstructed." Since *fu* (*bjegx) and *fou* (*pjegx) were phonetically close enough in the Han to be interchangeable, it has been assumed (by Zhang Liwen, for instance; *Zhouyi boshu jin zhu jin yi*, 59) that *fu* here is a phonetic loan for *fou*. However, comparing the manuscript version of the top line of this hexagram with that of the received text,

> M: 頃婦, 先不後喜

> Momentary wife; at first negative, later happy.

> R: 傾否, 先否後喜

> Inclined negation; first nugatory, later happy,

we find, instead of the two occurrences of *pi* in the received text, two distinct graphs: *fu* 婦 and *bu* 不, "negative." This might suggest that the reading *fu* was distinct, at least in the mind of the manuscript's copyist, from the notion of negation.

2. For *ba* 犮, "to scamper (the manner in which a dog runs)," the received text reads *ba* 拔, "to pluck."

3. For *hui* 胃, "root," the received text reads *hui* 彙, "root," of which the *Jingdian shiwen* 經典釋文 says the archaic form is 胃.

4. Here and in the Six in the Third line, for *fu* 枹, "drumstick," the received text reads *bao* 包, "to wrap."

5. For *you* 憂, "sadness," the received text reads *xiu* 羞, "a prepared offering; shame."

6. For *tao* 檮, "split-log," *luo* 羅, "net," and *chi* 齒, "teeth," the received text reads *chou* 疇, "field division," *li* 離, "to fasten," and *zhi* 祉, "blessing."

7. For *ji* 繫, "to hit," the received text reads *xi* 繫, "to tie," which is recommended by the following prepositional *yu* 于.

8. For *fu* 枹, "drumstick," the received text reads *bao* 苞, "thick-leafed; bushy."

9. For *qing* 頃, "moment, instant," the received text reads *qing* 傾, "aslant, inclined."

10. For *bu* 不, "not, negative," the received text reads *pi* 否, "not, negative, nugatory."

288

3. *YUAN,* "WIELDING"

1. Throughout this hexagram, for *yuan* 掾, "to wield," the received text, in which this is hexagram 33, reads *dun* 遯, "to retreat."

2. For *gong* 共, "to uphold," the received text reads *zhi* 執, "to shackle."

3. For *le* 勒, "bridle; to compel," the received text reads *ge* 革, "leather; to revolt."

4. For *duo* 奪, "to overturn," the received text reads (*yue* 說:) *tuo* 脫, "to peel off."

5. For *wei* 爲, "to do, to serve as," the received text reads *xi* 係, "to tie, to tether."

6. For *pu* 僕, "servant," the received text reads *chen* 臣, "retainer."

7. For *bu* 不, "not, negative," the received text reads *fou* (or *pi*) 否, "not, negative, nugatory."

8. For *xian* 先, "first," the received text reads *wu* 旡, "nothing." The formulaic usage of the phrase "there is nothing not beneficial" (*wu bu li* 旡不利) throughout the text suggests a miscopying here, the two graphs being quite similar in appearance.

4. *LI,* "TREADING"

1. Throughout this hexagram, for *li* 禮, "ritual," the received text, in which this is hexagram 10, reads *lü* 履, "to tread," which context shows sometimes to be the only appropriate reading.

2. Here and in the Six in the Third line, for *zhen* 眞, "real," the received text reads *die* 咥, "to bite."

3. For *cuo* 錯, "counter; mistaken," the received text reads *su* 素, "plain."

4. For *dan* 亶, "sincere; full," the received text reads *dan* 坦, "smooth."

5. For *li* 利, "benefit," the received text reads *lü* 履, "to tread, to walk," which the contrast with the preceding phrase recommends.

6. For *tong* 迵, "to penetrate; unified," the received text reads *wei* 爲, "to do; to serve as; on behalf of."

7. For *shuo* 朔, "to begin; beginning of the month," the received text reads *su* 愬, "panicky."

8. For *shi* 史, "scribe; historian," the received text reads *guai* 夬, understood as *jue* 決, "to resolve; to be resolved." 史 and 夬 being very similar in appearance, this is probably a case of a miscopying on the part of the manuscript's scribe.

9. For *qiao* 巧, "crafty," the received text reads *kao* 考, "deceased-father; to inspect."

10. For *xiang* 翔, "to soar," the received text reads *xiang* 祥, "auspice."

11. For *huan* 圜, "circular, revolve," the received text reads *xuan* 旋, "turn about, return."

5. *SONG,* "LAWSUIT"

1. In the received text, this is hexagram 6.

2. For *fu* 復, "return," the received text reads *fu* 孚, "to capture; sincerity."

3. For *xu* 洫, "moat," which I here interpret as *xu* 恤, "to pity," the received text reads *zhi* 窒, "blocked; afraid."

4. For *ning* 寧, "tranquil," the received text reads *ti* 惕, "afraid."

5. For *ke* 克, "to succeed, to be able," the received text reads *zhong* 中, "middle."

6. Here and in the Initial Six line, for *dong* 冬, "winter," the received text reads *zhong* 終, "end."

7. The word "herewith" (*yong* 用) is absent from the received text.

8. For *shao* 少, "few; small," the received text reads *xiao* 小, "little."

9. For *sheng* 省, "to inspect," the received text reads *sheng* 眚, "calamity."

10. The received text here adds the words "in the end auspicious" (*zhong ji* 終吉).

11. For *yu* 俞, "to answer in the affirmative," the received text reads *yu* 渝, "to change."

12. For *ci* 賜, "to award," the received text reads *xi* 錫, "to award."

13. For *ban* 般, "type," the received text reads *pan* 鞶, "leather belt."

14. For the unknown graph 搋, which is composed of a "hand" signific and probably the phonetic *shi* 市, the received text reads *chi* 褫, "to take away."

6. *TONGREN,* "GATHERING MEN"

1. In the received text, this is hexagram 13.

2. Here and throughout the text, for *lin* 鄰, "chickadee," the received text reads *lin* 吝, "distress."

3. For *fu* 服, "clothing; to surrender," the received text reads *fu* 伏, "to crouch; to hide in ambush; to submit."

4. For *rong* 容, "appearance; to contain," the received text reads *rong* 戎, "belligerent."

5. For *deng* 登, "to climb," the received text reads *sheng* 升, "to ascend."

6. Before the word "later" (*hou* 後), the received text has the copula *er* 而.

7. For *jiao* 茭, "pasture," the received text reads *jiao* 郊, "suburb."

7. *WUMENG,* "PESTILENCE"

1. For *wumeng* 无孟, "pestilence," the received text, in which this is hexagram 25, reads *wuwang* 无妄, "pestilence." For the meaning "pestilence," see Arthur Waley, "The Book of Changes," 131–32.

2. Before the negative *fei* 匪, the received text has the pronoun *qi* 其, "it."

3. Here and in the Elevated Nine line, for *sheng* 省, "to inspect," the received text reads *sheng* 眚, "calamity."

4. For *yu* 餘, "excess," the received text reads *yu* 畬, "to work old fields."

5. The received text has the conditional *ze* 則, "then," at the head of this final clause.

6. For *ji* 擊, "to hit," the received text reads *xi* 繫, "to tie, to tether."

7. For *zi* 茲, "this," the received text reads *zai* 災, "disaster."

8. In the received text, the possessive particle *zhi* 之 before the word "motion" (*xing* 行) is absent, so that the received text reads "The pestilence moves."

8. *GOU,* "MEETING"

1. For *gou* 狗, "dog," the received text, in which this is hexagram 44, reads *gou* 姤, "to meet." In the only occurrence of the word in this hexagram, in the Elevated Nine line, "to meet" makes better sense of the context.

2. For *ji* 擊, "to hit," the received text reads *xi* 繫, "to tie, to tether."

3. For *ti* 梯, "ladder; stairs," the received text reads *ni* 柅, "spindle."

4. For *xi* 豨, "young pig," the received text reads *shi* 豕, "pig."

5. For *fu* 復, "to return," the received text reads *fu* 孚, "to capture; sincerity."

6. Here and in the Nine in the Fifth line, for *fu* 枹, "drumstick," the received text reads *bao* 包, "to enfold, to wrap."

7. For *zheng* 正, "upright," the received text reads *qi* 起, "to stand up."

8. The manuscript mistakenly reads *wu* 五, "five" instead of *jiu* 九, "nine."

9. For *ji* 忌, "jealousy," the received text reads *qi* 杞, "willow tree."

10. For *huo* 或, "something," the received text reads *you* 有, "there is."

11. For *sun* 損, "to decrease," the received text reads *yun* 隕, "to fall."

9. *GEN,* "STILLING"

1. For *gen* 根, "root," the received text, in which this is hexagram 52, reads *gen* 艮, understood as "to make still."

2. For *fei* 肥, "fat," the received text reads *fei* 腓, "calf (of the leg)," which is parallel with the body parts mentioned in the other line statements, suggesting it should be the original reading.

3. For *deng* 登, "to climb; to raise aloft," the received text reads *zheng* 拯, "to hold up; to help."

4. For *li* 戾, "perverse; go against the grain," the received text reads *lie* 列, "to rip, to rend."

5. For *shen* 肿, "flesh over the spine" (the graph of which, however, is not clear in the manuscript), the received text reads *yin* 夤, "flesh over the spine."

6. For *gong* 躬 (i.e., 躳), "torso," the received text reads *shen* 身, "body." Also, the received text of this line statement includes a final "there is no trouble" (*wu jiu* 无咎).

10. *TAIXU,* "GREAT STORAGE"

1. For *tai xu* 泰蓄, "great storage," the received text, in which this is hexagram 26, reads *da chu* 大畜, "great domestic animals."

2. For *che* 車, "cart," the received text reads *yu* 輿, "cart."

3. For the unknown graph 縨, which is composed of the "silk" signific and the phonetic *fu* 复, the received text reads *fu* 輹, "axlestrut."

4. For *sui* 遂, "to follow," the received text reads *zhu* 逐, "to chase, pursue."

5. For *gen* 根, "root," the received text reads *jian* 艱, "difficulty."

6. The received text concludes this clause with the word *wei* 衛, "to protect; defend."

7. For *ju* 鞠, "to interrogate; to bow; to nurture," the received text reads *gu* 牿, "ox headboard."

8. For *ku* 哭, "to cry," the received text reads *fen* 豶, "gelded."

9. For *xi* 豨, "pig" (said in *Fang yan* 方言 to be a Chu 楚 dialect word), the received text reads *shi* 豕, "pig."

10. For *ju* 瞿 (i.e., 懼), "frightened, wary," the received text reads *qu* 衢, "pervasive."

11. *BO,* "FLAYING"

1. In the received text, this is hexagram 23.

2. Here and in the Six in the Second and Six in the Fourth lines, for *zang* 臧, "good," the received text reads *chuang* 牀, "bed."

3. For *bian* 辯, "to dispute," the received text reads *bian* 辨, "to divide."

4. In the received text, "to flay" (*bo* 剝) is followed by the pronoun "it" (*zhi* 之); thus, "flaying it."

5. For *shi* 食, "to eat," the received text reads *yi* 以, "to take; together with."

6. For *long* 籠, "steamer," the received text reads *chong* 寵, "favor."

7. For *shi* 石, "stone," the received text reads *shi* 碩, "eminent."

8. For *che* 車, "chariot," the received text reads *yu* 輿, "cart."

9. For *lu* 蘆, "gourd," the received text reads *lu* 廬, "hut."

12. *SUN,* "DECREASE"

1. In the received text, this is hexagram 41.

2. For *fu* 復, "to return," the received text reads *fu* 孚, "to capture; sincerity."

3. As Yu Haoliang ("Boshu Zhouyi," 19) has argued, 𥝢 is an abbreviated form of *xia* 轄, "linchpin of a chariot's draftpole," for which the received text reads *he* 曷, "why." See too its usage as *hai* 害, "harm," in the Initial Nine line of *Dayou* 大有, hexagram 50.

4. For *qiao* 巧, "craft," the received text reads *gui* 簋, "tureen."

5. For *fang* 芳, "aromatic grass," the received text reads *xiang* 享, "to make offering."

6. Because of confusion between the graphs *yi* 已, "to stop; already," and *si* 巳: 祀, "to sacrifice," among commentators of the received text there have been two readings of this line: "The finished service quickly goes" (e.g., Wang Bi 王弼, *Zhouyi zhu* 周易注) or "The sacrificial service quickly goes" (e.g., Li Dingzuo 李鼎祚, *Zhouyi jijie* 周易集解). The manuscript seems not to resolve this confusion.

7. Here and in the Six in the Fourth line, for *duan* 端, "ends," the received text reads *chuan* 遄, "quickly."

8. For *zheng* 正, "upright," the received text reads *zheng* 征, "to campaign."

9. For *shi* 事, "to serve, to attend to," the received text reads *shi* 使, "to cause."

10. In the received text, this is prefaced by the word "someone" (*huo* 或).

293

11. For *hui* 回, "circular; return," the received text reads *wei* 違, "to disobey."

12. The received text reads "beneficial (*li* 利) to have someplace to go."

13. For *pu* 僕, "servant," the received text reads *chen* 臣, "retainer."

13. *MENG,* "FOLLY"

1. In the received text, this is hexagram 4

2. Both here and below in this hexagram statement, for *ji* 吉, "auspicious," the received text reads *gao* 告, "to report."

3. For *tu* 擉, "to draw out," the received text reads *du* 瀆, "muddled."

4. For *ji* 即, "then," the received text reads *ze* 則, "then."

5. For *fei* 廢, "to discard," the received text reads *fa* 發, "to develop."

6. For *yi* 已, "to stop; already," the received text reads *yi* 以, "to take; in order to."

7. For *fu* 枹, "drumstick," the received text reads *bao* 包, "to wrap."

8. For *ru* 入, "to enter; to cause to enter," the received text reads *na* 納, "to take in."

9. For the relative particle *suo* 所, the received text reads *yu* 禦, "to parry, to drive off."

14. *FAN,* "LUXURIANCE"

1. Throughout this hexagram, for *fan* 繁, "luxuriant," the received text, in which this is hexagram 22, reads *bi* 賁, "decorated."

2. Here and in the Six in the Fourth line, for *ru* 茹, "entangled roots; to eat," the received text reads *ru* 如, "to resemble."

3. For *fan* 蕃, "lush," the received text reads *po* 皤, "white."

4. For *min* 閩, "confused," the received text reads *hun* 婚, "to marry."

5. For *gou* 詬, "to slander," the received text reads *gou* 媾, "to have intercourse with."

6. For *bai* 白, "white," the received text reads *bo* 帛, "silk."

15. *YI,* "JAWS"

1. In the received text, this is hexagram 27.

2. For *duan* 短, "short," the received text reads *duo* 朵, "moving; hanging."

3. The received text does not have this *yue* 曰, "to say."

4. For *fu* 枡, "thresher," the received text reads *fu* 拂, "to thresh."

5. For *bei* 北, "north," the received text reads *qiu* 丘, "mound."

6. For *zheng* 正, "upright," the received text reads *zheng* 征, "to campaign."

7. For *chenchen* 沈沈, "submerged," the received text reads *dandan* 耽耽, "to look with eyes downcast."

8. For *rong* 容, "appearance; content," the received text reads *yu* 欲, "desire."

9. For *di* 笛, "a type of flute," the received text reads *zhu* 逐, "to pursue," but there are variant readings of *you* 攸, "long," and *you* 悠, "sad"; for these see Xu Qinting, *Zhouyi yiwen kao*, 57.

16. *GU,* "BRANCH"

1. Throughout this hexagram, for *gu* 箇, "branch," the received text, in which this is hexagram 18, reads *gu* 蠱, "disorder."

2. The received text does not have this *ji* 吉, "auspicious."

3. For *qiao* 巧, "crafty," the received text reads *kao* 考, "deceased-father; to inspect."

4. For *yu* 浴, "to bathe," the received text reads *yu* 裕, "abundant; magnanimous."

5. For *yu* 輿, "cart," the received text reads *yu* 譽, "praise."

6. For *de* 德, "virtue," the received text reads *shi* 事, "service."

7. The received text does not have this *xiong* 凶, "inauspicious."

17. *XI GAN,* "REPEATED ENTRAPMENT"

1. For *xi gan* 習贛, "repeated entrapment," the received text, in which this is hexagram 29, reads *kan* 坎, "entrapment."

2. The received text does not have this *xi* 習, "repeated."

3. For *fu* 復, "to return," the received text reads *fu* 孚, "to capture; sincerity."

4. For *xi/sui* 纗, "cords of a net; appended," the received text reads *wei* 維, "tied."

5. Both here and in the Six in the Third line, in the received text *ru* 入, "to enter," is followed by *yu* 于, "in."

6. For *shen* 訦, "trustworthy," but doubtless to be read as *chen* 沈, "deep," the received text reads *xian* 險, "precipitous; dangerous."

7. For *yan* 唅, "the appearance of a fish breathing," the received text reads *xian* 險, "precipitous; dangerous."

8. For *shen* 訦, "trustworthy," but doubtless to be read as *chen* 沈, "deep," the received text reads *zhen* 枕, "pillow."

9. For *dian* 奠, "to offer libations," the received text reads *zun* 樽, "a wine vessel."

10. For *qiao* 巧, "craft," the received text reads *gui* 簋, "tureen."

11. For *ji* 詠, the meaning of which is unclear, the received text reads *er* 貳, "two." The meaning of this line has long been an enigma, which unfortunately the manuscript does not help to explain. The transcription *fu* 訣, understood as a phonetic loan for *fu* 簠, "a square tureen," proposed by Yu Haoliang ("Boshu Zhouyi," 18), though inviting, is inconsistent with the way *fu* 夫 is written in the manuscript, as can be seen for instance in the Six in the Second and Six in the Third lines of *Sui* 隋, hexagram 47.

12. For *ru* 入, "to enter; to send in," the received text reads *na* 納, "to take in."

13. For *yao* 葯, "angelica," the received text reads *yue* 約, "bonds; restrained."

14. As Zhang Liwen, *Zhouyi boshu jin zhu jin yi*, 238–39, points out, the unknown graph 塭 of the manuscript is probably a miswriting of *ti* 禔, "sandbar," which is also written as *zhi* 坻. The received text reads *zhi* 祗, "blessing; sprite," showing classifier variation with *zhi* 坻.

15. For *hui* 諱, "taboo," the received text reads *hui* 徽, "three-strand braid." Here *hui* 諱 doubtless derives from classifier variation with *hui* 禕, which various early glosses equate with *hui* 徽.

16. For *qin* (*tshjen) 親, "to draw near; close; related," the received text reads *zhi* (*tsje) 寘, "to place."

17. For *cong* 蘴, "azure," the received text reads *cong* 叢, "clump of trees."

18. For *le* 勒, "bridle," the received text reads *ji* 棘, "thornbush."

18. *RU* (SHORT COAT:), "MOISTENED"

1. Throughout this hexagram, for *ru* 襦, "a short coat," but understood as *ru* 濡, "moist," the received text, in which this is hexagram 5, reads *xu* 需, "to await."

2. For *fu* 復, "to return," the received text reads *fu* 孚, "to capture; sincerity."

3. For *jiao* 茭, "pasture," the received text reads *jiao* 郊, "suburb."

4. The manuscript here mistakenly writes *liu* 六, "six," instead of *jiu* 九, "nine."

5. For *chu* 楚, "thornwood," the received text reads *su* 速, "to bid, summon; to urge." After *su*, the received text includes the possessive particle *zhi* 之.

19. *BI,* "ALLIANCE"

1. In the received text, this is hexagram 8.

2. Both here and below, for *fu* 復, "to return," the received text reads *fu* 孚, "to capture; sincerity."

3. For *dong* 冬, "winter," the received text reads *zhong* 終, "end."

4. For *chi* 池, "pond," the received text reads *ta* 它, "other; harm."

5. For *jie* 戒, "to warn," the received text reads *jie* 誡, "to frighten; frightened." The Han Stone Classic text, Yu Fan's 虞翻 text, and the *Zhouyi jijie* text all also read *jie* 誡; see Xu Qinting, *Zhouyi yiwen kao*, 28.

6. The received text reads "ally with him" (*bi zhi* 比之).

20. *JIAN,* "AFOOT"

1. For *jian* 蹇, "afoot," the received text, in which this is hexagram 39, reads *jian* 蹇, "hobbled."

2. For *yu* 輿, "cart; to ride in a cart," the received text reads *yu* 譽, "praise."

3. For *pu* 僕, "servant," the received text reads *chen* 臣, "retainer."

4. According to the *Wenwu* transcription, there is a *jin* 今, "current," here; according to both Zhang Liwen and Han Zhongmin's transcriptions, there is no graph. The photograph published in *Mawangdui Han mu wenwu* shows a tear at this point. The received text reads *gong* 躬, "torso, body."

5. The manuscript is defective for this entire line, but based on the other line texts I maintain the reading "afoot" for *jian* 蹇 instead of "hobbled" for *jian* 蹇.

6. As Zhang Liwen, *Zhouyi boshu jin zhu jin yi*, 273, points out, it would seem that the manucript's 倗, which is an unknown graph, is a miswriting of *beng* 崩 (written elsewhere in the manuscript as 備; e.g., the Nine in the Fourth line of *Yu* 餘, "Excess," hexagram 27), apparently identical with *peng* 朋, "friend," the reading of the received text.

7. For *shi* 石, "stone," the received text reads *shi (shuo)* 碩, "big head; eminent."

21. *JIE,* "MODERATION"

1. In the received text, this is hexagram 60.

2. Here and in the Elevated Six line, for *ku* 枯, "withered," the received text reads *ku* 苦, "bitter."

3. For *you* 牖, "window," the received text reads *ting* 庭, "courtyard."

22. *JIJI*, "ALREADY COMPLETED"

1. In the received text, this is hexagram 63.

2. For *dong* 冬, "winter," the received text reads *zhong* 終, "end."

3. For *ru* 乳, "nipple; breast-milk," the received text reads *luan* 亂, "disorder."

4. The manuscript mistakenly writes *liu* 六, "six," instead of *jiu* 九, "nine."

5. For *yi* 拽, "to drag," the received text reads *yi* 曳, "to drag."

6. For *lun* 綸, "azure-colored silk ribbon," the received text reads *lun* 輪, "spoked wheel."

7. For *wang* 亡, "to vanish; to lose," the received text reads *sang* 喪, "to die; to lose."

8. For *fa* (發:) 髮, "hair," the received text reads *fu* 茀, "hair ornament."

9. For *sui* 遂, "to follow," the received text reads *zhu* 逐, "to pursue."

10. For *ru* 襦, "a short coat," the received text reads *xu* 繻, "gauze." The *Jingdian shiwen* cites the Zi Xia 子夏 text as also reading *ru* 襦; see Xu Qinting, *Zhouyi yiwen kao*, 113.

11. For *ru* 茹, "waste silk; wadding," the received text reads *nü* 袽, "waste silk; wadding." The *Jingdian shiwen* cites the Zi Xia 子夏 text as also reading *ru* 茹; see Xu Qinting, *Zhouyi yiwen kao*, 113.

12. For *dong* 冬, "winter," the received text reads *zhong* 終, "end."

13. The words *yi ji* 以祭, "in order to sacrifice," are not found in the received text.

14. For *ruo* 若, "to be like," the received text reads *ru* 如, "to be like."

15. For *zhuo* (*drekw) 濯, "to rinse," the received text reads *yue* (*rekw) 禴, "spring sacrifice."

16. The received text does not have this *ji* 吉, "auspicious."

23. *ZHUN,* "HOARDING"

1. In the received text, this is hexagram 3.

2. For *lü* 律, "regulated," the received text reads *jian* 建, "to establish," as does the manuscript in the initial line of this hexagram.

3. For *ban yuan* 半遠, "half distant," the received text reads *panhuan* 磐桓, "to and fro; not making headway." *Ban* 半 is presumably a protograph for *pan* 砰, "a large rock," which is interchangeable with *pan* 磐, while *yuan* (*gwjanx) and *huan* (*gwən) are also phonetically close.

4. For *tan* 壇, "earthen mound, altar," the received text reads *zhan* 邅, "to turn around," though Yan Shigu 顏師古 (579–645) quotes his text of the *Yijing* as reading *dan* 亶, "sincere"; see his comment at *Han shu*, 100A.4216.

5. For *fan* 煩, "vexatious," the received text reads *ban* 班, "arrayed."

6. Here and in the Six in the Fourth line, for *min* 閩, "confused," the received text reads *hun* 婚, "to marry."

7. Here and in the Six in the Fourth line, for *hou* 厚, "thick; to enrich," the received text reads *gou* 媾, "to have intercourse with." In the Six in the Fourth line of *Fan* 蘩, "Luxuriant" (hexagram 14), where the received text also reads *gou* 媾, "to have intercourse with," the manuscript reads *gou* 詬, "to slander."

8. For *hua* 華, "flower; ornamentation," the received text reads *yu* 虞, "gamekeeper; deceit."

9. For *ji* 汲, "to dip water," the received text reads *qi* 泣, "to weep."

10. For *lian* 連, "connected," the received text reads *lian* 漣, "streaming."

24. *JING,* "THE WELL"

1. In the received text, this is hexagram 48.

2. For the unknown graph 茞, the phonetic of which is *ji* 己, the received text reads *gai* 改, "to change."

3. For *wang* 亡, "loss," the received text reads *sang* 喪, "death; loss."

4. For the unknown graph 氜, which is composed of components meaning "to exhaust, to dry up," and "vapor," the received text reads *xi* 汔, "water drying up."

5. For *ji* 汲, "to draw water," the received text reads *yu* 繘, "well-rope."

6. For *lei* 纍, "to burden," the received text reads *lei* 羸, "to weaken."

7. The received text does not have this *xing* 刑, "punishment; form."

8. For *du* 瀆, "ditch; murky," the received text reads *gu* 谷, "valley."

9. For *wei bi gou* 唯 敝 (句:) 笱, "it is only the worn-out fish-trap," the received text reads *weng bi lou* 甕敝漏, "the pot is worn out and leaking."

10. For *se* 塞, "to block, to stop up," the received text reads *ce* 惻, "pained."

11. For *jiao* 椒, "pepper tree," the received text reads *zhou* 甃, "masonry wall of a well."

12. For *li* 戾, "against the grain; perverse," the received text reads *lie* 冽, "clear water."

13. For *fu* 復, "to return," the received text reads *fu* 孚, "to capture; sincerity."

25. *CHEN,* "THUNDER"

1. Here and throughout this hexagram text, for *chen* 辰, "the fifth chronogram corresponding to the third month of spring," the received text, in which this is hexagram 51, reads *zhen* 震, "thunder."

2. For *shuo* 朔, "the first day of a new moon; a new beginning," the received text reads *xi* 虩, "a clap of thunder; to startle." According to *Jingdian shiwen*, Xun Shuang's 荀爽 text read *shuo* 愬, "startled"; see Xu Qinting, *Zhouyi yiwen kao*, 97.

3. For *yao* 芺, "a plant with bitter leaves," the received text reads *xiao* 笑, "to laugh."

4. For *jing* 敬, "to respect," the received text reads *jing* 驚, "to alarm."

5. Here and in the Six in the Second and the Six in the Fifth lines, for *wang* 亡, "to lose," the received text reads *sang* 喪, "to die; to lose."

6. For *shang* 觴, "a wine vessel," the received text reads *chang* 鬯, "fragrant wine."

7. For *qi* 齎, "a grain sacrifice," the received text reads *ji* 躋, "to ascend."

8. For *sui* 遂, "to follow," the received text reads *zhu* 逐, "to pursue."

9. For *shu* 疏, "slow," the received text reads *su* 蘇, "the sound of rolling thunder."

10. For *sheng* 省, "to inspect," the received text reads *sheng* 眚, "imperfection; fault."

11. For *xi* 昔, "ancient; former," the received text reads *suo* 索, "the sound of a thunderclap."

12. For *ju* 懼, "to be scared," the received text reads *jue* 矍, "to glance all about."

13. For *zheng* 正, "upright," the received text reads *zheng* 征, "to campaign."

14. The word "going" (*wang* 往) is not found in the received text.

15. For *min gou* 聞詬, "confused slander," the received text reads *hun gou* 婚媾, "marital intercourse."

26. *TAIZHUANG,* "GREAT MATURITY"

1. For *tai* 泰, "great," the received text, in which this is hexagram 34, reads *da* 大, "great."

2. For *zheng* 正, "upright," the received text reads *zheng* 征, "to campaign."

3. For *fu* 復, "to return," the received text reads *fu* 孚, "to capture; sincerity.

4. For *wang* 亡, "to lose," the received text reads *wang* 罔, "to be without."

5. For the unknown graph 璠, which is composed of a "jade" signific and the phonetic *fan* 番, the received text reads *fan* 藩, "fence."

6. For *kuai* 块, "block," the received text reads *jue* 决, "to break."

7. For *che* 車, "chariot," the received text reads *yu* 輿, "wagon."

8. For the unknown graph 緮, the phonetic of which is *fu* 复, the received text reads *fu* 輹, "axlestrut."

9. For *wang* 亡, "to lose," the received text reads *sang* 喪, "to die; to lose."

10. For *gen* 根, "root," the received text reads *jian* 艱, "difficult."

27. *YU,* "EXCESS"

1. Throughout this hexagram, for *yu* 餘, "excess," the received text, in which this is hexagram 16, reads *yu* 豫, "comfort."

2. For *jie* 疥, "to scratch," the received text reads *jie* 介, "border; to make sturdy."

3. For *yu* 杅, "bowl; self-satisfied," the received text reads *xu* 盱, "wide-eyed."

4. For *yun* 允, "really," the received text reads *you* 由, "source."

5. For *jia* 甲, "shell (of a turtle, for instance); armor; first (of the Chinese denary system)," the received text reads *he* 盍, "what, why not; to cover."

6. For *chan* 讒, "to slander," the received text (though with many variants) reads *zan* 簪, "hair-pin." Since *zen* 譖, "to slander," which shares the same phonetic as *zan* 簪, writes the same word as *chan* 讒, it seems clear that the manuscript reading here is preferable.

7. For *huo* 或, "perhaps," the received text reads *you* 有, "there is."

8. For *yu* 諭, "to inform," the received text reads *yu* 渝, "to change for the worse."

28. *SHAOGUO,* "SMALL SURPASSING"

1. For *shao* 少, "small," the received text, in which this is hexagram 62, reads *xiao* 小, "little."

2. For *tai* 泰, "great," the received text reads *da* 大, "great."

3. Here and below, for *yu* 愚, "stupid," the received text reads *yu* 遇, "to meet."

4. For *bi* 比, "ally," the received text reads *bi* 妣, "grandmother."

5. For *pu* 僕, "servant," the received text reads *chen* 臣, "retainer."

6. For *fang* 仿, "to imitate," the received text reads *fang* 防, "to repel."

7. For *zang* 臧, "good; to treat as good," the received text reads *qiang* 戕, "to cut; to injure." I base the choice between the two readings, and consequently the translation, in large part on the final "inauspicious," consistency with which suggests that the received text is superior.

8. For *ge* 革, "to revolt," the received text reads *jie* 戒, "to warn; to be on guard."

9. For *jiao* 茭, "pasture," the received text reads *jiao* 郊, "suburb."

10. For *she* 射, "to shoot," the received text reads *yi* 弋, "to shoot an arrow with attached string."

11. For *pi* 皮, "skin," the received text reads *bi* 彼, "that."

12. For *luo* 羅, "net," the received text reads *li* 離, "to fasten (in a net)."

13. For *zi* 茲, "this," the received text reads *zai* 災, "calamity, disaster."

14. For *sheng* 省, "to inspect," the received text reads *sheng* 眚, "imperfection."

29. *GUIMEI,* "RETURNING MAIDEN"

1. In the received text, this is hexagram 54.

2. Here and in the Initial Nine line, for *zheng* 正, "upright," the received text reads *zheng* 征, "to campaign."

3. For *di* 弟, "younger brother," the received text reads *di* 娣, "younger sister."

4. For *li* 利, "benefit," the received text reads *lü* 履, "to tread, to walk."

5. The received text here anomalously includes an attributive particle *zhi* 之 before the word *zhen* 貞, "to determine," thus nominalizing it: *viz.* "beneficial for a dark man's determination."

6. For *ru* 嬬, "consort," the received text reads *xu* 須, "to await; to require," though several early texts also read *ru* 嬬 (see Xu Qinting, *Zhouyi yiwen kao,* 101–2), corroborating the manuscript's reading.

7. For *ti* 苐, "a type of grass," both here and in the Six in the Fifth line below, the received text reads *di* 娣, "younger sister," as in the Initial Nine line above.

8. For *yan* 衍, "to overflow; to exceed," the received text reads *qian* 愆, "fault, mistake."

9. In the received text, the word *ri* 日, "sun; day," is absent, which comparison with the Elevated Nine line of *Shaoshu* 少蓄, "Small Har-

vest" (hexagram 58), and the Six in the Fourth line of *Zhong Fu* 中孚, "Central Return" (hexagram 61), shows probably to be correct.

10. For *ji* 既, "to finish," the received text reads *ji* 幾, "almost."

30. *JIE*, "UNTANGLED"

1. In the received text, this is hexagram 40.

2. For *su* 宿, "to spend the night," the received text reads *su* 夙, "early, morning."

3. For *qi* 其, "his," the received text reads *er* 而, "and; your."

4. For *mu* 栂, "hemlock," the received text reads *mu* 拇, "thumb."

5. For *fu* 復, "to return," the received text reads *fu* 孚, "to capture; sincerity."

6. For *ci* 此, "this," the received text reads *si* 斯, "this."

7. For *wei* 唯, "only," the received text reads *wei* 維, "to be."

8. For *fu* 復, "to return," the received text reads *fu* 孚, "to capture; sincerity."

9. As Zhang Liwen points out (*Zhouyi boshu jin zhu jin yi*, 385), the unknown graph 夐 is plausibly an elaboration of the received text's *sun* 隼, "hawk."

31. *FENG*, "ABUNDANCE"

1. In the received text, this is hexagram 55.

2. For *yu* 禺, "monkey," here and in the Nine in the Fourth line below, the received text reads *yu* 遇, "to meet."

3. For the unknown graph 肥, which is easily confused with *fei* 肥, "fat; affluent," the received text reads *pei* 配, "companion; spouse," though there is also a variant reading of *fei* 妃, "consort."

4. For *wei* 唯, "only," the received text reads *sui* 雖, "although."

5. For *pou* 剖, "to tear open," here and in the Nine in the Fourth line below, the received text reads *bu* 蔀, "curtain."

6. For *fu* 復, "to return," the received text reads *fu* 孚, "to capture; sincerity."

7. For *xu* 沍, "drainage ditch; to leak," the received text reads *fa* 發, "to emit, to develop." At the end of this line, the received text has a *ji* 吉, "auspicious," that is absent in the manuscript.

8. For *fan* 蕂, "a type of sedge," here and in the Elevated Six line below, the received text reads *pei* 沛, "lofty, abundant; screen," with such variants as *pei* 旆, "banner," *fei* 芾, "lush," and *wei* 韋, "leather" (for all of which, see Xu Qinting, *Zhouyi yiwen kao*, 104).

9. For *mo* 茉, "white jasmine," the received text reads *mo* 沬, "tiny

bubbles," explained in various commentaries as referring to the small stars behind the handle of the celestial Dipper.

10. For *gong* 弓, "bow (i.e., the weapon)," the received text reads *gong* 肱, "arm."

11. For *ju* 舉, "to raise, lift up," the received text reads *yu* 譽, "praise."

12. For *gui* 闈, "a window rectangular on the bottom and arched on the top," the received text reads *kui* 闚, "to peep" (as through a crack in a door).

13. As Yu Haoliang ("Boshu Zhouyi," 20), argues, the unknown graph 㒟 may be a miswriting of *xi* 瞁, "to look with alarm," which is the phonetic of the received text's *qu* 閴, "tranquil; vacant."

14. For *sui* 遂, "to follow," the received text reads *di* 覿, "to see."

32. *HENG,* "CONSTANCY"

1. In the received text, this is also hexagram 32.

2. For *xiong* 敻, "distant; to seek," the received text reads *jun* 浚 (also written 濬), "deep; to dredge."

3. For *xiong* 敻, "distant; to seek," the received text reads *zhen* 振, "to shake; to incite."

33. *CHUAN,* "THE FLOW"

1. For *chuan* 川, "river," the received text, in which this is hexagram 2, reads *kun* 坤, generally understood as "The Earthly Principle," but also routinely glossed as *shun* 順, "in the flow; compliant." Since *chuan* 川 is the phonetic component of *shun* 順, it would seem that their combined sense of "water flowing smoothly within a channel" leads to the original sense of this name.

2. For *wang* 亡, "to lose," the received text reads *sang* 喪, "to die; to lose."

3. For *li* 禮, "ritual," the received text reads *lü* 履, "to tread, to walk."

4. For *he* 合, "to close," the received text reads *han* 含, "to contain."

5. For *chang* 常, "constant," the received text reads *shang* 裳, "skirt, lower garment."

6. For *tong* 迵, "to penetrate; unified," the received text reads *yong* 用, "use" (i.e., Use of the Six).

34. *TAI,* "GREATNESS"

1. In the received text, this is hexagram 11.

2. For *ba* 犮, "to scamper (the manner in which a dog runs)," the received text reads *ba* 拔, "to pluck."

3. For *wei* 胃, "stomach, gizzard," the received text reads *hui* 彙, "root." In the Initial Six line of *Fu* 婦, "The Wife" (hexagram 2), with which this line is otherwise identical, this word is written *hui* 胃, said by the *Shuo wen* 說文 to be an archaic form of *hui* 彙.

4. Although the manuscript is defective here and the received text here reads *zheng* 征, "to campaign," since all other cases of this formula in the manuscript read *zheng* 正, "upright," I retain this reading here as well.

5. For *fu* 枹, "drumstick," the received text reads *bao* 包, "to wrap."

6. For *wang* 妄, "reckless," the received text reads *huang* 荒, "wild, uncultivated."

7. For *xia* 騢, "roan horse," the received text reads *xia* 遐, "distant."

8. For *fu wang* 弗忘, "not forget it," the received text reads *peng wang* 朋亡, "the friend is lost."

9. For *bo* 波, "wave" (as in water), the received text reads *bei* 陂, "slope."

10. For *gen* 根, "root," the received text reads *jian* 艱, "difficulty."

11. For *fu* 復, "to return," the received text reads *fu* 孚, "to capture; sincerity."

12. Although the manuscript is defective here and the received text here reads *fu* 孚, "to capture; sincerity," since in all other cases the manuscript reads *fu* 復, "to return," I retain this reading here as well.

13. For *chi* 齒, "tooth; age" the received text reads *zhi* 祉, "blessing."

35. *QIAN*, "MODESTY"

1. Throughout this hexagram, for *qian* 嗛, "unsatisfied; hamster" or *xian*, "to hold in the mouth," the received text, in which this is hexagram 15, reads *qian* 謙, "modesty." The "mouth" 口 and "language" 言 significs are commonly interchangeable in early manuscripts.

2. For *e* 譌, "false, erroneous," the received text reads *hui* 撝, "to rip, tear."

36. *LIN*, "THE FOREST"

1. Throughout this hexagram, for *lin* 林, "forest," the received text, in which this is hexagram 19, reads *lin* 臨, "to look down upon."

2. Here and in the Nine in the Second line, for *jin* 禁, "to prohibit," the received text reads *xian* 咸, "in all cases."

37. *SHI*, "THE TROOPS"

1. In the received text, this is hexagram 7.

2. For *bu* 不, "not," the received text reads *fou* 否, "not."

3. For the unknown graph 湯 (which should be differentiated from *tang* 湯, "hot water"), the received text reads *xi* 錫, "to award."

4. For *yu* 與, "to join with; and; to give," the received text reads *yu* 輿, "cart; to carry in a cart." Note that in the Six in the Fifth line, the manuscript reads *yu* 輿, "to cart."

5. Here and in the Six in the Fifth line, for 屍, which seems to occur only in Chu 楚 epigraphic sources as part of the names of months (for which, see Li Ling, "Formulaic Structure of Chu Divinatory Slips," *Early China* 15 [1990], 80 n. b), the received text reads *shi* 尸, "corpse." It seems likely here that the extra 示 component serves as a phonetic marker.

6. The word *ren* 人, "man," is absent from the received text, giving the reading "the great lord."

7. For *qi* 啓, "to open," the received text reads *kai* 開, "to open," thus avoiding the tabooed name of Emperor Jing (r. 156–141 B.C.) of the Han.

38. *MINGYI,* "CALLING PHEASANT"

1. In the received text, this is hexagram 36.

2. For *gen* 根, "root," the received text reads *jian* 艱, "difficulty."

3. The word *zuo* 左, "left," is absent from the received text.

4. For *cheng* (or *sheng)* 撜, "to hold aloft" (said in the *Shuo wen* to be an alternate form of *zheng* 抍), the received text reads *zheng* 拯, "to hold aloft."

5. For *chuang* 牀, "bed," the received text reads *zhuang* 壯, "maturity; vitality."

6. For *shou* 守, "to maintain; defend," the received text reads *shou* 狩, "to hunt."

7. The words *ming yi* 明夷, "calling pheasant," are absent from the received text, and in place of the duplication mark, ⹀, that follows *yi* in the manuscript, the received text reads *ru* 入, "to enter."

8. For *hai* 海, "sea," the received text reads *hui* 晦, "darkness."

39. *FU,* "RETURNING"

1. In the received text, this is hexagram 24.

2. For *beng* 堋, "to bury," the received text reads *peng* 朋, "friend." Jing Fang's 京房 text read *beng* 崩, "to die," perhaps supporting the manuscript's reading; see Xu Qinting, *Zhouyi yiwen kao,* 50.

3. For *ti* 提, "to lift; to mention," the received text reads *qi* 祇, "earth god" (also read as *zhi* 祇, "only").

4. For *bian* 編, "to knit; to edit; to put in sequence," the received text reads *pin* 頻, "repeated; incessant."

5. For *zi sheng* 茲省, "this inspection," the received text reads *zai sheng* 災眚, "calamitous imperfection." For another occurrence of the term, see the Elevated Six line of *Shaoguo* 少過, "Small Harvest" (hexagram 62).

6. For *zheng* 正, "upright," the received text reads *zheng* 征, "to campaign."

40. *DENG,* "ASCENDING"

1. Here and throughout this hexagram, for *deng* 登, "to ascend," the received text, in which this is hexagram 46, reads *sheng* 升, "to ascend."

2. For *xue* 血, "blood," the received text reads *xu* 恤, "to pity."

3. For *zheng* 正, "upright," the received text reads *zheng* 征, "to campaign." Though elsewhere I have maintained the manuscript's reading of "upright," that the *zheng* is here qualified as "southern" suggests that it means "campaign."

4. For *fu* 復, "to return," the received text reads *fu* 孚, "to capture; sincerity."

5. For *zhuo* (*drekw) 濯, "to rinse," the received text reads *yue* (*rekw) 禴, "spring sacrifice." For another example of this usage, see the Nine in the Fifth line of *Jiji* 既濟, "Already Completed" (hexagram 22).

41. *DUO,* "USURPATION"

1. Throughout this hexagram, for *duo* 奪, "to usurp," the received text, in which this is hexagram 58, reads *dui* 兌, "joy; harmony."

2. The word *xiao* 小, "little," is absent from the received text.

3. For *xiu* 休, "beneficent," the received text reads *he* 和, "harmonious."

4. For the unknown graph 誜, composed of the signific for language 言 and the phonetic *fu* 孚, the received text reads *fu* 孚, "to capture; sincere." In the received text, this word is followed by *dui* 兌, "joy, harmony." Comparison with the other line statements suggests that the absence of *duo* 奪, "to usurp," in the manuscript is probably inadvertent.

5. The manuscript mistakenly reads *jiu* 九, "nine," instead of *liu* 六, "six."

6. For *zhang* 章, "pattern," the received text reads *shang* 商, "to measure; commerce."

7. For (*jing* 景:) *ying* 影, "shadow," the received text reads *yin* 引, "to draw, to extend."

42. *GUAI,* "RESOLUTION"

1. In the received text, this is hexagram 43.

2. For *yang* 陽, "sunny," the received text reads *yang* 揚, "to raise up."

3. For *fu* 復, "to return," the received text reads *fu* 孚, "to capture; sincerity."

4. For *jie* 節, "to regulate," the received text reads *ji* 即, "to approach."

5. Here and in the Nine in the Third line, for *chuang* 牀, "bed," the received text reads *zhuang* 壯, "mature."

6. For *zhi* 止, "foot," the received text reads *zhi* 趾, "toe."

7. For *yi* 傷, "light; slow," the received text reads *ti* 惕, "wary."

8. For *xue* 血, "blood," the received text reads *xu* 恤, "to pity."

9. For *kui* 頯, "cheekbones," the received text reads *qiu* 頄, "cheekbones."

10. Here and in the Nine in the Fifth line, for *que* 缺, "broken; deficient," the received text reads *guai* 夬, "resolute."

11. For *yu* 愚, "stupid, foolish," the received text reads *yu* 遇, "to meet."

12. For *ru* 如, "to be like," the received text reads *ruo* 若, "to be like."

13. For *wen* 溫, "hot-springs; warmth," the received text reads *yun* 慍, "to be angry, hot."

14. For *chun* (脤:) 脣, "the lips; labia," the received text reads *tun* 臀, "buttocks."

15. For *qixu* 郪胥, the received text reads (*ciqie* 次且:) *ziju* 趑趄, "moving but not advancing."

16. For the unknown graph 爇, which is composed of the signific for "fire" and *le* 勒, "bridle; to control," the received text reads *lu* 陸, "land" (but variously understood by *Yijing* commentators).

17. For *dong* 冬, "winter," the received text reads *zhong* 終, "end."

43. *ZU,* "FINISHED"

1. Throughout this hexagram, for *zu* 卒, "to end, finish," the received text, in which this is hexagram 45, reads *cui* 萃, "to bunch together."

2. For *sheng* 生, "life," the received text reads *sheng* 牲, "animal offering."

3. Here and in the Six in the Second and Nine in the Fifth lines, for *fu* 復, "to return," the received text reads *fu* 孚, "to capture; sincerity."

4. For *ru* 乳, "breast-milk," the received text reads *luan* 亂, "disorder."

5. The pronoun *qi* 其, "he," is absent from the received text.

6. For *wu* 屋, "room," the received text reads *wo* 握, "to clasp."

7. For *yu* 于, "in," the received text reads *wei* 爲, "to do; to be."

8. For *xue* 血, "blood," the received text reads *xu* 恤, "to pity."

9. For *zhuo* (*drekw) 濯, "to rinse," the received text reads *yue* (*rekw) 禴, "spring sacrifice."

10. According to *Erya* 爾雅 ("Shi gu, xia"; *Erya yishu* [Sibu beiyao ed.], A1+.22a), *jie* 吷 and 嗟 are orthographic variants for the same word, "a sound of sighing."

11. For *shao* 少, "small," the received text reads *xiao* 小, "little."

12. For *li* 立, "to stand," the received text reads *wei* 位, "position."

13. For *zizi* 粢欿, the received text reads *jizi* 齎咨, in both cases being understood as the sound of sighing or crying.

14. For *ji* 洎, "broth; to soak; until," the received text reads *yi* 洟, "snivel." As Yu Haoliang ("Boshu Zhouyi," 19) argues, *ji* 洎, considered as a *huiyi* 會意 graph combining components for "water" and "nose," with the "nose" (*zi* 自) component also serving as phonetic, should be the original form for the word "snivel."

44. *QIN,* "FEELINGS"

1. Throughout this hexagram, for *qin* 欽, "to respect," the received text, in which this is hexagram 31, reads *xian* 咸, "in all cases," but usually understood as the protograph for *gan* 感, "to feel." In the *Appended Statements* (*Xici* 繫辭) commentary, at the two places where the received text reads *gan* 感 and the context clearly requires the meaning "to feel," the manuscript reads *qin* 欽, suggesting that it does indeed represent the word *gan* "to feel."

2. For *mu* 栂, "hemlock," the received text reads *mu* 拇, "thumb," but *Jingdian shiwen* cites the Zi Xia 子夏 text as reading *mu* 踇, "big toe," which the bottom-to-top sequence of images in the line statements would suggest; see Xu Qinting, *Zhouyi yiwen kao*, 65.

3. For the unknown graph 躩, which is composed of the signific for "foot" and the phonetic *fei* 肥, the received text reads *fei* 腓, "calf," the two graphs clearly writing the same word.

4. The manuscript here repeats, apparently inadvertently, the unknown but decipherable graph 腓, "calf," of the Six in the Second line, while the received text reads *gu* 股, "thigh."

5. The received text reads "to go is distressful" (*wang lin* 往吝).

6. For *tongtong* 童童, the received text reads *chongchong* 憧憧, "undecided."

7. For *xi* 璽, "seal" (of office), the received text reads *er* 爾, "you."

8. For *gu* 股, "thigh," the received text reads *mei* 脢, "spinal cord," which the bottom-to-top sequence of images in the line statements would suggest.

9. For the unknown graph 肢, which is composed of the signific for "flesh" and the phonetic *fu* 父, the received text reads *fu* 輔, "cheek bones," the two graphs clearly writing the same word.

10. For *xia* 陜, "ravine," the received text reads *jia* 頰, "jowls."

45. *KUN*, "ENTANGLED"

1. In the received text, this is hexagram 47.

2. For *chen* 辰, understood as *chun* 脣, "the lips; labia" (for which compare the Nine in the Fourth line of *Guai*, "Resolution," hexagram 42), the received text reads *tun* 臀, "buttocks."

3. For *yao* 要, "to want," the received text reads *you* 幽, "dark."

4. For *yu* 浴, "bath," the received text reads *gu* 谷, "valley."

5. For *tu* 擯, "to draw out," the received text reads *di* 覿, "to see."

6. This "inauspicious" (*xiong* 凶) is absent from the received text.

7. For *zhu* 絑, "scarlet," the received text reads *zhu* 朱, "scarlet," the same word.

8. Here and in the Nine in the Fifth line, for *fa* 發, "to shoot; to develop," the received text reads *fu* 紱, "kneepads."

9. Here and in the Nine in the Fifth line, for *fang* 芳, "aromatic grass," the received text reads *xiang* 享, "to make offering."

10. For *zheng* 正, "upright," the received text reads *zheng* 征, "to campaign."

11. For *hao* 號, "to cry out," the received text reads *ju* 據, "embedded."

12. For *jili* 疾莉, the received text reads *jili* 蒺藜, "thistles."

13. In the received text, "slowly" (*xu* 徐) is repeated.

14. Here and in the Elevated Six line, for *er* 貳, "repeated; two," the received text reads *yi* 劓, "to cut off the nose."

15. Here and in the Elevated Six line, for *chuan* 椽, "rafter," the received text reads *yue* 跀, "to cut off the feet."

16. For *helei* 褐纍, the received text reads *gelei* 葛藟, "creeping vines."

17. For *hui yi* 悔夷, "regretting the level," the received text reads *dong hui* 動悔, "setting regret in motion."

18. For *zhen* 貞, "to determine," the received text reads *zheng* 征, "to campaign."

46. *LE*, "THE BRIDLE"

1. Throughout this hexagram, for *le* 勒, "bridle; to compel," the received text, in which this is hexagram 49, reads *ge* 革, "leather; to revolt."

2. Throughout this hexagram, for *fu* 復, "to return," the received text reads *fu* 孚, "to capture; sincerity."

3. For *gong* 共, "common; together," the received text reads *gong* 鞏, "to strengthen."

4. For *zheng* 正, "upright," the received text reads *zheng* 征, "to campaign."

5. Although the received text here and in the Elevated Six line reads *zheng* 征, "to campaign," since other examples of this formula in the manuscript read *zheng* 正, "upright," that should probably also be the reading here as well.

6. For the unknown graph 苣, the phonetic of which is *ji* 己, the received text reads *gai* 改, "to change." For another example, see the hexagram statement of *Jing* 井, "The Well" (hexagram 24).

7. Here and in the Elevated Six line, for *bian* 便, "convenience," the received text reads *bian* 變, "to change; alternate," though the Han Stone Classic text reads *bian* 辯, "to dispute"; see Xu Qinting, *Zhouyi yiwen kao*, 95.

47. *SUI*, "FOLLOWING"

1. Throughout this hexagram, for *sui* 隋, "ripped flesh," the received text, in which this is hexagram 17, reads *sui* 隨, "to follow."

2. For *huo* 或, "someone; perhaps," the received text reads *you* 有, "to have."

3. For *yu* 諭, "to notify, inform," the received text reads *yu* 渝, "to change."

4. For *fu* 復, "to return," the received text reads *fu* 孚, "to capture; sincerity."

5. For *yi* 已, "to finish, end," the received text reads *yi* 以, "to take; by way of."

6. For *fu* 復, "to return," the received text reads *fu* 孚, "to capture; sincerity."

7. The manuscript mistakenly reads *jiu* 九, "nine," instead of *liu* 六, "six."

8. For *gou* 枸, "medlar tree," the received text reads *ju* 拘, "to grab, to arrest."

9. For *hua* 罣, "strings of a net; to bind," the received text reads *wei* 維, "to bind."

10. For *fang* 芳, "aromatic grass," the received text reads *heng* 亨, "receipt," understood as *xiang* 享, "to make offering."

48. *TAIGUO,* "GREAT SURPASSING"

1. For *tai* 泰, "great," the received text, in which this is hexagram 28, reads *da* 大, "great."

2. For *long* 朧, "draftpole of a chariot; to bow upward," the received text reads *nao* 橈, "to sag." In the Nine in the Fourth line, for the same graph the received text reads *long* 隆, "flourishing; lofty."

3. Here and in the Nine in the Fifth line, for *hu* 楛, "name of a tree," loan for *ku* 苦, "bitter," the received text reads *ku* 枯, "withered."

4. For *yi* 荑, "to weed, to mow," the received text reads *ti* 稊, "sprouts, shoots."

5. For *long* 朧, "draftpole of a chariot; to bow upward," the received text reads *long* 隆, "flourishing; lofty."

6. The manuscript mistakenly reads *liu* 六, "six," instead of *jiu* 九, "nine."

7. The manuscript mistakenly reads *jiu* 九, "nine," instead of *liu* 六, "six."

8. For *ding* 釘, "nail," the received text reads *ding* 頂, "top of the head."

49. *LUO,* "THE NET"

1. Throughout this hexagram, for *luo* 羅, "net," the received text, in which this is hexagram 30, reads *li* 離, "to fasten."

2. For *li* 禮, "ritual," the received text reads *lü* 履, "to tread, to walk."

3. For *xi* 昔, "ancient; formerly," the received text reads *cuo* 錯, "reverse, counter."

4. For the unknown graph 禝, which is doubtless a miswritten form of *ji* 禝, which is a variant form of *ji* 稷, "millet," which in turn is an attested loan for *ze* 昃, "declining sun," the received text reads *ze* 則 "then."

5. For *ji* 即, "to approach; then," the received text reads *ze* 則, "then."

6. Here and in the Six in the Fifth line below, for *jie* 跓 the received text reads *jie* 嗟, "to sigh," two graphs that *Erya* ("Shi gu, xia"; *Erya yishu* [Sibu beiyao ed.], A1+.22a) identifies as graphic variants.

312

7. For *die* 絰, "kerchief worn in mourning," the received text reads *die* 耋, "old," though *Jingdian shiwen* cites Jing Fang's 京房 text as also reading *die* 絰; see Xu Qinting, *Zhouyi yiwen kao*, 63.

8. For *chu* 出, "to go out," the received text reads *tu* 突, "abrupt."

9. In the received text, this "coming-like" (*lai ru* 來如) is preceded by the pronoun *qi* 其, "his."

10. For *fen* 紛, "confused," the received text reads *fen* 焚, "to burn."

11. For *zheng* 正, "upright," the received text reads *zheng* 征, "to campaign."

12. For the negative particle *bu* 不, the received text reads *fei* 匪, "not," and adds the pronoun *qi* 其. Also, for the unknown graph 戳, which is composed of the "dagger-ax" signific (on the right) and the phonetic *shou* 壽, the received text reads *chou* 醜, also written 魗, "hate; type; masses."

50. *DAYOU,* "THE GREAT POSSESSION"

1. In the received text, this is hexagram 14.

2. As Yu Haoliang ("Boshu Zhouyi," 19) has argued, 离 is an abbreviated form of *xia* 轄, "linchpin of a chariot's draftpole," for which the received text reads *hai* 害, "to harm." See too its usage as *he* 曷, "why," in the hexagram statement of *Sun* 損, "Decrease," hexagram 12.

3. For *gen* 根, "root," the received text reads *jian* 艱, "difficulty."

4. For *fang* 芳, "aromatic grass," the received text reads *heng* 亨, understood as *xiang* 享, "to make offering."

5. For *que* 闕, "gatetower," the received text reads *jue* 厥, "his."

6. For *fu* 復, "to return," the received text reads *fu* 孚, "to capture; sincerity."

7. For *wei* 委, "stooped," the received text reads *wei* 威, "awed; dignified."

8. For *you* 右, "right; to the right," the received text reads *you* 祐, "blessing."

51. *JIN,* "AQUAS"

1. Throughout this hexagram, for *jin* 溍, "aquatic," the received text, in which this is hexagram 35, reads *jin* 晉, usually understood in *Yijing* commentaries to mean "to advance."

2. For 昜, probably an abbreviation of *ti* 鬄, "bangs," the received text reads *xi* 錫, "to award."

3. For *jie* 綏, "to continue," the received text reads *jie* 接, "to connect."

313

4. The manuscript mistakenly reads *jiu* 九, "nine," instead of *liu* 六, "six."

5. For *jun* 浚, "deep water," the received text reads *cui* 摧, "to cut; to break."

6. For this "regret is gone" (*hui wang* 悔亡), the received text has only the negative particle *wang* 亡.

7. For *fu* 復, "to return," the received text reads *fu* 孚, "to capture; sincerity."

8. For *yu* 浴, "bath," the received text reads *yu* 裕, "abundance."

9. For *zhishu* 炙鼠, "mole cricket," the received text reads *shishu* 鼫鼠, "vole-mouse."

10. For *shi* 矢, "arrow," the received text reads *shi* 失, "to lose."

11. For *xue* 血, "blood," the received text reads *xu* 恤, "to pity."

12. For *wei* 唯, "only," the received text reads *wei* 維, "to be."

52. *LÜ,* "TRAVELING"

1. In the received text, this is hexagram 56.

2. For *shao* 少, "small," the received text reads *xiao* 小, "little."

3. For *ci* 此, "this," the received text reads *si* 斯, "this."

4. For *huo* 火, "fire," the received text reads *zai* 災, "calamity."

5. For *ji* 既, "to finish; already," the received text reads *ji* 即, "to approach; just about."

6. For *huai* 壞, "bad; to decay," the received text reads *huai* 懷, "to cherish."

7. For *ci* 茨, "to collect, amass," the received text reads *zi* 資, "goods; capital."

8. For *bo* 剝, "to flay," the received text reads *pu* 僕, "servant."

9. For *jin* 溍, "aquatic," the received text reads *zi* 資, "goods; capital." The manuscript's copyist apparently mistakenly copied the graph *jin* from the preceding hexagram, in the manuscript the column to the immediate right of this column.

10. For *dong* 冬, "winter," the received text reads *zhong* 終, "end."

11. For *ju* 舉, "to raise, to present," the received text reads *yu* 譽, "to praise."

12. For *wu* 烏, "crow," the received text reads *niao* 鳥, "bird."

13. For *fen* 棼, "to disorder wood or string," the received text reads *fen* 焚, "to burn."

14. For *guo* 摼, "to hit," the received text reads *hao* 號, "to cry out; to weep."

15. For *tao* 桃, "peachtree," the received text reads *tao* 咷, "to wail."

314

53. *GUAI,* "PERVERSION"

1. Throughout this hexagram, for *guai* 乖, "perverse," the received text, in which this is hexagram 38, reads *kui* 睽, "the two eyes seeing differently; to see incorrectly," but often understood in the *Yijing* tradition as meaning "perverse."

2. For *wang* 亡, "to lose," the received text reads *sang* 喪, "to lose, to die."

3. For *sui* 遂, "to follow," the received text reads *zhu* 逐, "to chase, pursue."

4. For *ya* 亞, "secondary; ugly," the received text reads *e* 惡, "ugly; distasteful."

5. After the first Nine in the Second (*jiu er* 九二), the manuscript's copyist apparently made an eye-skip back to the "there is no trouble" (*wu jiu* 无咎) at the end of the Initial Nine line statement, mistakenly recopying it, and then copying again "Nine in the Second."

6. Here and in the Nine in the Fourth and the Elevated Nine lines, for *yu* 愚, "stupid, foolish," the received text reads *yu* 遇, "to meet."

7. For *che* 車, "cart," the received text reads *yu* 輿, "wagon, cart."

8. The received text here reads "See the wagon dragging, its cow with one horn upturned." For the manuscript's *jia* 恕, "unconcerned; anxious," the corresponding word in the received text would seem to be *che* 掣, but according to *Jingdian shiwen* written in Zheng Xuan's 鄭玄 text as 觢, the phonetic component being the same as that of the manuscript's *jia* 恕; see Xu Qinting, *Zhouyi yiwen kao*, 74. For the unknown graph 詍, the phonetic of which is *shi* 世, the corresponding word in the received text is *yi* 曳, "to drag," which, as Yu Haoliang ("Boshu Zhouyi," 20) points out, has an archaic form of 抴, the phonetic component being the same as the manuscript's 世. It would seem that the manuscript's copyist here mistakenly reversed these two words.

9. Here and in the Elevated Nine line, for *qiao* 苆, "mustard-seed," the received text reads *gu* 孤, "solitary."

10. For *fu* 復, "to return," the received text reads *fu* 孚, "to capture; sincerity."

11. For *deng* 登, "to climb," the received text reads *jue* 厥, "his."

12. For *shi* 筮, "to divine by milfoil," the received text reads *shi* 噬, "to bite."

13. For *xi* 豨, "pig," the received text reads *shi* 豕, "pig."

14. For *xiao* 柧, "thorn," the received text reads *hu* 弧, "bow."

15. For *hu* 壺, "jar," the received text reads *hu* 弧, "bow."

16. For the unknown graph 闃, which is composed of the signific

for "gate" and a variant of the graph for "evening," *mo* 莫, which may also serve as the phonetic, the received text reads *hun* 婚, "to marry," but the phonetic of which, *hun* 昏, means "dusk."

17. For *hou* 厚, "thick; rich," the received text reads *gou* 媾, "to have intercourse."

18. For *ji* 即, "to approach; then," the received text reads *ze* 則, "then."

54. *WEIJI,* "NOT YET COMPLETED"

1. In the received text, this is hexagram 64.

2. For *qi* 气, "vapor," the received text reads *qi* 汔, "at the point of."

3. For *she* 涉, "to ford," the received text reads *ji* 濟, "to cross; to complete."

4. For *yi* 拽, "to drag," the received text reads *yi* 曳, "to drag," the modern form of the graph.

5. For *lun* 綸, "sash; string," the received text reads *lun* 輪, "wheel."

6. The received text ends with the word "auspicious" (*ji* 吉), which the formulaic usage "determination is auspicious" would suggest is correct.

7. For *zheng* 正, "upright," the received text reads *zheng* 征, "to campaign."

8. For *shang* 商, "commerce," the received text reads *shang* 賞, "to reward."

9. For "regret is gone" (*hui wang* 悔亡), the received text reads "there is no regret" (*wu hui* 无悔).

10. Here and in the Elevated Nine line, for *fu* 復, "to return," the received text reads *fu* 孚, "to capture; sincerity."

55. *SHI KE,* "BITING AND CHEWING"

1. The manuscript is defective at this point at which the hexagram name would normally come. In the received text, in which this is hexagram 21, the hexagram name is *Shi Ke* 噬嗑, "Biting and Chewing." The word *shi* 噬, "to bite," occurs throughout the hexagram, in the manuscript written as *shi* 筮, "to divine using milfoil."

2. For *ju* 句, "crooked," the received text reads *ju* 屨, "to wear on the feet."

3. For *zhi* 止, "foot; to stop," the received text reads *zhi* 趾, "foot."

4. Here and in the Six in the Fifth line, for *yu* 愚, "stupid, foolish," the received text reads *yu* 遇, "to meet."

5. For *shao* 少, "small," the received text reads *xiao* 小, "little."

6. For the unknown graph 瓄, which is composed of the "jade"

signific and the phonetic *feng* (*phjung) 豊, the received text reads *zi* 胾, "meat with bone in," but for which *Jingdian shiwen* cites Zi Xia's 子夏 text as reading *fu* (*pju) 脯, "preserved meat"; see Xu Qinting, *Zhouyi yiwen kao*, 46.

7. For *gen* 根, "root," the received text reads *jian* 艱, "difficulty."

8. For *du* 毒, "poison," the received text reads *huang jin* 黃金, "yellow metal; gold."

9. For *he* 荷, "to carry on the shoulders," the received text reads *he* 何, "what," but understood as a loan word for *he*, "to carry."

56. *DING,* "THE CAULDRON"

1. In the received text, this is hexagram 50.

2. For *tian* 塡, "to fill in," the received text reads *dian* 顛, "to overturn."

3. For *zhi* 止, "foot; to stop," the received text reads *zhi* 趾, "foot."

4. For *bu* 不, "not, negative," the received text reads *pi* 否, "not; negative, nugatory."

5. For the unknown graph 戕, which is composed of the "dagger-ax" signific and the phonetic *qiu* 求, the received text reads *chou* 仇, "enemy; mate," for which the *Ji yun* 集韻 gives 扏 as a variant writing.

6. For *jie* 節, "to regulate," the received text reads *ji* 即, "to approach."

7. For *le* 勒, "bridle; to compel," the received text reads *ge* 革, "leather; to revolt."

8. For *fu* 復, "to return," the received text reads *fu* 覆, "to cover; to reverse."

9. For the unknown graph 茫, which is composed of the "grass" signific and the phonetic *xu* 疋, the received text reads *su* 餗, "stew."

10. For *xing* 刑, "punishment," the received text reads *xing* 形, "form," but several sources read *xing* 刑, "punishment"; see Xu Qinting, *Zhouyi yiwen kao*, 96.

11. For *wu* 屋, "room," the received text reads *wo* 渥, "glossy," but several sources read *wu* 剭, "punishment-in-chamber" (for this translation, see Kunst, "The Original 'Yijing,'" 435); see Xu Qinting, *Zhouyi yiwen kao*, 96–97.

57. *SUAN,* "CALCULATIONS"

1. The manuscript is defective at this point, at which the hexagram name would normally come, but the word *suan* 筭, "to calculate," occurs throughout the hexagram, whereas the received text, in which this is hexagram 57, reads *xun* 巽, "compliance."

2. For *nei* 內, "inside," the received text reads *tui* 退, "to with-draw."

3. For *shi* 事, "to serve; to cause to serve," the received text reads *shi* 史, "scribe."

4. For *fen* 忿, "indignant, furious," the received text reads *fen* 紛, "disordered, entangled."

5. For *bian* 編, "to knit; to edit; to put in sequence," the received text reads *pin* 頻, "repeated; incessant."

6. For *wang* 亡, "to lose," the received text reads *sang* 喪, "to lose; to die."

7. For *jin* 潜, "aquatic," the received text reads *zi* 資, "goods; capital." For another case, see the Nine in the Fourth line of *Lü* 旅, "Traveling" (hexagram 52).

58. *SHAOSHU*, "SMALL HARVEST"

1. For the unknown graph 菽, which is composed of the "grass" signific and the phonetic *shu* 埶 (*zjuk*), the received text's hexagram 9 reads *chu* 畜, "domestic animals." Although it is possible that the manuscript's reading is but a phonetic loan for the *chu* of the received text (as suggested by Zhang Liwen, *Zhouyi boshu jin zhu jin yi*, 675), that the other hexagram in the received text whose name includes *chu*, *Da chu* (hexagram 26 in the received sequence), also reads *chu* in the manuscript (hexagram 10), which is to say differently from the present hexagram, suggests that this name should be differentiated from that of the received text. So as to maintain this differentiation, I would like to suggest that the graph here, 菽, stands for *shu* (*sjuk*) 叔/菽, "soybean"/ "to harvest," especially considering that the graph's phonetic element *shu* 埶 is a protograph for the word *shu* 熟, "ripe."

2. For *jiao* 菱, "pasture," the received text reads *jiao* 郊, "suburb."

3. For *jian* 堅, "firm," the received text reads *qian* 牽, "to lead, to draw."

4. For *che* 車, "cart," the received text reads *yu* 輿, "wagon."

5. For the unknown graph 緮, which is composed of the "silk" signific and the phonetic *fu* 复, the received text reads *fu* 輻, "spoke," but with numerous texts reading *fu* 輹, "axlestrut" (for which, see Xu Qinting, *Zhouyi yiwen kao*, 28–29).

6. Here and in the next line, for *fu* 復, "to return," the received text reads *fu* 孚, "to capture; sincerity."

7. For the unknown graph 湯, which is composed of a "water" signific and the phonetic *yi* 易, the received text reads *ti* 惕, "wary."

8. For *luan* 䜌, "entangled; linked," the received text reads *luan* 攣, "linked."

9. For *de* 得, "to get, obtain," the received text reads *de* 德, "virtue."

10. For *nü* 女, "woman, young girl," the received text reads *fu* 婦, "wife."

11. For *zheng* 正, "upright," the received text reads *zheng* 征, "to campaign."

59. *GUAN,* "LOOKING UP"

1. In the received text, this is hexagram 20.

2. For *zun* 尊, "to raise up; to make offering," the received text reads *jian* 薦, "to offer in sacrifice."

3. For *fu* 復, "to return," the received text reads *fu* 孚, "to capture; sincerity."

4. For the unknown graph 覝, which is composed of the "sight" signific and the phonetic *gui* 圭, the received text reads *kui* 闚, "to peek."

60. *JIAN,* "ADVANCING"

1. In the received text, this is hexagram 53.

2. For *yuan* 淵, "watery depths," the received text reads *gan* 干, "bank of a stream," with a variant *jian* 澗, "mountain stream."

3. For *li* 癘, "critical illness," the received text reads *li* 厲, "danger."

4. For *ban* 坂, "slope," the received text reads *pan* 磐, "boulder."

5. For *jiu* 酒, "wine," the received text reads *yin* 飲, "to drink."

6. For *yan* 衍, "water flowing; overflowing," the received text reads *kan* 衎, "joy."

7. Here and in the Nine in the Fifth line, for *sheng* (*ying*) 繩, "rope, cord," the received text reads *yun* 孕 (with the variant *cheng* 乘), "to be pregnant."

8. For *suo* 所, "place; relative pronoun," the received text reads *yu* 禦, "to parry; to drive off." For a similar case, see the Elevated Nine line of *Meng* 蒙, "Folly" (hexagram 13).

9. For *zhi* 直, "straight," the received text reads *de* 得, "to get, obtain."

10. For *kou* 寇, "robber," the received text reads *jue* 桷, "perch." The word *chou* 鼗, "to reject," is not found in the received text. Although the rhyme between *mu* (*muk) 木, "tree," and *jue* (*kuk) 桷, "perch," favors the received text's reading (the manuscript's copyist perhaps

mistakenly copying the *kou*, "robber," from the end of the Nine in the Third line), given the presence of *chou*, "to reject," I translate the manuscript as it is written.

11. For *yi* 宜, "appropriate," the received text reads *yi* 儀, "emblem."

61. *ZHONGFU,* "CENTRAL RETURN"

1. For *fu* 復, "to return," the received text, in which this is also hexagram 61, reads *fu* 孚, "to capture; sincerity."

2. *He* 和, "harmonious," here is obviously a mistake for *li* 利, "beneficial," which is the reading of the received text.

3. For *yu* 杆, "bowl; self-satisfied," the received text reads *yu* 虞, "to be at ease; burial ritual."

4. For *ning* 寧, "tranquil," the received text reads *yan* 燕, "calm."

5. For *lei* 羸, "weak, thin," the received text reads *mi* 靡, "to erase, to empty."

6. For *pi* 皮, "skin," but probably to be understood as *pi* 疲, "weary," the received text reads *ba* 罷, "to put down; to rest."

7. For *ji* 汲, "to ladle water," the received text reads *qi* 泣, "to cry."

8. For *bi* 必, "necessary," the received text reads *pi* 匹, "counter for horses."

9. For *lun* 論, "to assay; essay," the received text reads *luan* 孿, "linked."

10. For the unknown graph 鸣, which is composed of the "bird" signific and the phonetic *wei* 韋, the received text reads *han* 翰, "golden pheasant."

62. *HUAN,* "DISPERSAL"

1. In the received text, this is hexagram 59.

2. For *yu* 于, "in," the received text reads *you* 有, "to have."

3. For *cheng* (or *sheng)* 撜, "to hold aloft" (said in the *Shuo wen* to be an alternate form of *zheng* 抍), the received text reads *zheng* 拯, "to hold aloft."

4. In the received text, this phrase reads "Herewith hold aloft a horse's maturity" (*yong zheng ma zhuang* 用拯馬壯).

5. This "regret is gone" (*hui wang* 悔亡) is absent in the received text.

6. For *ben* 賁, "to rush," the received text reads *ben* 奔, "to rush."

7. For *jie* 階, "stairs," the received text reads *ji* 機, "bench; apparatus."

8. The manuscript mistakenly reads *jiu* 九, "nine," instead of *liu* 六, "six."

9. For *di* 娣, "younger sister," the received text reads *yi* 夷, "level; eastern barbarian."

10. The received text reads "Dispersing the liver, it greatly cries" (*huan gan qi da hao* 渙肝其大號).

11. For the unknown graph 湯, which is composed of a "water" signific and the phonetic *yi* 易, which elsewhere stands for *ti* 惕, "wary" (see the parallel in the Six in the Fourth line of *Shaoshu* 少藑, "Small Harvest," hexagram 58), the received text reads *ti* 逖, "far-away."

12. The received text concludes with the formula "there is no trouble" (*wu jiu* 旡咎), which is absent in the manuscript.

63. *JIAREN,* "FAMILY MEMBERS"

1. In the received text, this is hexagram 37.

2. For *men* 門, "gate," the received text reads *xian* 閑, "barricade."

3. For *gui* 貴, "esteemed," the received text reads *kui* 饋, "food."

4. For the unknown graph 樂, which is composed of the "fire" signific and the phonetic *le* (which means "joy" and may lend itself to the word's meaning), the received text reads *xiao* 嗃 (for which the *Jingdian shiwen* cites a variorum of 熇; see Xu Qinting, *Zhouyi yiwen kao,* 74), which is variously—and contradictorally—defined as either "(a sound of) happiness" or "(a sound of) angry severity." With the translation "excited," I attempt to retain something of this ambiguity.

5. For *li* 裏, "internal, interior," the received text reads *xi* 嘻, "the sound of happiness; giggling."

6. The word "going" (*wang* 往) is absent from the received text.

7. For *fu* 復, "to return," the received text reads *fu* 孚, "to capture; sincerity."

8. For *wei* 委, "stooped," the received text reads *wei* 威, "awed; dignified."

64. *YI,* "INCREASE"

1. In the received text, this is hexagram 42.

2. The manuscript mistakenly reads *jiu* 九, "nine," instead of *liu* 六, "six."

3. For *heng* 亨, "to offer," the received text reads *ke* 克, "to be able to," the manuscript apparently representing a miscopying.

4. For *hui* 回, "circular; return," the received text reads *wei* 違, "to disobey."

5. For *fang* 芳, "aromatic grass," the received text reads *xiang* 享, "to make offering."

6. For *gong* 工, "work; effort," the received text reads *xiong* 凶, "inauspicious."

7. Here and twice in the Nine in the Fifth line, for *fu* 復, "to return," the received text reads *fu* 孚, "to capture; sincerity."

8. For *gui* 閨, "a window rectangular on the bottom and arched on the top," the received text reads *gui* 圭, "tessera."

9. For *jia* 家, "family," the received text reads *yi* 依, "to rely upon."

THE SEVERAL DISCIPLES ASKED

1. "Yellow skirts" alludes to the Six in the Fifth line of *Chuan* 川, "The Flow," hexagram 33, which in the received text is called *Kun* 坤, "The Earthly Principle," and is hexagram 2.

2. This alludes to the Six in the Second line of *Chuan*, "The Flow."

3. This is the Initial Nine line of *Jian* 鍵, "The Key," hexagram 1, which in the received text is called *Qian* 乾, "The Heavenly Principle," and is also hexagram 1.

4. This is the Elevated Nine line of *Jian*, "The Key"; note that the reading *hang* 杭, "to raft," is different from both that of the manuscript (*kang* 抗, "to resist") and the received text (*gang* or *kang* 亢, "haughty, arrogant").

5. The transcription of Chen Songchang and Liao Mingchun does not indicate where the break between the fourth and fifth columns of text comes.

6. This is the Elevated Six line of *Chuan*, "The Flow."

7. This is the Six in the Second line of *Jian* 蹇, "Afoot," hexagram 20, which in the received text is called *Jian* 蹇, "Hobbled," and is hexagram 39; note that in all three variora between the manuscript text and the received text of this line (the manuscript's *pu* 僕, "vassal," as opposed to the received text's *chen* 臣, "retainer," *jian* 蹇, "afoot," as opposed to *jian* 蹇, "hobbled," and *gong* 躬, "body," as opposed to *jin* 今, "present"), this quotation matches the received text.

8. This is the Nine in the Fourth line of *Ding* 鼎, "The Cauldron," hexagram 56, which in the received text is hexagram 50; note that this quotation matches the manuscript text as opposed to that of the received text, especially of the third clause, which reads: "Its form (*xing* 形) is glistening (*wo* 渥)."

9. This is the Elevated Nine line of *Ding*, "The Cauldron."

10. This is the hexagram statement of *Jin* 溍, "Aquas," hexagram 51, which in the received text is called *Jin* 晉, "Advancing," and is hexagram 35.

11. This is the Six in the Fourth line of *Chuan,* "The Flow."

12. This is the Nine in the Second line of *Jian,* "The Key."

13. The text here inserts an extraneous verb complement *yi* 以, "to take; in order to."

14. This is the Nine in the Third line of *Jian,* "The Key"; the reading of *yi* 沂, the graph of which is taken from the concluding quotation below, is different from both that of the manuscript, *ni* 泥, "ashen," and also that of the received text, *ti* 惕, "wary," but it is likely that *yi* is a phonetic loan for *ti*, "wary."

15. This is the Nine in the Fifth line of *Jian,* "The Key"; note that the graph *fei* 蜚, "red-feathered sparrow," which is supplied from the concluding quotation, matches the reading of the manuscript, but both there and here should be understood as a phonetic loan for *fei* 飛, "to fly," the reading of the received text.

16. This is the Unified Nine line of *Jian,* "The Key."

17. This is the Initial Six line of *Chuan,* "The Flow."

18. On the basis of a suggestion by Qiu Xigui 裘錫圭 (personal communication, 18 August 1995), I here emend Chen Songchang's transcription of *tian chan xian* 田產濕 to *xi'nan wen* 西南溫.

19. This is the Six in the Third line of *Chuan,* "The Flow"; note that the reading of *han* 含, "to contain," matches that of the received text instead of the manuscript, which here reads *he* 合, "to enclose."

20. This is the Nine in the Fifth line of *Zhun* 屯, "Hoarding," hexagram 23, which in the received text is hexagram 3.

21. This is the hexagram statement of *Tongren* 同人, "Gathering Men," hexagram 6, which in the received text is hexagram 13.

22. This is the Initial Nine line of *Tongren,* "Gathering Men."

23. This is the Six in the Second line of *Tongren,* "Gathering Men"; note that neither the manuscript nor the received text includes the word "determination" (*zhen* 貞).

24. This is the Six in the Fifth line of *Dayou* 大有, "The Great Possession," hexagram 50, which in the received text is hexagram 14; note that the reading here matches that of the manuscript instead of that of the received text for both *jiao* 交, "intersected," and *wei* 威, "awe."

25. This is the hexagram statement of *Qian* 嗛, "Modesty,"

hexagram 35, which in the received text is called *Qian* 謙 and is hexagram 15; note that neither the manuscript nor the received text includes the word "auspicious" (*ji* 吉).

26. Here some portion of text has apparently been left out by the scribe.

27. This is the Six in the Third line of *Yu* 餘, "Excess," hexagram 27, which in the received text is called *Yu* 豫, "Comfort," and is hexagram 16; note that the quotation here is virtually identical with the received text (*yu* 予 being the protograph of *yu* 豫, "comfort") instead of the manuscript (which reads "A bowl's excess" [*yu yu* 杅餘]).

28. This is the Nine in the Second line of *Zhongfu* 中復, "Central Return," hexagram 61, which in the received text is called *Zhongfu* 中孚, "Central Sincerity," and is also hexagram 61; note that the quotation matches the manuscript in reading *lei* 纍, "thin; to down," instead of the *mi* 靡, "erase," of the received text.

29. This is the Six in the Fifth line of *Shaoguo* 少過, "Small Surpassing," hexagram 28, which in the received text is called *Xiaoguo* 小過, "Little Surpassing," and is hexagram 62; note that the quotation matches the received text in reading *pi* 皮, "skin," instead of the *bi* 彼, "that," of the manuscript.

30. This is the Nine in the Third line of *Heng* 恆, "Constancy," hexagram 32 in both the manuscript and received text; note that this quotation differs from both the manuscript and the received text in reading *you* 憂, "sadness," instead of *xiu* 羞, "disgrace."

31. This is the Elevated Six line of *Jie* 解, "Untangled," hexagram 30, which in the received text is hexagram 40; note that the quotation lacks the words "bagging it" (*huo zhi* 獲之) that are present in both the manuscript and the received text.

32. This is the hexagram statement of *Gen* 根, "Stilling," hexagram 9, which in the received text is called *Gen* 艮 and is hexagram 52.

33. On the basis of a suggestion by Qiu Xigui (personal communication, 18 August 1995), I here emend Chen Songchang and Liao Mingchun's transcription of 𣪠 to *zhang zhong* 長眾.

34. This is the Six in the Fifth line of *Gen*, "Stilling."

35. This is the hexagram statement of *Feng* 豐, "Abundance," hexagram 31, which in the received text is hexagram 55; note that neither the manuscript nor the received text, nor, for that matter, Confucius's comment quoted below, includes the word "self" (*zi* 自) given in this quotation.

36. This is the hexagram statement of *Weiji* 未濟, "Not Yet Com-

pleted," hexagram 54, which in the received text is hexagram 64; note that whereas this quotation reads "the little fox fording the river and almost completed wets his tail" (*xiao hu she chuan ji ji xu qi wei* 小狐涉川幾濟濡其尾), both the manuscript and the received text (with the minor variation of *she* 涉, "to ford," instead of *ji* 濟, "to complete; to ford") read "the little fox at the point of fording wets his tail" (*xiao hu qi she xu qi wei* 小狐乞涉濡其尾).

APPENDED STATEMENTS

1. This refers to *Jian* 鍵, "The Key," hexagram 1, which in the received text is called *Qian* 乾, understood as "The Heavenly Principle" or "Vigor," and is also hexagram 1.

2. This refers to *Chuan* 川, "The Flow," hexagram 33, which in the received text is called *Kun* 坤, understood as "The Earthly Principle" or "Compliance," and is hexagram 2.

3. In the received text this phrase reads "'Vigor' through change (or ease) knows" (*qian yi yi zhi* 乾以易知); it is likely that the manuscript's copyist inadvertently left out the verb "to know."

4. For *jian* 閒, "crack," the received text reads *jian* 簡, "simple."

5. In the received text, the two words *yi*, "to change" (or "the *Changes*") and *yi*, "ease," are written with the same graph, lending this passage a certain pregnant ambiguity. In the manuscript, the two words are disambiguated, the "to change" written 易, and "ease" written 傷.

6. Here and throughout the text, for *ma* 馬, "horse," the received text reads *xiang* 象, "image."

7. For *sui* 遂, "to follow," the received text reads *tui* 推, "to push"; i.e., "The hard and the soft *push* each other."

8. The manuscript is unclear here. Although Huang Peirong is correct in pointing out that the remnants of the graph do not resemble *xu* 序, "sequence," the reading of the received text, they also do not resemble *xiang*, "image," which is his suggestion, the same reading *Jingdian shiwen* cites for Yu Fan's 虞翻 text; see "Mawangdui boshu Xici zhuan jiaodu," *Zhouyi yanjiu* 14 [1992], 4 and n. 11. For the time being, it seems best to retain the reading of the received text.

9. For *shi* 始, "beginning," the received text reads *ci* 辭, "statement."

10. Here and regularly, though not invariably, throughout the text, for *jiao* 教, "teaching," the received text reads *yao* 爻, "line" (of a hexagram).

11. This is the Elevated Nine line of *Dayou* 大有, "The Great Possession," hexagram 50, which in the received text is hexagram 14.

12. For *ru* 如, "to be like," the received text reads *hu* 呼, "in"; i.e., "to be phrased *in* images."

13. For *yan* 言, "to be phrased," the received text reads *shan* 善, "to be good at."

14. For *ji* 極, "extreme; to go to the extreme," the received text reads *qi* 齊, "equal; to make equal"; i.e., "equalizing the great and little resides in the hexagrams."

15. For *fen* 分, "division," the received text reads *jie* 介, "border, interstice."

16. For *shun* 順, "to flow with; to comply," the received text reads *zhun* 準, "level."

17. For *guan* 觀, "to observe," the received text reads *yuan* 原, "source; to go to the source"; i.e., "Going to the source of the beginning."

18. For *jing* 精, "semen; essence," the received text reads *qing* 情, "characteristics; phenomenal nature." Since the two words are commonly written with the same graph, either reading is possible.

19. For *jiao* 校, "to compare," the received text reads *si* 似, "to resemble."

20. For *hui* 回, "turn around; to deflect," the received text reads *wei* 違, "to disobey."

21. For *qi* 齊, "to be equal," the received text reads *ji* 濟, "to cross; to complete; to help."

22. For *yi* 遺, "to leave out or behind," the received text reads *liu* 流, "to flow" (out of bounds).

23. For the unknown graph 㥈, the meaning of which is unclear, the received text reads *ai* 愛, "to love."

24. For *xi* 係, "to tie," the received text reads *ji* 繼, "to continue."

25. For *sheng* 生, "life," the received text reads *xing* 性, "inborn nature"; since 生 is the protograph of 性, either reading is possible.

26. For *shengzhe ren yong* 聖者仁用, "The sage's humane use," the received text reads *xian zhu ren cang zhu yong* 顯諸仁藏諸用, "manifest in humanity and stored in use"; for some discussion of this variorum (including the possibility that the graphs *cang zhu* 藏諸, "to be stored in," were copied after the fact between the graphs *ren* 仁 and *yong* 用), see Shaughnessy, "A First Reading of the Mawangdui *Yijing* Manuscript," 61–62.

27. For *zhongren* 眾人, "masses of men," the received text reads

shengren 聖人, "sage." This variorum effectively shifts the topic of the sentence from the "sage" in the Manuscript to the Way (*dao* 道) in the received text.

28. For *ji* 幾, "almost," the received text reads *yi* 矣, "indeed."

29. For *cheng* 誠, "sincere," the received text reads *sheng* 盛, "full."

30. For *sheng* 生, "life; to give life," the received text reads *sheng sheng* 生生, "to give life and to give life," seemingly putting greater emphasis on the generative capacity of the Way.

31. For *jiao* 敎, "to teach," the received text reads *xiao* 效, "to imitate."

32. The received text here adds the words *buce* 不測, "unfathomable"; i.e., "the yin and yang's unfathomability."

33. For *guo* 過, "to surpass," the received text reads *yu* 禦, "to defend; to drive off."

34. For *jing* 精, "semen; essence," the received text reads *jing* 靜, "tranquil."

35. For *juan* 圈, "curly," the received text reads *zhuan* 專, "concentrated" (translated in Wilhelm, *The I Ching*, 301, as "one"), but as I have argued elsewhere even that reading should be understood as a phonetic loan for *juan*, "curled"; see Xia Hanyi, "Shuo *Qian* zhuan zhi *Kun* xi pi xiang yi," *Wenshi* 30 (1988), 24.

36. For *yao* 榣, "the shaking of a tree," but doubtless to be read as *yao* 搖, "to shake, to move; to impregnate," the received text reads *zhi* 直, "straight"; it seems to me that the manuscript focuses on the function here, while the received text focuses on the description.

37. For *lian* 斂, "to gather," the received text reads *xi* 翕, "to close."

38. For *he* 合, "to close; to join," the received text reads *yi* 義, "propriety."

39. For *ti* 體, "body; to embody," the received text reads *li* 禮, "ritual," though *Jingdian shiwen* cites the Shu Cai 蜀才 text as also reading *ti* 體; see Xu Qinting, *Zhouyi yiwen kao*, 122. In this case, either reading makes sense, and so I translate the manuscript literally as it is written. Elsewhere, the manuscript's consistent reading of *ti* for *li* does not seem to make good sense in context.

40. For *ju* 具, "complete," the received text reads *you* 有, "to have."

41. For *ye* 業, "enterprise," the received text reads *ji* 蹟, "manifestation."

42. There is space for two graphs here (though the manuscript is defective at this point), but only the single graph *ni* 擬, "to imitate," in the received text. It is possible that here, as in column 28, the manu-

script read *buyi* 不疑, "not doubt"; i.e., "does not doubt it in its form and appearance."

43. For *ji ti* 疾體, "ill body," the received text reads *dian li* 典禮, "canons and rituals."

44. For *ye* 業, "enterprise," the received text reads *dong* 動, "movement."

45. Here and throughout the text, for *ru* 乳, "breast-milk," the received text reads *luan* 亂, "disorder; to disorder."

46. For *zhi* 知, "to know," the received text reads *ni* 擬, "to imitate."

47. For *yi* 義, "proper; to make proper," the received text reads *yi* 議, "to deliberate."

48. At this point in the manuscript, there is a round black dot occupying the space of a single graph; perhaps it is intended to mark a chapter division.

49. This is the Nine in the Second line of *Zhongfu* 中復, "Central Return," hexagram 61, which in the received text is called *Zhongfu* 中孚, "Central Sincerity," and is also hexagram 61. Note that this quotation accords with the manuscript in reading *lei* 羸, "thin" (here translated as "down"), rather than the *mi* 靡, "to erase," of the received text.

50. In the received text, before the word *yue* 曰, "to say; to mean," there is the word *zi* 子, "son; master; Confucius."

51. The received text here adds the words "puts forth his" (*chu qi* 出其); i.e., "puts forth his words well."

52. For *ying chen zhi dou* 營辰之斗, "construction star's dipper," the received text reads *rong ru zhi zhu* 榮辱之主, "master of renown and disgrace." By reparsing the manuscript, it might be possible to derive a reading such as "The pivot and fulcrum's developing work is (like) the Dipper of the stars."

53. The received text here concludes with the exclamation "Can one not be careful about it!" (*ke bushen hu* 可不慎乎).

54. This is the Nine in the Fifth line of *Tongren* 同人, "Gathering Men," hexagram 6, which in the received text is hexagram 13. Note that for *ku* 哭, "crying," here, both the manuscript and the received text (of both the *Zhouyi* and the *Xici*) read *xiao* 笑, "laughing."

55. For *mou* 謀, "to plan; to plot," the received text reads *mo* 默, "silent."

56. This is the Initial Six line of *Taiguo* 泰過, "Great Surpassing," hexagram 48, which in the received text is called *Daguo* 大過 and is hexagram 28.

57. For *zu* 足, "foot," the received text reads *cuo* 錯, "wrong; to grind."

58. This is the Six in the Second line of *Qian* 嗛, "Modesty," hexagram 35, which in the received text is written 謙 and is hexagram 15.

59. For *dai* 代, "to substitute," the received text reads *fa* 伐, "to cut, to attack; to brag"; *dai* appears to represent a scribal error, the manuscript's copyist failing to write the final stroke of the graph.

60. For *cheng* 成, "completion," the received text reads *sheng* 盛, "full."

61. For *gong* 共, "common; collective," the received text reads *gong* 恭, "respectful."

62. This is the Elevated Nine line of *Jian* 鍵, "The Key," hexagram 1, which in the received text is called *Qian* 乾 and is also hexagram 1. Note that the reading here *kang* 抗, "to resist," matches that of the manuscript, but differs from the *gang* (or *kang*) 亢, "haughty; arrogant," of the received text.

63. The received text here reads "The worthy man is in the lower position but is without support" (*xian ren zai xia wei er wu fu* 賢人在下而无輔).

64. This is the Initial Nine line of *Jie* 節, "Moderation," hexagram 21, which in the received text is hexagram 60. Note that the reading here of *you* 牖, "window," matches that of the manuscript, but differs from the *ting* 庭, "courtyard," of the received text.

65. For *ying* 盈, "fullness," the received text reads *cheng* 成, "completion."

66. This is the Six in the Third line of *Jie* 解, "Untangled," hexagram 30, which in the received text is hexagram 40.

67. The received text here reads "Arrogant storage induces bandits, and seductive appearance induces licentiousness" (*man zang hui dao, ye rong hui yin* 慢藏誨盜, 冶容誨淫).

68. For *cuo* 錯, "mistake; counter," the received text reads *xiang* 響, "echo."

69. For *xian* 險, "precipitous," the received text reads *shen* 深, "deep."

70. For *qin* 欽, "to respect," the received text reads *gan* 感, "to feel, feeling."

71. In the received text, this sentence comes before the preceding paragraph, and is then followed by an extended passage, generally known as the "Da yan" 大衍 or "Great Exposition," that purports to describe the method of milfoil divination.

72. The received text here reads "The *Changes* opens beings and completes responsibilities" (*fu yi kai wu cheng wu* 夫易開物成務).

73. For *yao* 樂, "to take pleasure in," the received text reads *mao* 冒, "to cover."

74. For *da* 達, "to penetrate," the received text reads *ding* 定, "to settle."

75. For *gong* 工, "work," but also *gong* 功, "accomplishment," the received text reads *gong* 貢, "to present."

76. For *yi* 佚, "to ease, to comfort," the received text reads *xi* 洗, "to wash, to clean."

77. For *nei* 內, "internal," the received text reads *tui* 退, "to retreat."

78. For *yuan* 願, "to wish," the received text reads huan 患, "anxiety."

79. For *wei* 爲, "to act; to do," the received text reads *yu* 與, "to participate; to partake."

80. For *yang* 恙, "to worry," the received text reads *sha* 殺, "to kill."

81. For *he* 闔, "to close," the received text reads *xing* 興, "to evoke; to cause to rise."

82. "People" (*min* 民) is repeated here, apparently a scribal error.

83. For *da heng* 大恒, "great constancy," the received text reads *tai ji* 太極, "great extreme." For discussion of this variorum and its philosophical significance, see Jao Tsung-i (Rao Zongyi), "Boshu Xici zhuan Da Heng shuo," *Daojia wenhua yanjiu* 3 (1993), 6–19.

84. For *sheng* 生, "life; to give life," the received text reads *ding* 定, "to settle."

85. For *rong* 榮, "renown," the received text reads *chong gao* 崇高, "exalted and high."

86. In the received text this reads "to explore the manifestations and to draw out the hidden" (*tan ji suo yin* 探賾索隱).

87. For *ding* 定, "to settle," the received text reads *cheng* 成, "to complete."

88. For *wuwu* 勿勿, "diligent," the received text reads *min min* 亹亹, also understood as "diligent."

89. For *shan* 善, "good," the received text reads *da* 大, "great."

90. For "heaven" here, the received text reads "heaven and earth" (*tian di* 天地).

91. In the received text, this clause is introduced with the words "Confucius said" (*zi yue* 子曰).

92. In the received text, this clause reads "can they not be seen!" (*qi buke jian hu* 其不可見乎).

93. At this point in the manuscript, there is an extraneous possessive particle *zhi* 之, which, when coupled with the writing of *li* 立, "to establish," as *wei* 位, "position," creates the ungrammatical "The sage's position images in order fully to express ideas."

94. The manuscript here omits the word "words" (*yan* 言), causing this passage to read: "appended statements to them in order fully to express their alternations, and connected them in order fully to express their benefit," which is certainly a possible reading. However, it seems to me that the received reading with the word "words" still makes the best sense of the passage.

95. For *jing* 經, "warp (or weaving); classic," the received text reads *yun* 縕, "loose hemp; confused" (but translated by Wilhelm as "secret"; *The I Ching or Book of Changes,* 322).

96. This redundant "then 'The Key' and 'The Flow' could not be seen. If 'The Key' and 'The Flow' could not be seen" is not found in the received text.

97. For *wei* 爲, "to act; to do," the received text reads *hua* 化, "to transform."

98. For *shi* 施, "to put into action," the received text reads *zai* 裁, "to cut; to control."

99. The received text here reads "to push and put them into motion is called penetration, and to lift and intersperse them among (*tui er xing zhi wei zhi tong, ju er cuo zhi* 推而行之謂之通,舉而錯之) the people under heaven is called service and enterprise."

100. For *qing* (請:) 情, "characteristics," the received text reads *ji* 賾, "manifestation."

101. For *bu yi* 不疑, "not to doubt," the received text reads *ni* 擬, "to imitate."

102. For *zhi* 制, "to regulate," the received text reads *cai* 裁, "to cut; to control."

103. For *mou* 謀, "to plan, to plot," the received text reads *mo* 默, "silent."

104. For *dong* 動, "to move," the received text reads *chong* 重, "to double." Either reading makes sense in the context.

105. For *qi* 齊, "equal; to equalize," the received text reads *ming* 命, "to command."

106. For *juzhe* 聚者, "what gathers," the received text reads "what moves time along" (*qu shi zhe* 趣時者), which perhaps makes better sense of the context.

107. Here and in the next three phrases, for *shang* 上, "high: to raise on high," the received text reads *zhen* 貞, "determination"; i.e., "what is victorious through determination."

108. For *xing* 行, "motion," the received text reads *dao* 道, "way."

109. For *shang guan tian zhe* 上觀天者, "what on high observes

331

heaven," the received text reads *zhen fu yi zhe* 貞夫一者, "the determined unity."

110. For *gaoran* 藃然, "loftily," the received text reads *queran* 確然, "decisively."

111. For *si* 思, "to think; thought," the received text reads *de* 德, "virtue."

112. For *fei* 費, "expenditure," the received text reads *bao* 寶, "treasure."

113. For *li (li:) wei* 立(立:)位, "to establish position," the received text reads just *wei* 位, "position."

114. For *ren* 人, "man," the received text reads *ren* 仁, "humaneness."

115. For *ai min an xing* 愛民安行, "to love the people and to pacify actions," the received text reads *jin min wei fei* 禁民爲非, "to prohibit the people from doing wrong."

116. This is hexagram 49, which in the received text is called *Li* 離, "Fastening," and is hexagram 30.

117. This is hexagram 64, which in the received text is hexagram 42.

118. In the received text, this *yu* 欲, "to wish, to desire," is absent, causing the sentence to read "each getting his place."

119. This is hexagram 55, which in the received text is hexagram 21.

120. For (*ru* 乳, "breast-milk":) *luan* 亂, "disorder," the received text reads *juan* 倦, "tired, exhausted."

121. For (*dong* 冬, "winter":) *zhong* 終, "end; to end," the received text reads *qiong* 窮, "to deplete." Also, the received text here adds the phrase "alternating then it penetrates" (*bian ze tong* 變則通).

122. The received text here adds the phrase "the benefit of boats and oars" (*zhou ji zhi li* 舟楫之利).

123. This is hexagram 62, which in the received text is hexagram 59.

124. This is hexagram 47, which in the received text is hexagram 17.

125. For *lü* 旅, "to travel," the received text reads *bao* 暴, "violent."

126. This is hexagram 27, which in the received text is called *Yu* 豫, "Comfort," and is hexagram 16.

127. This is hexagram 28, which in the received text is called *Xiaoguo* 小過, "Little Surpassing," and is hexagram 62.

128. This is hexagram 53 (though note that here the graph is written with the addition of a "speech" signific), which in the received text is called *Kui* 睽, "Perverse," and is hexagram 38.

129. This is hexagram 26 (though note that in the manuscript the hexagram name is written as *Taizhuang* 泰壯), which in the received text is hexagram 34.

130. For *li* 裏, "interior; to inter," the received text reads *yi* 衣, "clothing; to clothe."

131. This is hexagram 48 (though note that in the manuscript the hexagram name is written as *Taiguo* 泰過), which in the received text is hexagram 28.

132. This is hexagram 50, which in the received text is hexagram 14. Note, however, that in the received *Xici*, this is attributed to *Guai* 夬, "Resolution," hexagram 42 in the manuscript or 43 in the received text.

133. In the received text, the two occurrences of *xiang* 象, "image," (in the manuscript written as 馬) are differentiated, the first written 象 and the second 像, "to image."

134. For *zhi* 制, "to regulate," the received text reads *cai* 財, "material."

135. This is from the Nine in the Fourth line of *Qin* 欽, "Feelings," hexagram 44, which in the received text is called *Xian* 咸 and is hexagram 31.

136. This is the Six in the Third line of *Kun* 困, "Entangled," hexagram 45, which in the received text is hexagram 47.

137. This is the Elevated Six line of *Jie* 解, "Untangled," hexagram 30, which in the received text is hexagram 40.

138. For the nominal particle *zhe* 者, the received text reads *shi* 時, "time"; i.e., "waits for the (proper) time."

139. For *zeng* 矰, "an arrow with a line attached," the received text reads *kuo* 括, "to bind."

140. In the received text, the word *ju* 舉, "to raise up," is absent, causing the sentence to read "speaks of one who completes implements and moves."

141. This is the Initial Nine line of *Shi Ke* 噬嗑, "Biting and Chewing," hexagram 55, which in the received text is hexagram 21 (though note that the reading of *gou* 構, "to frame; to form," differs from both that of the maunscript [*ju* 句, "crooked"] and also that of the received text [*ju* 屨, "to wear on the feet"]).

142. This is the Elevated Nine line of *Shi Ke* 噬嗑, "Biting and Chewing," hexagram 55, or in the received text hexagram 21.

143. For *wei* 位, "position," the received text reads *si* 俟, "to wait for."

144. This is the Six in the Second line of *Yu* 餘, "Excess," hexagram 27, which in the received text is called *Yu* 豫, "Comfort," and is hexagram 16 (though note that the reading here of *jie* 介, "border; to make

sturdy," matches that of the received text but differs from the *jie* 疥, "to scratch," of the manuscript).

145. For *wu* 毋, "do not," the received text reads *ning* 寧, "tranquil."

146. For *wu* 物, "beings," the received text reads *wei* 微, "subtle."

147. Following this the received text contains a passage of more than five hundred graphs (537), which is found in the Mawangdui manuscript *Yao*, "Essentials."

148. The received manuscript here reads: "If it were not for the middle lines it would not be complete. Oh, also the importance of existence and loss, auspiciousness and inauspiciousness, then dwelling it can be known" (*ze fei qi zhong yao bu bei, yi yi yao cun wang ji xiong ze ju ke zhi yi* 則非其中爻不備,噫亦要存亡吉凶則居可知矣). As Chen Songchang, "Boshu Xici chutan," *Daojia wenhua yanjiu* 3 (1993), 155–164, argues, the manuscript reading placing importance on the first line of a hexagram is consistent with the preceding quotations and argumentation that the beginning of affairs is most important; for further discussion of this variorum, see Shaughnessy, "A First Reading of the Mawangdui *Yijing* Manuscript," 60–61. Note too that the received text continues from this point with a passage of almost two hundred graphs that is found in the Mawangdui manuscript *Yi zhi yi*, *The Properties of the* Changes.

149. In the received text, this sentence is prefaced with the words "As for *Qian* (i.e., *Jian*), it is the most vigorous of all under heaven" (*fu qian, tianxia zhi zhi jian ye* 夫乾,天下之至健也).

150. For *shu* 數, "number; to count," the received text reads *yan* 研, "to research."

151. For *ju* 具, "complete, thorough," the received text reads *yun* 云, "cloudlike; billowingly."

152. For *shun* 順, "to comply," the received text reads *tuan* 彖, "hexagram statement."

153. For *lun* 論, "essay; to assay," the received text reads *qing* 情, "characteristics."

154. For *dong zuo* 動作, "movements and actions," the received text reads *bian dong* 變動, "alternations and movements."

155. For *fan* 反, "to turn about," the received text reads *ban* 叛, "to rebel."

156. For (*ru* 乳, "breast-milk":) *luan* 亂, "disorder," the received text reads *can* 慙, "mortified." Note too that the received text continues here with the phrase "who in his heart has doubts, his statements will be (branched:) forked" (*zhong xin yizhe qi ci zhi* 中心疑者其辭枝).

THE PROPERTIES OF THE CHANGES

1. This is the Six in the Second line of *Chuan* 川, "The Flow," hexagram 33, which in the received text is called *Kun* 坤, "The Earthly Principle," and is hexagram 2.

2. This is the Unified Nine line of *Jian* 鍵, "The Key," hexagram 1, which in the received text is called *Qian* 乾, "The Heavenly Principle," and is also hexagram 1.

3. This is hexagram 1; in the received text, in which it is called *Qian* 乾, "The Heavenly Principle," it is also hexagram 1.

4. The hexagram here referred to as *Rong* 容, "Appearance," is called *Song* 訟, "Lawsuit," in both the manuscript, in which it is hexagram 5, and in the received text, in which it is hexagram 6.

5. This is hexagram 37, or in the received text hexagram 7.

6. This is hexagram 19, or in the received text hexagram 8.

7. The hexagram here referred to as *Xiaoxu* 小蓄, "Little Storage," is called *Shaoshu* 少薮, "Small Harvest," in the manuscript, in which it is hexagram 58, and *Xiaochu* 小畜, "Little Livestock," in the received text, in which it is hexagram 9.

8. The hexagram here referred to as *Lü* 履 is called *Li* 禮, (Ritual:) "Treading," in the manuscript, in which it is hexagram 4, but in the received text, in which it is hexagram 10, it is also written *Lü* 履.

9. This is hexagram 64, or in the received text hexagram 42.

10. This is hexagram 2, or in the received text, in which it is called *Pi* 否, "Negation," hexagram 12.

11. This is hexagram 7, or in the received text, in which it is called *Wuwang* 无妄, "Pestilence," hexagram 25.

12. The hexagram here referred to as *Ru* 嬬, "Weakness," is called *Ru* 襦, "Short Coat," but understood as *Ru* 濡 "Moistened," in the manuscript, in which it is hexagram 18, and *Xu* 需, "Awaiting," in the received text, in which it is hexagram 5.

13. This is hexagram 50, or in the received text hexagram 14.

14. Here and below, the hexagram referred to as *Dachuang* 大牀, "Great Bed," is called *Taizhuang* 泰壯, "Great Maturity," in the manuscript, in which it is hexagram 26, or *Dazhuang* 大壯 in the received text, in which it is hexagram 34.

15. The hexagram here referred to as *Daxu* 大蓄, "Great Storage," is called *Taixu* 泰蓄 in the manuscript, in which it is hexagram 10, or *Dachu* 大畜, "Great Domestic Animals," in the received text, in which it is hexagram 26.

16. This is hexagram 47, or in the received text hexagram 17.

17. The hexagram here referred to as *Jin* 謹, "Caution," apparently refers to *Gen* (根 "Roots":) 艮, "Stilling," hexagram 9, or in the received text hexagram 52.

18. This refers to hexagram 63, or in the received text hexagram 37.

19. This refers to hexagram 24, or in the received text hexagram 48.

20. The hexagram here referred to as *Gou* 垢, "Dirt," is called *Gou* 狗, (Dog:) "Meeting," in the manuscript, in which it is hexagram 8, and *Gou* 姤, "Meeting," in the received text, in which it is hexagram 44.

21. This is hexagram 31, or in the received text hexagram 55.

22. This is hexagram 36, or in the received text, in which it is called *Lin* 臨, "Looking Down," hexagram 19.

23. This is hexagram 59, or in the received text hexagram 20.

24. The hexagram here called *Ji* 齎, "Clutching," apparently refers to *Jin* 溍, "Aquas," hexagram 51, or in the received text, in which it is called *Jin* 晉, "To Advance," hexagram 35.

25. This saying does not occur either elsewhere in the manuscript or in the received *Yijing*.

26. This refers to hexagram 55, or in the received text hexagram 21.

27. This is hexagram 12, or in the received text hexagram 41.

28. This is hexagram 29, or in the received text hexagram 54.

29. This is hexagram 22, or in the received text hexagram 63.

30. This is the Six in the Second line of *Jin* 溍, "Aquas," hexagram 51, which in the received text is called *Jin* 晉, "Advance," and is hexagram 35.

31. This is the Elevated Nine line of *Gu* 箇, "Branch," hexagram 16, which in the received text is called *Gu* 蠱, "Disorder," and is hexagram 18.

32. This is from the Elevated Nine line of *Shi Ke* 噬嗑, "Biting and Chewing," hexagram 55, which in the received text is hexagram 21.

33. This is from the Initial Nine line of *Shi Ke*, "Biting and Chewing," hexagram 55, which in the received text is hexagram 21.

34. Virtually all of this paragraph, beginning with the top of line 14, corresponds to the first three sections of the *Shuo gua* 說卦, *Explanation of the Hexagrams,* commentary in the received *Yijing*. The most important discrepancy between this and the received text is the phrase which here reads "fire and water assault each other," but in the received text reads "fire and water do not assault each other" (*huo shui bu xiang she* 水火不相射).

35. This refers to the Elevated Nine line of *Jian* 鍵, "The Key," hexagram 1, which in the received text is called *Qian* 乾, "The Heav-

enly Principle," and is also hexagram 1; note that the word *kang* here is written 炕, "blazing," instead of 抗, "resisting," as it is in the manuscript of the text, or as *gang* or *kang* 亢, "haughty, arrogant," as it is in the received text.

36. This refers to the Elevated Six line of *Taizhuang* 泰壯, "Great Maturity," hexagram 26, which in the received text is called *Dazhuang* 大壯 and is hexagram 34.

37. This refers to the Elevated Nine line of *Gou* 狗, "Meeting," hexagram 8, which in the received text is called *Gou* 姤 and is hexagram 44.

38. This refers to the Nine in the Fourth line of *Ding* 鼎, "Cauldron," hexagram 56, which in the received text is hexagram 50.

39. This apparently alludes to the Elevated Six line of *Feng* 豐, "Abundance," hexagram 31 (in the received text hexagram 55), which reads: "Making abundant his room, screening his house, and arching his window; he is alarmed at his having no people; for three years he does not follow; inauspicious."

40. This refers to the hexagram statement of *Chuan* 川, "The Flow," hexagram 33, which in the received text is called *Kun* 坤, "The Earthly Principle," and is hexagram 2.

41. This refers to the hexagram statement of *Shaoshu* 少蓺, "Small Harvest," hexagram 58, which in the received text is called *Xiaochu* 小畜, "Little Domestic Animals," and is hexagram 9.

42. This refers to the Initial Six line of *Gou* 狗, "Meeting," hexagram 8, which in the received text is called *Gou* 姤 and is hexagram 44.

43. This alludes to the Nine in the Third line of *Jian* 漸, "Advancing," hexagram 60, which in the received text is hexagram 53.

44. This refers to the Elevated Six line of *Zhun* 屯, "Hoarding," hexagram 23, which in the received text is hexagram 3.

45. This is again the Six in the Second line of *Chuan*, "The Flow," hexagram 33.

46. This refers to the Initial Nine line of *Jian*, "The Key," hexagram 1, which in the received text is called *Qian* 乾, "The Heavenly Principle," and is also hexagram 1; note that the reading of *qian* 潛, "to submerge," here matches that of the received text instead of the *qin* 浸, "to submerse," of the manuscript.

47. This refers to the Nine in the Second line of *Jian*, "The Key," hexagram 1.

48. This refers to the Nine in the Third line of *Jian*, "The Key," hexagram 1.

49. This also refers to the Nine in the Third line of *Jian*, "The

Key," hexagram 1; note that while the reading *yi* 沂 here varies from both the *ni* 泥, "ashen," of the manuscript and also the *ti* 惕, "wary," of the received text, it is likely a phonetic loan for the latter.

50. This refers to the Nine in the Fourth line of *Jian*, "The Key," hexagram 1.

51. This refers to the Nine in the Fifth line of *Jian*, "The Key," hexagram 1.

52. This refers to the Elevated Nine line of *Jian*, "The Key," hexagram 1.

53. This refers to the Unified Nine line of *Jian*, "The Key," hexagram 1.

54. This refers to the hexagram statement of *Chuan*, "The Flow," hexagram 33, which in the received text is called *Kun* 坤, "The Earthly Principle," and is hexagram 2.

55. This also refers to the hexagram statement of *Chuan*, "The Flow," hexagram 33.

56. This refers to the Initial Six line of *Chuan*, "The Flow," hexagram 33.

57. This refers to the Six in the Second line of *Chuan*, "The Flow," hexagram 33.

58. This refers to the Six in the Third line of *Chuan*, "The Flow," hexagram 33; note that the reading *han* 含, "to contain," matches that of the received text (hexagram 2) instead of the *he* 合, "to enclose," of the manuscript.

59. This refers to the Six in the Fourth line of *Chuan*, "The Flow," hexagram 33.

60. This refers to the Six in the Fifth line of *Chuan*, "The Flow," hexagram 33.

61. This refers to the Elevated Six line of *Chuan*, "The Flow," hexagram 33.

62. This also refers to the Six in the Third line of *Chuan*, "The Flow," hexagram 33.

63. This again refers to the Elevated Nine line of *Shi Ke*, "Biting and Chewing," hexagram 55, or in the received text hexagram 21.

64. This refers to the Six in the Second line of *Qian* 嗛, "Modesty," hexagram 35, which in the received text is written *Qian* 謙, and is hexagram 15.

65. This refers to the Six in the Second line of *Yuan* 掾, "Wielding," hexagram 3, which in the received text is called *Dun* 遯, "To Retreat," and is hexagram 33.

66. *Huan* 渙, "Dispersal," is hexagram 62, or in the received text hexagram 59.

67. This graph seems to be extraneous.

68. This refers to the hexagram statement of *Chuan*, "The Flow," hexagram 33.

69. An alternative translation of this phrase might be: "silently does not turn away even after seeing ugliness."

70. This also refers to the hexagram statement of *Chuan*, "The Flow," hexagram 33.

71. This again refers to the Initial Six line of *Chuan*, "The Flow," hexagram 33.

72. The graph here, 新, is a *hapax legomenon* composed of *bo* or *bei* 孛, "comet," and *jin* 斤, "ax." The word family based on *bo* shares elements of abrupt and transgressive action.

73. This again refers to the hexagram statement of *Chuan*, "The Flow." Based on the comment that Confucius makes, it would seem that he here understands *peng* 朋, "double strand of cowries; friend," in its original sense of a "double strand of cowries."

74. This again refers to the Six in the Second line of *Chuan*, "The Flow"; note that for *ji* 吉, "auspicious," both the manuscript and the received text read *wu jiu* 无咎, "there is no trouble."

75. This again refers to the Six in the Third line of *Chuan*, "The Flow."

76. This again refers to the Six in the Third line of *Chuan*, "The Flow"; note that both the manuscript and the received text read "Someone follows the king's service" (*huo cong wang shi* 或從王事).

77. The italicized passage here corresponds with the first lines of Section B6 of the received *Xici* 繫辭 commentary. The passage then continues, with some interruptions, through the rest of B6, B7, B8 and most of B9 of the received *Xici*. I italicize the passages that correspond, noting significant variora.

78. This again refers to the Six in the Fourth line of *Chuan*, "The Flow."

79. This again refers to the Six in the Fifth line of *Chuan*, "The Flow."

80. This again refers to the Elevated Six line of *Chuan*, "The Flow."

81. For *bian* (辯:) 辨, "to discriminate," the received text of the *Xici* reads *cheng* 稱, "to raise up; to praise."

82. The received text of the *Xici* here reads "in examining into its categories" (*yu qi qi lei* 於稽其類).

83. For *tong* 童, "young boy; debased," but perhaps to be understood

as *dong* 動, "to move; movement," the received text of the *Xici* reads *yi* 意, "idea; sense." It is also possible that it is a scribal error, 童 and 意 being similar in appearance.

84. For *zan jue* 贊絕, "to praise what is cut off," the received text of the *Xici* reads *chan you* 闡幽, "to elaborate the dark."

85. The text here mistakenly writes *song* 宋 instead of *kun* 困, "entangled."

86. For *guo* 果, "fruit," the received text reads *he* 和, "to harmonize."

87. The received text of the *Xici* here reads "As a book the *Changes* cannot be distanced, as a way it frequently shifts" (*Yi zhi wei shu ye bu ke yuan, wei dao ye ju qian* 易之爲書也不可遠, 爲道也屢遷).

88. The three spaces in the manuscript here correspond to just the one word "alternates" (*bian* 變) in the received text of the *Xici*.

89. For *xu* 序, "sequence," the received text of the *Xici* here reads *shi* 適, "to go"; i.e., "It only alternates where it goes."

THE ESSENTIALS

1. This is from the Nine in the Fifth line of *Fu* 婦, "The Wife," hexagram 2, which in the received text is called *Pi* 否, "Negation," and is hexagram 12.

2. This is the Nine in the Fourth line of *Ding* 鼎, "The Cauldron," hexagram 56, which in the received text is hexagram 50.

3. The preceding highlighted passage corresponds closely with part of section B5 of the received *Xici* commentary.

4. This is the Initial Nine line of *Fu* 復, "Returning," hexagram 39, which in the received text is hexagram 24.

5. This is the Six in the Third line of *Sun* 損, "Decrease," hexagram 12, which in the received text is hexagram 41.

6. This is the Elevated Nine line of *Yi* 益, "Increase," hexagram 64, which in the received text is hexagram 42.

7. This highlighted passage corresponds closely with the final passage of section B5 of the received *Xici* commentary.

8. According to Ikeda Tomohisa 池田知久, "Maōtei Kan bo hakusho Shūeki Yō hen no shisō" 馬王堆漢墓帛書周易要篇の思想, *Tōyō bunka kenkyūjo kiyō* 東洋文化研究所紀要 126 (1995), 11, the final *gang* 剛, "hard," here should read instead *tu* 圖, "illustration."

9. This reading is based on the transcription of Ikeda, "Maōtei Kan

bo hakusho Shūeki Yō hen no shisō," 12, giving *hou* 後, "to put last," instead of *fu* 復, "to return to; to restore."

10. The passage "milfoil, and yet knows auspiciousness and inauspiciousness and complies with heaven" has been added on the basis of Ikeda, "Maōtei Kan bo hakusho Shūeki Yō hen no shisō," 14.

M U H E and *Z H A O L I*

MU HE

1. These lines do not appear in the extant *Shijing* or *Classic of Poetry*.

2. This is the hexagram statement of *Kun* 困, "Entangled," hexagram 45, which in the received text is hexagram 47.

3. This is the Nine in the Third line of *Qian* 嗛, "Modesty," hexagram 35, which in the received text is written 謙 and is hexagram 15.

4. This is the hexagram statement of *Meng* 蒙, "Folly," hexagram 13, which in the received text is hexagram 4; note that the text here reads *du* 讀, "to read," whereas the manuscript reads *tu* 攢, "drawn out," and the received text reads *du* 瀆, "muddled."

5. *Qian*, "Modesty," hexagram 35, is here written 溓 as opposed to the 嗛 of the manuscript and 謙 of the received text.

6. This refers to the hexagram *Mingyi* 明夷, "Calling Pheasant," hexagram 38, which in the received text is hexagram 36; its hexagram picture, ䷣, differs from that of *Qian* ䷎, "modesty," by only the single line here mentioned (i.e., the initial or bottom line). Before line tags such as Initial Six came to be used, the standard way of referring to a given line was to juxtapose two different hexagrams in this way.

7. This refers to the hexagram ䷝, called *Luo* 羅, "The Net," hexagram 49 in the manuscript and, as here, *Li* 離 in the received text, in which it is hexagram 30; it is composed of the doubled trigram ☲.

8. This refers to the hexagram *Chuan* 川, "The Flow," hexagram 33, which in the received text is called *Kun* 坤, "The Earthly Principle," and is hexagram 2; it is composed of the doubled trigram ☷.

9. For *shang* 上, "high, top," here, which matches the reading of the received text, the manuscript invariably writes *shang* 尚, "elevated." While there is very little difference between the two words, I have tried to maintain the distinction in the translations.

10. This is the Six in the Third line of *Song* 訟, "Lawsuit," hexagram 5, which in the received text is hexagram 6.

11. This is the Nine in the Fifth line of *Bi* 比, "Alliance," hexagram 19, which in the received text is hexagram 8.

12. Chen Songshang's transcription here repeats *cai* 財, "resources," but this must be an error. For this story, see *Shiji* 44 ("Wei shijia"), 1839.

13. This is the Nine in the Fifth line of *Yi* 益, "Increase," hexagram 64, which in the received text is hexagram 42.

14. This is the Elevated Six line of *Qian* 嗛, "Modesty," hexagram 35, which in the received text is written 謙 and is hexagram 15. Note that whereas the quote here reads "to campaign against the state" (*zheng guo* 征國), the received text reads "to campaign against the city and state" (*zheng yi guo* 征邑國); the manuscript is defective at that point and does not allow comparison.

15. This is from the Elevated Nine line of *Guai* 乖, "Perversion," hexagram 53, which in the received text is called *Kui* 睽, "To Observe," and is hexagram 38.

16. This is from the Six in the Fourth line of *Mingyi* 明夷, "Calling Pheasant," hexagram 38, which in the received text is hexagram 36.

17. This is the Six in the Fourth line of *Guan* 觀, "Looking Up," hexagram 59, which in the received text is hexagram 20.

18. This is from the Nine in the Fourth line of *Qin* 欽, "Feelings," hexagram 44, which in the received text is called *Xian* 咸 and is hexagram 31.

19. This is from the Elevated Six line of *Fu* 復, "Returning," hexagram 39, which in the received text is hexagram 24. Note that the word *zheng* 征, "to campaign," is here written 徰, probably similar to the reading of the received text, whereas the manuscript reads *zheng* 正, "to be upright."

20. This is from the Nine in the Third line of *Ding* 鼎, "The Cauldron," hexagram 56, which in the received text is hexagram 50.

21. This is from the Elevated Six line of *Mingyi* 明夷, "Calling Pheasant," hexagram 38, which in the received text is hexagram 36.

22. This is from the Elevated Six line of *Tai* 泰, "Greatness," hexagram 34, which in the received text is hexagram 11.

23. This is again from the Six in the Fourth line of *Guan*, "Looking Up," hexagram 59, which in the received text is hexagram 20.

ZHAO LI

24. This is from the Six in the Fourth line of *Shi* 師, "The Troops," hexagram 37, which in the received text is hexagram 7.

25. This is from the Nine in the Third line of *Taixu* 泰蓄, "Great Storage," hexagram 10, which in the received text is called *Dachu* 大畜, "Great Domestic Animals," and is hexagram 26.

26. This is from in the Six in the Fifth line of *Taixu*.

27. This is from the Nine in the Second line of *Shi* 師, "The Troops," hexagram 37, which in the received text is hexagram 7.

28. This is from the Nine in the Fifth line of *Bi* 比, "Alliance," hexagram 19, which in the received text is hexagram 8.

29. This is from the Elevated Six line of *Tai* 泰, "Greatness," hexagram 34, which in the received text is hexagram 11.

30. This probably refers to the Nine in the Fourth line of *Lü* 旅, "Traveling," hexagram 52, which in the received text is hexagram 56, but the image also occurs in the Elevated Nine line of *Suan* 箅, "Calculations," hexagram 57, which in the received text is called *Xun* 巽, "Compliance," and is also hexagram 57.

31. This refers to the Six in the Second line of *Wumeng* 无孟, "Pestilence," hexagram 7, which in the received text is called *Wuwang* 无妄, and is hexagram 25.

32. This probably refers to the Elevated Nine line of *Shaoshu* 少蓺, "Small Harvest," hexagram 58, which in the received text is called *Xiaochu* 小畜, "Little Domestic Animals," and is hexagram 9. In the received text, there are two other lines that share this image (the Six in the Fifth line of *Guimei* 歸妹, "Returning Maiden," hexagram 54, and the Six in the Fourth line of *Zhongfu* 中孚, "Central Sincerity," hexagram 61), but in the corresponding lines in the manuscript (of *Guimei*, "Returning Maiden," hexagram 29, and *Zhongfu* 中復, "Central Return," also hexagram 61) the *ji* 幾, "almost," is written instead as *ji* 既, "already."

Baoshan Chu jian 包山楚簡. Ed. Hubei sheng Jingsha tielu kaogudui. Beijing: Wenwu chubanshe, 1991.

William G. Boltz. "Manuscripts with Received Counterparts." In *New Sources of Early Chinese History: An Introduction to Reading Inscriptions and Manuscripts*. Ed. Edward L. Shaughnessy. Berkeley: Society for the Study of Early China, 1996. In press.

Chen Guying 陳鼓應. "Yi zhuan Xici suoshou Laozi sixiang ying-xiang—jianlun Yi zhuan nai Daojia xitong zhi zuo" 易傳繫辭所受老子思想影嚮———兼論易傳乃道家系統之作. *Zhexue yanjiu* 哲學研究 1989.1, 34–42, 52.

Chen Guying 陳鼓應. *Lao Zhuang xinlun* 老莊新論. Hong Kong: Zhonghua shuju, 1991.

Chen Guying 陳鼓應. "Yi Zhuan yu Chuxue Qixue" 易傳與楚學齊學. *Daojia wenhua yanjiu* 道家文化研究 1 (June, 1992), 143–156.

Chen Songchang 陳松長. "Boshu Xici chutan" 帛書繫辭初談. *Daojia wenhua yanjiu* 道家文化研究 3 (1993), 155–164.

Chen Songchang 陳松長. "Boshu Xici shiwen" 帛書繫辭釋文. *Daojia wenhua yanjiu* 道家文化研究 3 (1993), 416–423.

Chen Songchang 陳松長. "Mawangdui Boshu Mu He Zhao Li shiwen" 馬王堆帛書《穆和》、《昭力》釋文. *Daojia wenhua yanjiu* 道家文化研究 6 (1995), 367–380.

Chen Songchang 陳松長 and Liao Mingchun 繆名春. "Boshu Ersanzi wen Yi zhi yi Yao shiwen" 帛書《二三子問》、《易之義》、《要》釋文. *Daojia wenhua yanjiu* 道家文化研究 3 (1993), 424–435.

Deng Qiubo 鄧球柏. *Baihua boshu Zhouyi* 白話帛書周易. Changsha: Yuelu shushe, 1995.

Han Zhongmin 韓仲民. *Bo Yi shuolüe* 帛易說略. Beijing: Beijing Shi-fan daxue chubanshe, 1992.

Henricks, Robert G. *Lao-tzu Te-Tao Ching: A New Translation Based on the Recently Discovered Ma-wang-tui Texts.* New York: Ballantine Books, 1989.

Hu Jiacong 胡家聰. "Yi Zhuan Xici sixiang yu Daojia Huang-Lao zhi xue xiangtong" 易傳繫辭與道家黃老之學相通. *Daojia wenhua yanjiu* 道家文化研究 1 (June, 1992), 157–174.

Huang Peirong 黃沛榮. "Mawangdui boshu Xici zhuan jiaodu" 馬王堆帛書繫辭傳校讀. *Zhouyi yanjiu* 周易研究 1992.4, 1–9.

Ikeda Tomohisa 池田知久. "Maōtei Kan bo hakusho Shūeki Yō hen no kenkyū" 馬王堆漢墓帛書周易要篇の研究. *Tōyō bunka kenkyūjo kiyō* 東洋文化研究所紀要 123 (1994), 111–207.

Ikeda Tomohisa 池田知久. "Maōtei Kan bo hakusho Shūeki Yō hen no shisō" 馬王堆漢墓帛書周易要篇の思想. *Tōyō bunka kenkyūjo kiyō* 東洋文化研究所紀要 126 (1995), 1–105.

Jiaguwen heji 甲骨文合集. Ed. Hu Houxuan 胡厚宣. 13 vols. Beijing: Zhonghua shuju, 1982.

Jao Tsung-i 饒宗頤. "Boshu Xici zhuan Da Heng shuo" 帛書繫辭傳大恒說. *Daojia wenhua yanjiu* 道家文化研究 3 (1993), 6–19.

Keightley, David N. *Sources of Shang History: The Oracle-Bone Inscriptions of Bronze Age China.* Berkeley: University of California Press, 1978.

Kunst, Richard A. "The Original 'Yijing': A Text, Phonetic Transcription, Translation, and Indexes, with Sample Glosses." Ph.D. diss.: University of California, Berkeley, 1985.

Legge, James. *The Chinese Classics*, Vol. 5: *The Ch'un Ts'ew with the Tso Chuen.* 1872; Rpt. Hong Kong: Hong Kong University Press, 1960.

Li, Ling. "Formulaic Structure of Chu Divinatory Bamboo Slips." *Early China* 15 (1990), 71–86.

Li Meili 李梅鹿. *Mawangdui Han mu yanjiu mulu* 馬王堆漢墓研究目錄. Changsha: Hunan sheng bowuguan, 1992.

Li Xueqin 李學勤. "Boshu Zhouyi de jidian yanjiu" 帛書周易的幾點研究. *Wenwu* 文物 1994.1, 45.

Li Xueqin 李學勤. *Zhouyi jing zhuan suyuan* 周易經傳溯源. Chang-chun: Changchun chubanshe, 1992.

Liao Mingchun 繆名春. "Boshu Ersanzi wen jianshuo" 帛書二三子問簡說. *Daojia wenhua yanjiu* 道家文化研究 3 (1993), 190–195.

Liao Mingchun 繆名春. "Boshu Mu He Zhao Li jianshuo" 帛書繆和昭力簡說. *Daojia wenhua yanjiu* 道家文化研究 3 (1993), 207–215.

Liao Mingchun 繆名春. "Boshu Yi zhi yi jianshuo" 帛書易之義簡說. *Daojia wenhua yanjiu* 道家文化研究 3 (1993), 196–201.

Liao Mingchun 繆名春. "Boshu Yao jianshuo" 帛書要簡說. *Daojia wenhua yanjiu* 道家文化研究 3 (1993), 202–206.

Liao Mingchun 繆名春. "Lun boshu Xici yu jinben Xici de guanxi" 論帛書繫辭與今本繫辭的關係. *Daojia wenhua yanjiu* 道家文化研究 3 (1993), 133–143.

Liu Dajun 劉大鈞. "Bo Yi chutan" 帛易初談. *Wenshizhe* 文史哲 1985.4, 53–60. Translated as "A Preliminary Investigation of the Silk Manuscript Yijing." *Zhouyi Network* 1 (Jan. 1986), 13–26.

Liu Zhaozhuan 劉昭瑞. "Lun *Yi* zhi ming Yi—Jiantan boshu Yao pian" 論易之名易———兼論帛書要篇. *Daojia wenhua yanjiu* 道家文化研究 6 (1995), 329–335.

Lynn, Richard John. *The Classic of Changes: A New Translation of the I Ching as Interpreted by Wang Bi*. New York: Columbia University Press, 1994.

Ma Heng 馬亨. *Han shi jing jicun* 漢石經集存. Beijing: Kexue chubanshe, 1957.

Mawangdui Han mu boshu zhengli xiaozu. "Mawangdui boshu 'Liushisi gua' shiwen" 馬王堆帛書六十四卦釋文. *Wenwu* 文物, 1984.3, 1–8.

Mawangdui Han mu wenwu 馬王堆漢墓文物 (Added English title: The Cultural Relics Unearthed from the Han Tombs at Mawangdui). Ed. Fu Juyou 傅舉有 and Chen Songchang 陳松長. Changsha: Hunan chubanshe, 1992.

Qu Wanli 屈萬里. *Han shi jing Zhouyi canzi jicheng* 漢石經周易殘字集成. Nangang: Academia Sinica, 1961.

Roth, Harold D. "Redaction Criticism and the Early History of Taoism." *Early China* 19 (1994), 1–46.

Shaughnessy, Edward L. "The Composition of the *Zhouyi*." Ph.D. dissertation: Stanford University, 1983.

Shaughnessy, Edward L. "A First Reading of the Mawangdui *Yijing* Manuscript." *Early China* 19 (1994), 47–73.

Shaughnessy, Edward L. "The Key and the Flow: Drying Out the Wet Woman of the *Yijing's Xici Zhuan*." Paper presented to the annual meeting of the Association for Asian Studies, 11 April 1996, Honolulu, Hawaii.

Shaughnessy, Edward L. "Marriage, Divorce, and Revolution: Reading between the Lines of the *Book of Changes*." *The Journal of Asian Studies* 51.3 (August 1992), 594.

Shaughnessy, Edward L. "The Origins of an *Yijing* Line Statement." *Early China* 20 (1995), 223–40.

Shaughnessy, Edward L. "Zhouyuan Oracle–Bone Inscriptions: Entering the Research Stage?" *Early China* 11–12 (1985–87), 146–163.

Waley, Arthur. *The Book of Changes. Bulletin of the Museum of Far Eastern Antiquities* 5 (1933), 121–142.

Wang Baoxuan 王葆玹. "Boshu Xici yu Zhanguo Qin Han Daojia Yi xue" 帛書繫辭與戰國秦漢道家易學. *Daojia wenhua yanjiu* 道家文化研究 3 (1993), 73–88.

Wang Baoxuan 王葆玹. "Cong Mawangdui boshu ben kan Xici yu Laozi xuepai de guanxi" 從馬王堆帛書本看繫辭與老子學派的關係. *Daojia wenhua yanjiu* 道家文化研究 1 (1992), 175–187.

Wang Bo 王博. "Yao pian lüelun" 要篇略論. *Daojia wenhua yanjiu* 道家文化研究 6 (1995), 320–328.

Wilhelm, Richard. *The I Ching or Book of Changes.* Translated by Cary F. Baynes. Princeton: Princeton University Press, 1967.

Xing Wen 邢文. "*Heguanzi* yu boshu Yao" 鶡冠子與帛書要. *Daojia wenhua yanjiu* 道家文化研究 6 (1995), 336–349.

Xu Qinting 徐芹庭. *Zhouyi yiwen kao* 周易異文考. Taipei: Wuzhou chubanshe, n.d.

Xu Xitai 徐錫台. *Zhouyuan jiaguwen zongshu* 周原甲骨文綜述. Xi'an: San Qin chubanshe, 1987.

Yates, Robin D. S. "The Yin–Yang Texts from Yinqueshan: An Introduction and Partial Reconstruction, with Notes on their Significance in Relation to Huang–Lao Daoism." *Early China* 19 (1994), 75–144.

Yu Haoliang 于豪亮. "Boshu Zhouyi" 帛書周易. *Wenwu* 文物 1984.3, 15–24.

Zhang Liwen 張立文. *Zhouyi boshu jin zhu jin yi* 周易帛書今注今譯. 2 vols. Taipei: Xuesheng shuju, 1991.

Zhang Zhenglang 張政烺. "Mawangdui boshu Zhouyi Xici jiaodu" 馬王堆帛書周易繫辭校讀. *Daojia wenhua yanjiu* 道家文化研究 3 (1993), 27–35.

Zhang Zhenglang 張政烺. "Shishi Zhouchu qingtongqi mingwen zhong de Yi gua" 試釋周初青銅器銘文中的易卦. *Kaogu xuebao* 考古學報 1980.4, 404–415. Translated as "An Interpretation of the Divinatory Inscriptions on Early Zhou Bronzes." H. Huber, R. Yates, *et al. Early China* 6 (1980–81), 80–96.

Zuo Songchao 左松超. "Mawangdui Han mu yanjiu ziliao mulu suoyin" 馬王堆漢墓研究資料目錄索引. *Zhongguo shumu jikan* 中國書目季刊 23 (1989), 95–115.

"Zuotan Changsha Mawangdui Han mu boshu" 座談長沙馬王堆漢墓帛書. *Wenwu* 1974.9, 45–57.

EDWARD L. SHAUGHNESSY is professor of East Asian Languages and Civilizations at the University of Chicago. His *Sources of Western Zhou History: Inscribed Bronze Vessels* (1991) is widely recognized as the seminal history of the period during which the *I Ching* was originally composed.